DRAMACONTEMPORARY

Germany

PAJ Books

Bonnie Marranca and Gautam Dasgupta,
Series Editors

DRAMACONTEMPORARY

Germany

PLAYS BY
BOTHO STRAUSS · GEORGE TABORI
GEORG SEIDEL · KLAUS POHL
TANKRED DORST · ELFRIEDE JELINEK
HEINER MÜLLER

Edited by Carl Weber

The Johns Hopkins University Press

BALTIMORE AND LONDON

Publication of this book was made possible in part
by a grant from the Consulate General of the Federal
Republic of Germany (New York).

The Johns Hopkins University Press, 2715 North Charles Street
Baltimore, Maryland 21218-4319
The Johns Hopkins University Press Ltd., London

Library of Congress Cataloging-in-Publication Data will be found at the end of this book.
A catalog record for this book is available from the British Library.

ISBN 0-8018-5279-X   ISBN 0-8018-5280-3 (pbk.)

Contents

●

Preface

"The Very Age and Body of the Time"

•

During the ten years between 1985 and 1995, the German people witnessed the most momentous changes in their history since the end of World War II. The implosion of the (East) German Socialist state in 1989 and its quick absorption by the Federal Republic of (West) Germany a year later marked the middle of a decade during which the plays in this volume either were written or premiered. The latter half of this truly historic decade failed to deliver the glorious results anticipated by most Germans on that euphoric night when the Berlin Wall fell, heralding an end to the nation's nearly half-century partition.

At present, unified Germany is in a precarious and still inconclusive state, beleaguered by a host of new social, economic, political, and cultural problems. Business as usual—that is, the way the citizens of the Federal Republic were accustomed to conduct their political and economic affairs—does not work any longer. New ideas, new perspectives, and a new agenda are needed for the powerhouse of eighty million people in the center of Europe. A peculiarly fumbling and confused search for such an agenda has been conducted in recent years. Any look into German newspapers and journals, or viewing of German TV and radio, or glance at the repertoire of German theater provides evidence of the ongoing investigation of the nation's position in a profoundly changed world.

The German stage has been confronting social and historical issues since the mid-eighteenth century, when it became the preferred site for the debates of an emerging nation. The authors who shaped the evolution of German drama always accepted this challenge. Lessing, Goethe, Schiller during the eighteenth century; Kleist, Büchner, Hauptmann in the nineteenth century; Brecht, Weiss, and Müller during ours (and these are only a few of the many who contributed to the tradition)—all regarded the stage as a public arena where issues that concerned the nation could be presented for scrutiny and judgment.

Quite in this tradition, the authors whose plays were selected for this anthology responded to the events of a turbulent decade, from 1985, when early stirrings began to unsettle the stagnation of European as well as German affairs, to 1995, when the high hopes for a unified Germany's future were undermined by a profound feeling of insecurity. Some of the texts reflect on the nation's condition in an outspoken, even aggressive, manner. Others explore in a more tentative and subtle way what might be called the private realm, a realm that nevertheless has been touched by history's shifts and society's pressures.

All of these playwrights are by now solidly established in the repertoire of the German theater. Three of them, Tankred Dorst, Klaus Pohl, and Botho Strauss, have been citizens of the Federal Republic, while Heiner Müller and Georg Seidel carried the passport of the now-extinct GDR. Elfriede Jelinek is an Austrian. George Tabori, Hungarian born, returned to Central Europe in 1971, after a thirty-five-year exile in England and the United States, and has arguably been the most successful in emulating the model of the late Brecht as a playwright/director with a major impact on the German theater. The lives and careers of these authors have been as different as they could be, and so is their work, marked as it is by their individual age and aesthetics, ideologies and tastes. They all, however, appear to share an intention that is more or less openly expressed in their texts, namely, to respond to the social and ideological forces that shaped the life of the German people in the twentieth century. Their plays indeed reveal "the very age and body of the time, his form and pressure," to quote Hamlet's instruction to the players.

Many playwrights in the language have made outstanding contributions to contemporary German drama: Thomas Bernhard, Peter Handke, Franz Xaver Kroetz, Gerlind Reinshagen, and Friederike Roth, for instance, immediately come to mind. However, this anthology presents authors who have never, or very rarely, been published in the United States. For the same reason, only one play by a woman is included, since a comprehensive volume of contemporary German women playwrights, *The Divided home/land,* edited by Sue Ellen Case, has recently been published. And Heiner Müller's latest brief theater text is included because it was the first published effort to explore the postunification "blues" so strongly experienced by many East Germans and so insistently articulated and attacked in the German media.* If there is any equivalent in the American historical experience, it would be the period after the Civil War, with its carpetbaggers, the Southern resentment of defeat by the

---

*Three volumes of Heiner Müller's writings were published by PAJ Books: *The Battle, Hamlet Machine,* and *Explosion of a Memory,* edited by Carl Weber.

Union, and the Northern assumption of moral superiority. In a way, one might compare the present German situation with that of the United States in the late 1860s. A German "cold civil war" has ended with the voluntary submission of one segment of the split nation to its much more affluent and powerful opposite part.

A playscript can, of course, be appreciated by the solitary reader, and it can be thoroughly analyzed and interpreted in an academic seminar. Yet only when performed by actors in front of an audience will a theater text come to what aptly is called *life*. So the selection for this anthology was also guided by practical considerations—that is, by the specifics each play requires for a staging: size of the cast, implied scope of sets and costumes, and in most instances, accessibility of topic and textual structure for American audiences, who lack an intimate knowledge of contemporary German history and culture.

The selections range from outspoken sociopolitical attacks to minutely detailed investigations of intimate relationships, from no-holds-barred melodrama to poetic metaphors of the toll alienation exacts in contemporary life. In their form, the texts run the gamut from a realistic linear narrative to a highly abstract construct of language and imagery. The spectrum of topics and styles could hardly be wider, and it is representative of the great number of new plays that were premiered by German theaters between 1985 and 1995.

Of all the texts, Heiner Müller's *Mommsen's Block* is the most unusual, given its nondiscursive, poetrylike, free-association mode. It might be read as a sarcastic and grim reckoning of the changes unification has wrought in the life of East Germans, as a wry comment on the futility of any effort to capture the complexity of history between the covers of a book, or in many other ways. Klaus Pohl's *The Beautiful Stranger* confronts its audience with the upsurge of xenophobia and anti-Semitism that shocked the world after the unification of 1990, by way of a spellbinding, melodramatic plot that unfolds in a small West German town close to the former intra-German border.

Georg Seidel's *Carmen Kittel* explores, in sharply focused scenes, the boredom and hypocrisy of everyday life in the former East Germany during the 1980s, especially the problematic situation of working-class women in a society that claims to have achieved complete equality of the sexes. Botho Strauss, in *The Tour Guide,* traces the self-discovery/self-destruction—the midlife crisis, if you will—of an aging teacher, a member of the so-called '68 generation, whose student revolt once shook West German society to its roots. Strauss's antihero becomes passionately involved with a young woman who was barely born by 1968. The play creates a bold metaphor for the resignation of the Old Left and the generational conflict in the West Germany of the 1980s.

The texts by Elfriede Jelinek and George Tabori dissect, in a satirical yet profoundly serious manner, two seminal figures of German twentieth-century ideology in its most notorious manifestations. In *Totenauberg (Death/Valley/Summit)*, it is the existentialist philosopher and unrepentant admirer of Hitler's historic project, Martin Heidegger, who after World War II encounters his former lover, the Jewish emigrant writer Hannah Arendt. In *Mein Kampf* it is the Führer himself, in his early years, when he was still dreaming of a glorious future as an artist while languishing in a squalid Vienna flophouse before World War I, where he is befriended by a Jewish roommate.

Finally, with *Fernando Krapp Wrote Me This Letter*, Tankred Dorst has fashioned (from one of the Spanish writer Unamuno's novellas of pre–World War I vintage) a poetic fairy tale about the mystery and fierceness of an amour fou in a decadent society where human identity has become as elusive and ever shifting as in a Pirandello play.

Thus, these texts span nearly all of the twentieth century, not only in terms of historical period but also in their literary style and mode of theatrical performance. In their variety of topics as well as their dramaturgic structure, they are representative examples of German drama in the decade under consideration. At its beginning, many dramatists were probing new frontiers within their respective societies of West and East Germany; Seidel's and Strauss's plays are from that time. After the Berlin Wall came down and the two German states were united, playwrights faced a completely new set of issues, issues of an urgency more burning than probably anything the German theater had to respond to during the forty years of the nation's partition. Some authors reacted quickly and aggressively, as Müller and Pohl demonstrate. Others, like Dorst, shrouded their response in metaphor. Others, again, were compelled to conjure a past when Germans either dreamt of an all-powerful Reich or refused to accept the Reich's demise, as Tabori and Jelinek let us see.

The diversity of content and form, the potential for performance in the American theater, and whether the prevailing issues of contemporary German theater are dealt with—these were the criteria that guided the play selections for the anthology. The volume offers a sampling of German drama that will, I hope, entice the reader to explore further the work of these and other contemporary playwrights. The collection is especially meant for the directors and dramaturgs of American regional theaters and university stages, where such plays have had and will have their chance for performance, a chance the texts surely deserve.

DRAMACONTEMPORARY

Germany

The Tour Guide

BOTHO STRAUSS

●

Translated by Carl Weber

Editor's Note

•

The Tour Guide (Die Fremdenführerin) was first performed at the Schaubühne am Lehninerplatz in Berlin on February 15, 1986.

In its opening scenes, the play appears to be a light-hearted comedy about the affair that a middle-aged teacher starts, during his sabbatical in Greece, with a young woman, a drifter who occasionally works as a tour guide. Quickly, the generational conflict moves to the fore, the incompatibility between the former student rebel of 1968, who is trying to cope with a midlife crisis, and his lover, who was barely born at a time when the teacher was embracing the idea of an enlightened progressive society.

Eventually, the plot takes a much more ominous turn. The teacher's apprehensive question: "Tour guide, whereto are you guiding me?" signals that "the play is a great game of questions. The answers are up to the spectator," as critic Rolf Michaelis has written. The tour guide leads her lover into a realm where love becomes a harrowing mythical ritual—a Strindbergian dance of death, if you will—until she dances away while he stays and seems to melt into the sun-baked primeval landscape where Pan reigns supreme.

Greece has exerted a strong attraction on German intellectuals and poets since the eighteenth century, when German classicism constructed its idealistic concept of ancient Greek culture. Classic Greek is still taught at many of the German high schools that bear the Greek name *gymnasium,* and the Mediterranean country remains a favorite of German tourists. It is an appropriate location for the encounter between Strauss's protagonists, who represent two generations that grew up as children of the postwar West German republic.

Luc Bondy, a friend of Strauss who has directed many of his plays, called the poet/playwright, in a 1989 speech, "a diagnostician of the present-day Federal Republic" and "a shy poet who keeps the monstrous in his view." There is, indeed, no other playwright who has presented onstage the West German middle class with comparable insight, precision, and recognition of their darker impulses. His tour guide, Kristina, at first appears to be a typical child of what Strauss once scathingly condemned as "this prevalent, goddamned fuck-and-throwaway society." However, she increasingly appears to resemble the incarnation of an ancient goddess, a playmate of Pan who

3

bewitches the intellectual Martin at a time when he arrives at his wit's—and Enlightenment's—end. In the play's final moment, while Martin is reading the tale of Pan and of the nymph, Syrinx, from Ovid's *Metamorphoses,* the spectator will remember an earlier scene when Kristina asks who was that frightening Pan-like apparition in the window and Martin enigmatically replies: "I." Have ancient Gods transformed him, also, into a being from another, primeval realm? The play poses many such riddles, while it raises issues of identity, perception, and the mysteries humans encounter when they truly "fall" in love.

Botho Strauss was born in 1944. He studied literature and sociology at Cologne and Munich universities. In 1967, he became a theater critic and editor for the journal *Theater Heute.* Strauss joined Peter Stein and his group of young actors when, in 1970, they established Germany's foremost experimental company at the Berlin Schaubühne. With Stein, he adapted plays by Labiche and Gorky for the group. The first of his own plays, *The Hypochondriacs,* was premiered at Hamburg Schauspielhaus in 1972. Since then, twelve more plays, many of them staged at the Schaubühne by Stein or Bondy, have established Strauss as the dramatist who captures the culture and lifestyles of West Germans more perceptively than anyone else.

Although several of Strauss's texts might be called realistic, they usually transcend realism's restrictions and explore in bold metaphors a territory where the mythic and the subconscious invade quotidian life. A number of his plays have been translated and internationally performed, foremost among them *Trilogy of a Reunion, Big and Little, The Park,* and *Time and the Room.* Strauss also has published several volumes of poetry and prose. Although during the 1970s he belonged to the left-leaning collective of the Schaubühne, he has moved since German unification toward an increasingly right-of-center, conservative position. Strauss has been living in Berlin since the 1960s.

Carl Weber

The Tour Guide

CHARACTERS

The Tour Guide
The Teacher
A Young Man
A Woman
A Tourist Couple

●

Act I

1

In the stadium of Olympia. Enter KRISTINA, *a young woman, the tour guide with her plastic ID badge pinned to the breast pocket of her blouse;* MARTIN, *approximately forty-five years of age.*

KRISTINA: Take a look if anyone else is coming.

MARTIN [*Looking back into the entranceway*]: No. No one else.

KRISTINA: Well. At the end of our tour we have arrived at the stadium of Olympia, spread out in front of us. For the people of classic antiquity, this site was the incarnation of the greatest glory. Not only were the Olympic Games referred to by the name of the athletes who won the races here—and who in that way entered the official account of historic events—but their glory was so elevated as to make them equal to the immortal gods.

Notice, first of all, the striking simplicity of the entire structure. You'll see how harmoniously it has been adapted to its natural environment. The slopes on all sides were created by the heaping up of enormous amounts of earth, and they served as grandstands for the spectators.

Notice the lack of any accommodations for seating—like, for instance, the stone steps you may know from other comparable sites for festive events. The stadium could accommodate up to forty thousand spectators, and a terrible pushing and shoving on the embankments must have been the rule at times. The games were held every four years, regularly, in the summer, during the dog days. This was done for ritual reasons, since the Olympic Games evolved from religious rites in honor of the God Zeus Olympios. So, it was incredibly hot. The wearing of any headgear wasn't allowed because of the obstruction of sight. You may well imagine that those five festive days of Olympia were also the cause of considerable hardship for some of the spectators.

It also should be mentioned that women were not admitted to the games, either as spectators or as athletes. Their presence at the festival site was even punishable by death. The only married woman attending the games was the priestess of Demeter. You see down there on the left, at the foot of the northern embankment, the remnants of a marble pedestal that used to be her seat. Right across from it on the southern wall you can recognize the remnants of the rostrum for the umpires. These were the only other seats in the stadium; they were occupied by the ten or twelve jurors.

Right before us—if you would step a bit closer—you can observe the well-preserved parts of the western winning post. The single stadium race, the oldest and most important Olympic discipline, started in the east, and the racers ran toward the holy precinct. The length of the track amounts to 630 feet and 10 inches, precisely. That was a standard measurement, one stadium, the length of a single stadium race. The double race was done in reverse direction and measured two stadia, once each way. That approximates our modern 440-yard dash. For this race the winning post served as the starting point. You can clearly see notched into the limestone plate the furrows that supported the racers' feet at the start.

The racers entered the contest naked. At the start they stood on the plate slightly bent forward, arms raised in front [*She demonstrates*], the posterior foot flat on the ground, the anterior slightly lifted at the heel. Today's familiar crouching start position wasn't yet known in those days. The start signal was given by a trumpet call. An early start was punished by a lash with the rod. The winner was he who first passed the winning post. Running time records were not taken.

MARTIN: By what means, after all?

KRISTINA: Besides the two short-distance races, there was, as the only long-distance race, the one of twenty-four stadia; that's approximately our five-thousand-yard race.

MARTIN: The only long distance, you mean, besides the marathon?

KRISTINA: The marathon race wasn't known in antiquity. The marathon is a modern contest. If you have any further questions, I'd be pleased to answer them later. The ancient spirit of sports attained its highest level of development with the creation of the so-called pentathlon. A high degree of technical skill as well as great strength, stamina, and speed were required for it. The five events included the disciplines of discus throw, broad jump, and javelin throw. Then there were the contests in the single stadium race and in wrestling.

MARTIN: Excuse me—You don't need to talk as if there were an audience. I'm only a single person. Not so loud. Do you understand?

KRISTINA: Yes, I will . . . There remains to be mentioned . . . Well, we were talking about the pentathlon—

MARTIN: It would be of interest to me, for instance: Were there also spiritual contests at Olympia? I mean, those competitions of bards and poets, like in Delphi or Athens?

KRISTINA: Spiritual contests, you mean . . . That's a question I can't answer right now. My . . . my brother could easily answer your question. He is an archeologist, you know. I'm doing this only pro tem. Because he's sick right now.

MARTIN: You're still a student?

KRISTINA: Not I, no.

MARTIN: What are you doing, if I may ask?

KRISTINA: I? Well, that depends. I'm a goldsmith by training.

MARTIN: Goldsmith. That's nice. Excuse me, I didn't want to embarrass you.

KRISTINA: No. You don't. I'm telling you: I've got to make money. [*Pause*] What do you think of the Greeks now, after you have done the guided tour?

MARTIN: What do I think? Oh, I think the Greeks were consumed by their greed for glory. I think many of them were exceedingly vain and arrogant people. Unbearable braggarts.

KRISTINA: You think so? Maybe I've given you the wrong impression.

MARTIN: Oh, you can read that in Plutarch.

KRISTINA: Where could I read that, please?

MARTIN: Plutarch. About great men.

KRISTINA: Did he write about the games?

MARTIN: You just have given me a long lecture on Olympia, you know something interesting about nearly every single stone here. You don't want to ask me now who Plutarch was, do you?

KRISTINA [*Laughs*]: I really don't know him!

MARTIN: I had a pupil in my class who passed his final exam with an A− average. But Mörike was to him only the name of a street.

KRISTINA: What about it? You're a teacher?

MARTIN: Of course I'm a teacher. Of course. What else should I be?

KRISTINA: I thought so. Teachers always ask these typical questions during the tour.

MARTIN: That isn't all. They also smell of floor polish all the time. They're always on vacation and drink too much cheap Provençal wine. Wait. I've got to sit down for a moment. I feel a bit weak in the knees. Probably the quick change of climate. I arrived only yesterday.

KRISTINA: As long as you can dance at night, I don't care how drunk you are.

MARTIN: I'm not drunk. Why? Where can you dance around here?

KRISTINA: Oh, you can dance all night if you care to.

MARTIN: It's rather hot. Don't you think so?

KRISTINA: Think about it. It will get much hotter. It's only early May. So. Do you want to hear about the pentathlon now?

2

Room in a vacation bungalow, viewed from the front garden through the open glass windows of the house. Morning. MARTIN, *half dressed, is sitting on the edge of the bed.* KRISTINA *stands before him.*

MARTIN: You're coming back?

KRISTINA: I don't know. Maybe. Can I use the telephone? [*She dials*] Hello. It's me . . . No . . . I'll tell you later. Fine, then go on sleeping. [*She hangs up*] I've met someone, you know. I think, I'm terribly in love.

MARTIN: Yes?

KRISTINA: Could be, this will turn into a long and difficult affair. That's what I'm afraid of.

MARTIN: Why do you think it will be difficult?

KRISTINA: Because he is a very difficult person. A very dear one.

MARTIN: Of whom are you talking?

KRISTINA: He is looking through all of us. He has, as the only one from our side, looked behind it all once more. What's behind that being human.

MARTIN: How can you sleep with me when you're in love with someone else?

KRISTINA: That's got to do with him. I can't explain it to you.

MARTIN: I don't believe there is this other person. Or else you're talking about me.

KRISTINA: I must go. Goodbye, teacher.

MARTIN: Can't you stay, only for this one day?

KRISTINA: Don't pressure me. Please. It's all still so new to me. We're still so new to each other.

MARTIN: Who?!

KRISTINA: Don't scream. I liked it with you. It was good the way it was.

MARTIN: You're cold. You're very careless.

KRISTINA: You can't say that. You don't know that. I'm not cold . . . I don't want to hear that anymore . . . I'm not cold when I'm really opening myself to another person.

MARTIN: Didn't you embrace me? Didn't you want me?

KRISTINA: But I don't know you at all!

MARTIN: Go! . . . Come back!

3

Same place. Several days later. KRISTINA *comes through the front garden.*

MARTIN: Hey, tour guide. How's life treating you? Are you looking again for someone to dance with?

KRISTINA: Life is round. Wherever you are, you're slipping off. Can I take a bath at your house? [*Pause*] I thought you wanted to see me again.

MARTIN: Don't talk so carelessly, Kristina.

KRISTINA: I—careless? How can you say such a thing?

MARTIN: Where have you been? Haven't you done any guided tours lately?

KRISTINA: No. I couldn't get away. I can't go on. I have no strength left.

MARTIN: You were with him, all the time?

KRISTINA: He's in very bad shape. The doctor came. He's trembling. He can hold a glass only with both hands, his mouth is always dry. He's had his life. There is nothing funny about someone who's come to the end. He's drinking. He's sick. And I can't help him. [*She cries*] He's still so young. He's a genius. He could do anything. He speaks six languages fluently. He knows whole books by heart. He's an archeologist. He always did the guided tours I'm doing now.

MARTIN: Didn't you say: your brother—?

KRISTINA: Yes. It wasn't true. It's he. Can I use your phone?

MARTIN: Please don't. Look at me. Be careful. You've got to be more careful with people.

KRISTINA: I am. I am careful. Very much so. [*Pause*]

MARTIN: Why did you come back?

KRISTINA: I'd like to know you better. You made me curious. I sensed so much understanding the first time, so much warmth.

MARTIN: Listen. I am, myself, in pretty poor shape. I'm not at all interested in playing cat and mouse with a nosey girl. I've come here to arrive at a decision. I've had some quite unpleasant times lately.

KRISTINA: A separation?

MARTIN: No.

KRISTINA: Oh, well. I'm also going through something like that right now. The man I'm living with drinks.

MARTIN: I thought you'd just fallen in love?

KRISTINA: I *am* in love! But I must get out of it again. It, anyway, doesn't work. He's destroying me and himself. There isn't much you can do. You watch how someone is killing himself, slowly but surely.

MARTIN: Even at the risk of boring you, my case is different. The problem is, Shall I go back to my school or not? Do I want to continue teaching or not?

KRISTINA: Ah, a teacher. That's what you are!

MARTIN: You've already forgotten?

KRISTINA: No, I haven't forgotten. I only thought . . . is it vacation now?

MARTIN: I've taken half a year off to think about it.

KRISTINA: What do you teach?

MARTIN: French and history.

KRISTINA: Do you enjoy it?

MARTIN: Do I enjoy it? Ha! There it is again, that dreary magic word! School is supposed to be enjoyable, teaching *must* be enjoyable. Joy, that's what I'm supposed to offer when I meet my class! Should I provide more joy, so that a seventeen-year-old doesn't try the second time to jump from the tenth floor? What am I supposed to do! *Whereto* am I educating my kids? For what kind of a world, against which world? I don't know it anymore. We're trying to *talk* them out of their despair. But there is no life without despair, and we haven't learned to console anyone.

KRISTINA: Yes, there's a lot to sort out. My, my. How true it is. You've told yourself, let's first take a break, so I can think before I'm going to lose it all. I like that.

MARTIN: To be reasonable! Reasonable. Yes, I hold onto that. I won't give an inch. I love argument and I hate punishment. All right, then. Because a number of things went wrong for me, I thought, why not go to the sources for a while, to the place where the world of our ideas came into being. Where everything was serene and sincere when it all began. In harmony. Reasonable. Simply experience the sources, experience the elements.

KRISTINA: I believe that, with you, I could succeed in achieving it, a real deep understanding, a mature and mutual appreciation. That's actually a very old wish I have had since childhood. I'd really like to use the phone—

MARTIN: Kristina, just a moment. What do you want from me?

KRISTINA: Would you run a bath for me?

MARTIN: What is behind all this? You're not interested in me. You're using me for something, something I don't see through.

KRISTINA: Give me some time, teacher. I'll come to you. Only not now, not right away. I am very sure that one day I'll belong to you. Wait for me. I'll come for sure.

KRISTINA, *in front garden, squatting next to* HER FRIEND, *who lies motionless on the ground. An embroidered bag hangs from his shoulder.*

MARTIN [*Stepping from the house*]: What are you doing here? Why do you drag the guy right in front of my house?

KRISTINA: I didn't drag him here. I wanted to see you. He ran after me.

MARTIN: Wake him up. Send him away.

KRISTINA: He can't. He's too far gone. Help me. We'll carry him into the bed.

MARTIN: Into which bed? No, Kristin, you can't be serious . . . You want to put your filthy Bacchus into my bed?

KRISTINA: Don't mock me! Take another route! He is beautiful. He's such a beautiful person. You have no idea what's whizzing through his mind, what he's hitting upon, what kind of ideas, when he is free and rising high. Really great, really great. Even if it's hard to endure. A head like a universe. He raises his arms high, and you're raised with them, if you want to or don't. But suddenly he's full. Suddenly he keels over, in the midst of the stream of things. Vassily, they love you because you are a poor giant. A cracked one. A giant whom one would like to protect, of course. Why is everything so easy for him? Nothing ever happens to him. He fails, forgets, betrays, neglects himself and others, he lies, he talks himself out of tight corners, he loves himself out of them. Everyone wants him, but I've got him. Women are buzzing around him, men and children, even the animals flock to him, they're purring, whimpering, scratching, and cackling, all the creatures turn docile when he appears, all the creatures lose their pride. Their indifference. Their callousness.

MARTIN: Your friend is sick. That's all. One of the many who have caught it. One of the many who are young and can't find anything to hold onto.

KRISTINA: Yes, he's sick. There he lies, and I must hold him.

MARTIN: It seems to me the picture is deceptive. In truth, it's rather you who are lying at his feet. You're obsessed with him.

KRISTINA: Stupid.

MARTIN: Don't say stupid to me.

KRISTINA: I help anyone who's down and out. I have learned that, holding a person's head when he's going to puke. If I don't feel pity for someone, I can't love him. I don't love what's strong; I love someone for what he can't help.

MARTIN: If you're so sure of that, then leave me in peace, please. I am not here as a nesting place for other people's passions.

KRISTINA: The way you always control yourself! Don't you ever make small mistakes? Don't you ever fall into the shit, too?

MARTIN: Get out of here. Both of you.

KRISTINA: All right, all right! I'm going. I'll drag him home all by myself. He can't stay here on the ground. It'll be cold soon.

[MARTIN *watches* KRISTINA *for a moment. Then he walks up to her and grabs her shoulders.*]

MARTIN: Listen, little person! I've had it with these young idiots who do everything possible to plunge themselves and others into misery. I've had it with you! I didn't come here to get myself entangled in another dismal affair.

KRISTINA: Don't worry. In the end I'll break with him. I've got to. Plain as hell. And I know that I'll pull it off, too.

MARTIN: You know nothing. You don't even notice the way you're cheating yourself. You completely depend on him. You haven't any will of your own left anymore.

KRISTINA: But I've got to help him! Someone has to help him. The restlessness, this horrible restlessness that's tearing him to shreds. He can't bear it that the earth turns. That round-and-round of the earth, that down-and-above of the sun. He can't step any longer in front of people and say, "Listen to me, this was earlier and that was later, this was the Greeks, that the Romans." He's knocking down everything. He can't do the tours anymore.

MARTIN: Why doesn't his family take care of him.

KRISTINA: But they do. What should they do? He's the son of a conductor.

MARTIN: What?

KRISTINA: Conductor. Someone who conducts an orchestra. [*She demonstrates with her arms*] The chief conductor of an orchestra, I believe.

MARTIN: All right. It's late, Kristin. I'd like to take a brief walk to the village.

KRISTINA: First we have to put him to bed.

MARTIN: Are you trying to fool me? Don't you realize that you're going a bit too far? Are you expecting me to sleep next to your drunk lover in my own bed? Or what is it you're thinking?

KRISTINA: You can come to my place, if you'd like to.

5

Next morning. Behind the glass window, VASSILY *nearly naked, sits on the edge of the bed. He rummages in his bag and pulls out cigarettes and a small liquor bottle.* KRISTINA *enters the front garden. Vassily gets up and steps to the window. Kristina moves both her palms across the glass and slides slowly down into a kneeling position.*

6

Later, inside the house. VASSILY *disappears into the bathroom.* KRISTINA *comes out from it with his washed clothes and lays them out on a chair, outside. Not knowing what else to do, she picks up the phone and dials.*

KRISTINA: Hello? It's me, Kristina . . . No, I just wanted to say hello. How are you anyway? . . . Fine, fine. Tell me, is Antonio there? Hm . . . I understand . . . I'll call . . . I'll call again, later. No, that's all right. Give him my regards. [*She immediately dials another number*] Lisa? [*In Greek*]: Can I talk to Elizabeth, please? [*She waits; then again in English*] Well? . . . As long as you can't explain to me the way you behaved?—I'll remain un-ad-dressable—I guess . . . Yes, good enough. *I* have called you, that's right. I thought I might hear something new. A mistake. What a pity . . . Oh, stop it! I can't hear that bull anymore! You know well enough that in such a situation he . . . But Vassily himself told me that! . . . Hm. Thanks a lot. Same here. [*She throws the receiver down*] Crow. [*Dials again. She speaks Greek.*] Yes, this is Kristina Richter. I'd like to make an appointment with Dr. . . . Next week? When? . . . Friday, 3 PM? Thanks. [*Dials again. No answer. She looks at her wristwatch. The entrance door opens.* MARTIN *enters.*]

MARTIN: Kristin! I was looking for you everywhere . . . Where have you been?

KRISTINA: You were still asleep when I left.

MARTIN [*Approaches* KRISTINA, *embraces her*]: Oh my love, I missed you . . .

KRISTINA: I missed you too.

MARTIN: But I wanted to wake up beside you. Kiss your hair, your shoulder . . .

KRISTINA: I thought I'd be someone who makes you happy and then disappears very quickly. Only once touch for real, and you'd be glad for a long time.

MARTIN: I am glad. Very glad. Because now the story of Martin and Kristin begins. Irrevocably. Too late now to think of anything else.

KRISTINA: I don't want to mourn, I don't want to weep. Do you understand?

MARTIN: Why are you saying that?

KRISTINA: I've had the experience, after all, that you can hurt yourself very badly.

MARTIN: You are Kristina, with whom I'd like to walk a long way.

KRISTINA: But who am I really?

MARTIN: You are this one and that one. Your are the one, the other, and the third one. You won't ask more precisely about it anymore. After all, one wants to give everything of oneself, one wants very slowly to become no one.

KRISTINA: Or one loves until one is empty. Then it will be bad.

MARTIN: Why are you talking with so little courage? Have you forgotten what happened?

KRISTINA: I haven't forgotten anything. But I do believe it has a very different meaning for me than it has for you.

MARTIN: Listen to me: I'm more than twenty years older than you are. Many a person would grab his head and say, "this can never go well. The affair at Olympia, well yes, nothing more," and that would be all there was to it. If experience and reason alone had their say. Only, there is an argument against this: I've never had affairs and will never have any.

KRISTINA: But you never know that.

MARTIN [*Turns and moves toward the bathroom*]: I do know it.

KRISTINA: Don't get upset—Vassily is just taking a bath.

MARTIN: Who's taking . . .

KRISTINA: But he was here . . . you knew that, didn't you?

MARTIN: Have you gone out of your mind, Kristina?

KRISTINA: I don't know what's wrong with you.

MARTIN: You're meeting him in my house. Are you mean? Are you bad? My God! What are you doing? Kick him out. Right away. Did you hear me?!

KRISTINA [*Meekly*]: Yes.

[MARTIN *goes outside, picks up the clothes of the young man, throws them at* KRISTINA]

KRISTINA: But you're free to use everything at my house, too, everything I have. I don't understand you.

7

Early morning. KRISTINA *sleeps on the grass in front of the window. The curtains are closed. Kristina wakes up, knocks on the windowpane.*

KRISTINA: Martin! Martin! Get up! Get up. [*She goes back to sleep again*]

8

The window curtains are open. KRISTINA *is encamped on the grass. She drinks through a straw from a paper bag.* MARTIN *steps through the door.*

MARTIN: What do you want?
KRISTINA: I've slept here. That's all. No one . . . Why don't you let me be with you? I have no idea where I should go.
MARTIN: Go away. Scram.
KRISTINA: I've got to talk to you.
MARTIN: Get a move on! [*He picks up a stone or a tuft of grass*]
KRISTINA: You're crazy! I'm not a dog! [*She ambles off*]

9

Night. KRISTINA *is sitting on the roof of the house and reading a book in the moonlight. Below,* MARTIN *stands in the room, at the window, smoking.*

10

Noon. MARTIN, *in the window.* KRISTINA's *camping spot is littered with remnants of meals and other utensils. She is trying to push a letter through a crack of the door. She doesn't succeed.*

KRISTINA: Just a letter! Just a letter! I've written you a letter so you won't misunderstand. So you know what to make of it. Take it, please . . .

[MARTIN *remains motionless.* KRISTINA *gets a small jar of honey, unfolds the letter, and sticks it to the window pane. Then she leaves.*]

11

Inside the house. KRISTINA *presents* MARTIN *with a small bunch of choco-lates shaped like flowers.*

KRISTINA: A hundred years of happiness!
MARTIN: Thanks. How pretty. Today, *you* are happy. So mellowed . . .
KRISTINA: Yes. I am quite happy.

MARTIN: Everything changes so rapidly. I can't quite grasp it. What's happening to me? How easily I'm saying thanks . . . Have I lost my conscience already to the degree that I don't resist you anymore? The constant one who's cracking . . . The clear beauty of an argument . . . effaced. Effaced tracks, effaced faces, an effaced story.

KRISTINA: We've got time. Plenty of time. We can think about everything in peace and quiet.

MARTIN: Tour guide, whereto are you guiding me?

KRISTINA: You've got to trust me. Then everything will be easy. Give me your hand. We've made quite a bit of progress, Vassily and I. Now I know that I'll be able to break with him. And he, too, knows that it will happen. Now it's like a slow, fatal bleeding.

MARTIN: That is good for you, Kristin.

KRISTINA: Yes. It is good. But it's very sad, too. I am in great fear that suddenly I'm all alone.

MARTIN: Haven't you ever lived alone?

KRISTINA: No. Not really. There was always someone.

MARTIN: You see. You're spoiled, a lightweight.

KRISTINA: I left home early. I moved in with a friend when I was still at school.

MARTIN: How old were you?

KRISTINA: Fourteen, when it started. We lived together for more than three years, after all.

MARTIN: Like husband and wife . . .

KRISTINA: Oh, well. I never wanted what he wanted. It was very uncomfortable, too. I did it only because of the boy. Him I liked very much. I was still quite little, after all. You know—the story with Vassily has still another catch. He has to go to a hospital right away. That is to say, he has to go back to Germany right away. He can't go on like this. He knows that, too. But we need the money for the plane fare, and we don't have it. I have to scratch up something like one thousand marks at once.

MARTIN: H'm.

KRISTINA: At the moment, I've no idea how I'd do that.

MARTIN: You mean, I should buy myself your separation?

KRISTINA: How can you say such a thing? How can anyone be so mean-spirited.

MARTIN: Maybe you should try imagining yourself in my situation, for once. Who, in the final analysis, is sitting here next to me? First of all, nothing but a small stray person who comes and goes and comes back at her whim. But I, I don't know for the life of me: What is she trying to do to me?

17

KRISTINA: You don't know? You don't know? After all that has happened, you don't know? A sorry result. I'm tearing myself apart, I really feel myself torn to pieces, I don't know anymore where I belong, and you talk to me in such a rude manner . . . so undignified! A stray person! Do you want to hurt me? I'd better leave, then, right away.

MARTIN: Stay!

KRISTINA: You're not a teacher. You are a disgusting pedant. A moralizing zealot. Without any active compassion. Without any serious concern for other human beings.

MARTIN: Kristin, please, stay! I can get the money cabled. I can write you a check. What would you like?

KRISTINA: A check. You really ought to try and think about what this means to me: I come here and I'm in dire need, I'm begging money from you, from you, whom I'd rather embrace, whom I'd like to approach in a totally straightforward manner, and you're doing everything to make me feel ashamed.

MARTIN: You don't need to be ashamed, my love. You should only make a definite decision about what you want and what you don't want.

KRISTINA: Without much ado, it will become very clear what I want and what I don't want. Anyway, it's all merely accidental. We've met by sheer accident. By sheer accident, something has happened between us. It's accidental what you learn and what you forget. Wanting something only destroys the accident.

MARTIN: It's too bad. I love you and I can't connect with you. You don't understand me. Or you do understand me and won't take anything to heart.

KRISTINA: You don't love me. You want to make me a terribly better person than I am. You don't love me, you just want to improve me. But you won't improve me. [*She takes the check, puts it on the bedside table, takes off her wristwatch and puts it on top of it*] Because I am not a lightweight. That is what keeps spinning in my mind, that you said to me: "Listen, you lightweight!" But I'm nothing of the kind. [*She stretches out on the bed*] I only have to be careful that I'm doing things that make sense. I've got to make a blot somewhere than no one can simply ignore. Something people can't simply forget and proceed to other current matters. I once used to attend the art academy, too. Originally, I wanted to study carpet weaving. But that's an art without any future. I know someone who has been weaving tapestries for fifteen years, beautiful patterns, really quite exquisite and valuable, and he has sold only two of these gigantic pieces, two pieces, in fifteen years. But he is a madman and works the night shift as a proofreader for a paper. I'm not really mad, you know. I'd very much like to do something important that'll open your eyes. That'll bowl you over. And I could do it, too; I'm just not mad enough.

12

Night. In front of the house. A WOMAN *appears. Knocks several times at the window.* KRISTINA *sits up in the bed. She pulls on jeans and a shirt, steps outside.*

KRISTINA: Is something wrong with Vassily? [*The* WOMAN *nods. They both run off.*]

13

In the stadium of Olympia. KRISTINA *is conducting a tour for one lonely tourist* COUPLE. MARTIN *enters. She abruptly leaves her clients and runs to him.*

KRISTINA: How nice of you to come. I really wanted to see you today.
MARTIN: I've come to ask you a question. I have thought about . . . I really wanted to leave. Even yesterday.
KRISTINA: Why?
MARTIN: I don't know . . . Come with me, Kristin.
KRISTINA [*Takes a step backward*]: I can't.
MARTIN: Is it because of the boy?
KRISTINA: His sister has arrived from Athens. She's taking care of him.
MARTIN: I see. Of course. So he didn't take the plane to Germany after all?
KRISTINA: Not now. Later. I can do these tours again. I don't need to be around him all the time.
MARTIN: At home I could take care of you. I could help you to find a real occupation. An independent job . . .
KRISTINA: I'm not interested in occupations, Martin.
MARTIN: And what are you interested in?
KRISTINA: What am I interested in? My imagination. My legs. My wholeness.
MARTIN: You're still very young.
KRISTINA: With my legs, I can hold someone tight and I can run away. You should be grateful to Zeus Olympios that you've met me. What would you be doing here all alone in a place far from home if you hadn't met me?

MARTIN: I'd be lying on my hotel bed staring at the ceiling, as I have done many times. I'd slowly disappear into an empty, white space. Probably I'd be somewhat unhappy.

KRISTINA: You'd be very unhappy.

MARTIN: But now I'm dissatisfied. That's much worse to bear. A second human being always creates excessive expectations.

KRISTINA: Isn't that a good thing?

MARTIN: Why have you been squatting before my house for nights on end? Why did you crawl into my bed? What is this kind of yes-and-no story? Whenever I take a step toward you, you retreat. When I retreat, you come closer.

KRISTINA: That's nearly like dancing, isn't it?

MARTIN: And that's the way it's supposed to continue?

KRISTINA: I don't know. Don't keep asking so much. Don't keep talking so much. It will become clear. Everything will become clear. Quite by itself.

MARTIN: But tell me what I should do!

KRISTINA: Why don't you wait?

MARTIN: Because I know for sure now: I want to leave and I want to take you with me.

KRISTINA: It's not possible now.

MARTIN: You could follow me, a bit later.

KRISTINA: No, Martin. I believe I won't come.

MARTIN: But if I'm absolutely sure of it! Why is it that I'm suddenly so damned sure?

KRISTINA: Will you go back to your school?

MARTIN: I can't. I can't.

KRISTINA: It's all because the three riders didn't arrive.

MARTIN: The three riders didn't arrive?

KRISTINA: It's because the end didn't happen. We had reckoned with the end, Vassily and I.

MARTIN: Oh, no! Let us quickly walk away from each other. We need to be separated, right away.

KRISTINA: You don't want to anymore? Ah! Not a story, only an affair after all? How petty.

MARTIN: What are you saying?

KRISTINA: There wasn't much you were able to do with me. Right?

MARTIN: Take care . . .

KRISTINA: You're going to hurt me?

MARTIN: Are you afraid?

KRISTINA: I'm not afraid of anything.

MARTIN: I can't go on haggling with you.

KRISTINA: Perhaps I've just stolen a bit of your time? I could have given you much more, so much more, if only you had accepted me.

MARTIN: But you didn't want it!

KRISTINA: I do want it. I do. One only has to take me truly seriously.

MARTIN: You want it and then again you don't want it. That's the truth.

KRISTINA: Don't you understand? This is no child's play. I've simply not yet discovered what I'm made of.

MARTIN: What you're made for, you mean?

KRISTINA: I'm making it difficult for myself . . .

MARTIN: I'll explain it for you: You're looking for total, blind dependence. You're not looking for a love that opens your eyes, a love between two clearly defined, self-assured human beings.

KRISTINA: Is there such a thing?

MARTIN: You will see. One simply cannot live according to one's whims and appetites. One day you'll stand there empty and without any form. Made mindless by your emotions. But every human life has to attain some kind of form, sooner or later. Of course, you've got to be careful that it won't turn out too small and narrow.

KRISTINA: You want to educate me? Please, start now!

MARTIN: How should I do that?

KRISTINA: Oh, there would be lots to do, and I wouldn't get tired of asking questions. I wouldn't get bored with you, because I'll hear a lot I'd like to take to heart.

MARTIN: No butterfly is aware of her own color. You are that what's happening to you. Pure coercion.

KRISTINA: No, tell me honestly: am I not too insignificant for you?

MARTIN: You're exhausting.

KRISTINA: You're exhausting.

14

In Martin's bungalow. MARTIN *opens the door because someone has knocked.* KRISTINA *enters and leans against the wall.*

MARTIN: Where are you coming from?

KRISTINA: Let me think. [*She presses her hand against her lips*]

MARTIN: What's the matter with you? Say something!

KRISTINA: I have to bring him his stuff . . . his razor and such.

MARTIN: There's nothing of his left here.

KRISTINA: No? Where could it be? Let me look . . . [*She rummages through a drawer*]

MARTIN: What are you looking for?

KRISTINA: There is something I didn't understand . . . Something he said I didn't understand. We wanted to go on a trip to Didyma, in Turkey. Everything had been readied. He wanted to see the newly discovered temple inscriptions that are so famous, a sensation . . . But that wasn't what he finally said. There was something he said at the end . . .

MARTIN: What are you talking about? Kristin! Do you hear me?

KRISTINA: It's my fault. I knew it; that he wouldn't pull through. I knew it for sure, that this time he wouldn't make it. It's my fault. I couldn't stop him.

MARTIN: When . . . when did it happen?

KRISTINA: He simply didn't get up anymore. He drank himself across to the other side. That was it. That was all. Sleep with me. Please. Now!

MARTIN: But that isn't possible . . .

KRISTINA: What are you doing? You don't want to? You don't want it?

MARTIN: Calm down. Be reasonable!

KRISTINA: Reasonable? Are you mad? Do you know what has happened to me? I'm waking up with a corpse! And I'm supposed to be reasonable?!

MARTIN: You're mourning, after all! You mustn't be so horrid . . .

KRISTINA: You know nothing nothing nothing!

MARTIN: Have you informed his parents?

KRISTINA: I want to feel you! I'm cold!

MARTIN: My dear—my dear little figure . . . you don't need to blame your-self. It's none of your fault. You see, he really was an unhappy boy, nobody could have stopped him. A young human being who had gone wide and far and still had to return home without having achieved any-thing, before he could fully force open the door to his life. You were at his side. You've endured with him in the darkness.

KRISTINA: My God! How do you talk to me? If that's all . . . If that's all there is.

MARTIN: What am I doing wrong? I'm trying to calm you down.

KRISTINA: Now, there's only you and me. I don't know who you really are. Perhaps only a braggart or a cheat. Perhaps a monster . . . but my man, my man.

MARTIN: One has to be credible. Everything depends on it. We have to become credible to each other. That won't come easy. There were too many truths already that have changed between us. How shall I know in what I can put my trust. Certainly not in words. The whole human being must talk to me . . . That's what it's like, if you look at it in broad daylight.

KRISTINA: And what's going to happen now?

MARTIN: That is, in broad daylight you don't see these things at all, of course . . .

Act II

A room in a primitive mountain cabin. A window in the back wall. Stage left, an entrance without a door. Stage right, the passage to another, smaller room. An old chair.

1

MARTIN *and* KRISTINA. *Their traveling bags are next to the chair.*

MARTIN: You see? This is it. A very small, a very poor house. Over there is a small room for sleeping, and here this single room. What do you think?

KRISTINA: Yes. I like it. Is there a phone?

MARTIN: No. No telephone.

KRISTINA: Ah!

MARTIN: Besides, it's very hot. The house has no protection from the sun. A few olive trees, out there; they provide little shade. Nothing else.

KRISTINA: I think the window is beautiful.

MARTIN: You can't see a thing. It's completely covered with filth.

KRISTINA: What kind of filth is it? It's beautiful.

MARTIN: I don't know. I'll take it down. [*He opens the window, wrenches the shutters loose, and puts them on the ground outside*]

KRISTINA: Is this a shepherd's house?

MARTIN: Maybe.

KRISTINA: It's very primitive.

MARTIN: That's why it's considerably cheaper than the previous one. There's no electricity. No running water. [*He steps into the other room*] It smells of old engine oil. Everywhere. [*He rummages about*] Aha! There's water only in the tank outside . . .

[KRISTINA *faces the wall and props herself against it with outstretched arms.* MARTIN *comes back.*]

MARTIN: What do you think? Shall we stay here?

KRISTINA [*Turns around, leans her back against the wall*]: Come!

23

[*Signal of time, light break. The calls of Pan and boomeranging voices; a whirling echo of sentences that Martin and Kristina have exchanged during the scene. The sound comes closer, enters the space, and moves away again.*]

2

MARTIN *squats.* KRISTINA *squats.*

KRISTINA: There's something within me that doesn't want to begin.

MARTIN: Begin with me?

KRISTINA: Begin with the task of clearing the past.

MARTIN: "Mourn out." Mourn out. That's what you wanted to do with this story. Like others fast for a week or cleanse their system.

KRISTINA: I'm made of him. Still. I'll remain made of him. Perhaps. I don't feel any grief.

MARTIN: The earth isn't turning only around your feelings, little person. There are also conventions one observes, so as to make life easier for oneself and other people.

KRISTINA: Oh, you know, other people have other worries.

MARTIN: You didn't even think of going to his funeral?

KRISTINA: To Germany? With what? I didn't know him that well, after all. And his family. How would you picture that, exactly? And he also is still living within me. I really don't know why you have to keep tutoring me.

MARTIN: One cannot make all decisions for a lifetime according to an infantile pattern of pleasure versus displeasure. You have to be careful that life isn't going to shrink deeper and deeper into yourself. Your emotion isn't any criterion at all. It borders on the meaningless.

KRISTINA: "One can, one is permitted to, one ought to."—And by which rule do I perceive you, you ideologist? How come we're together if you say it's worthless what I am feeling, and why are you falling upon me— am I falling upon you—to make bliss, helter-skelter, because I am something like a mummy, inward, or freeze-dried, or—what do you think? Probably simply because we feel like doing it, simply feel like it! . . . Sometimes you're a miserable drip. [*She puts a black sleeping mask over her eyes*]

MARTIN: Why do you put the sleeping mask on?

KRISTINA: It's too bright for me.

MARTIN: You don't want to see me. That's it.

KRISTINA: No. But I realize before our bliss you always talk in quite another way than afterward. Before, you're sweet. Afterward, miserable. I don't like that.

MARTIN: Proust was always wearing such a mask. Le masque anti lumière. So he could better remember.

KRISTINA [*Points at him*]: Come, stranger, let's not fight! It's time to act. Show me that you're no braggart. Let's only be man and woman. Nothing but that. Nothing else.

MARTIN: You mean, we should give ourselves a new law? Or do you mean, for two people anything is game?

KRISTINA: It's noon. It's much too hot to mean anything.

[*Pause*]

MARTIN: What did you think when you saw me for the first time?

KRISTINA: I thought, he drinks. He lies. He suffers.

MARTIN: I don't drink. I don't lie. That was the other one.

KRISTINA: Sometimes you're fibbing.

MARTIN: It's you who's doing that.

KRISTINA: Be quiet! What's calling there, outside? Don't you hear? Is it a human being or an animal that's screaming?

MARTIN: It's the silence. The almighty silence.

KRISTINA: There's no silence . . . the calls . . .

MARTIN: If only one could remember things precisely enough, hardly anything would then be worth remembering. But the past is pickled in the jelly of our losses . . . it tastes real good. Imagine a drug that won't cause a high, nor sleep, but the pure realization of the present—

KRISTINA [*Moves to the window*]: What's that? [MARTIN *steps behind her. Puts his hand on her shoulder.* KRISTINA *whirls around with a scream.*]

MARTIN: You're frightened? What makes you frightened?

[*Signal of time, light break.* MARTIN *and* KRISTINA *clutch each other.*]

3

In semidarkness MARTIN *and* KRISTINA *come from the other room and sit down facing each other, with their backs against the wall. Then it gets bright.*

KRISTINA: Up here, you never get any mail, I'm sure.

MARTIN: Mail? Oh. The light is a never-ceasing mail. What else would you like to know?

KRISTINA: Is it forever noon here? When we sleep, it's noon. When we get up, it's noon. How long have we been here now? A month? A week?

MARTIN: Some space of time. Spacious. Very spacious.

KRISTINA: All the things going on right now, without me.

MARTIN: Do you believe you're missing something?

KRISTINA: I'd like to make a call. Just that. Got to say that much.

MARTIN: You're restless.

KRISTINA: I'm not at all restless.

MARTIN: What are you waiting for?

KRISTINA: I? Don't know.

MARTIN: It's all over. That's what the situation is like. And we *are* the situation.

KRISTINA: Now it's completely still outside. I don't hear anything anymore. Sometimes I think I have to get out of here immediately. I can't breathe anymore. I've got no time—

MARTIN: I've got time enough . . . Time is all I've got. How much do you need?

KRISTINA: The air is so hot and heavy. Even our voices get caught in it.

MARTIN: The shepherds are groaning in their sleep under the olive trees.

KRISTINA: There are no shepherds around here.

MARTIN: Of course there are.

KRISTINA: Shepherds? Real ones? You're dreaming. In earlier times, sure. But today?

MARTIN: Where I was born, the farmers still believed in ghosts in the rye. The rye auntie. The noon witch. Because she came when a farmer kept working through the noon hour instead of taking a rest. Then she came and asked him questions to the death. She asked and asked until he dropped dead.

KRISTINA: Oh my. What else is there I could think about?

MARTIN: You don't listen to me.

KRISTINA: I do listen to you. Very much so.

MARTIN: You could, for instance, think about going to shop for a few things.

KRISTINA: I won't go alone!

MARTIN: I won't go at all.

KRISTINA: I won't stay here alone, and I won't go without you.

MARTIN: Fine. We're both going to stay here. Starve here. Go to seed within each other. Rot within each other.

KRISTINA: Rot! You think that's the right way to put it?

MARTIN: Putrefy into nothingness.

KRISTINA: Do something. Nobody is stopping you—

MARTIN: The house is wide open. No window, no door. Nothing that could keep you.

KRISTINA: What do you want to tell me? That I should go?

MARTIN: I don't care.

KRISTINA: I don't understand—make bliss again now?

MARTIN: Do *you* want bliss or do *I* want bliss?

KRISTINA: I thought we both want it.

MARTIN: Yes. But everyone in his own time.

KRISTINA: We aren't speaking the truth. Is it too much for you, or not enough?

MARTIN: The larvae of the silk fly, sticky and bristly as they are, grab the plant louse with their forcipate jaws and drink it empty. That's the way it goes. That's the way it went.

KRISTINA: Maybe it's because I'm just having a phase when I very much need protection. [*Pause*] And what's going to happen now?

MARTIN: There's nothing that would be next in turn. The next Now has been canceled.

KRISTINA: Hmm. I'd like to know what would make you walk once around the house. An earthquake. Perhaps. Perhaps a suspicious noise? I'd like to experience for once that precious minute when you aren't here. Just one minute! When you're outside. When I hear you outside as you're walking around the house. When you're listening to the air. And that moment when you appear in the door, when you enter again. When you come back again! [*She rises in front of him*] I'd like you to be happy. I don't care what else you think of me. I believe only those things should be important that define a man and a woman. Everything else—forget it. Martin? Are you already destroyed? Already kaput? No—you aren't?

[*Signal of time, light break*]

4

KRISTINA *on the chair*

MARTIN: What are you doing?

KRISTINA: I'm painting my toenails.

MARTIN: Black?

KRISTINA: He doesn't like it very much.

MARTIN: *Didn't. Didn't* like it very much.

KRISTINA: I tell him, lie down, lie down flat on your stomach. It's better if you're lying than standing in this ridiculous posture before me. You aren't able to stand! Stay here! You can't do the tour like that! "No problem" he says . . .

MARTIN: Bang Bang Bang. My God, I'd like to shoot up the sky!

KRISTINA: And I . . . I'd like to make a phone call right now. Either make a call right now or hear something knocking at the house.

MARTIN: Did he also prostrate himself at your feet? Were you also invited to place your dainty foot on his nape? Or did he only torment you all the time?

KRISTINA: Oh, well. That power thing was quite important in the beginning . . .

MARTIN: Be quiet! Shut up! Why do you answer? You're hiding from me the thousand humiliations he made you suffer. Not a trace has been left in your smile, in your flirting, of all the abominable degradations, of the accusations born out of hate and vulgarity with which he defiled you. With which he wanted to brand you forever. With which he wanted to make you worthless and trivial. You're radiant with revenge! You believe I'm now in your place and you're in his? What kind of a newfangled breed are you? What type of woman? You're no Lulu, you're no Lola. Merely a wisp of a body, but your sexual appetite is a rhinoceros. You're merely a phantom who's scurrying from man to man, desiring protection. A phantom, afraid and craving pleasure, a phantom of a panicky clinging vine. Hey! Say something!

KRISTINA: I don't want to say anything. You amaze me.

MARTIN: Sometimes you look at me as if you were thinking, "he's at the end of his tether. He won't make it much longer." Ha! Don't you deceive yourself! You haven't got the slightest idea who I am . . . I've shown courage enough in my lifetime. I've toppled the president of a state government. I've gone on a hunt for the Yeti, the Abominable Snowman, in Tibet! I'm a good teacher. My methods are beyond reproach. Besides, I wield quite an impressive pen. Those in power have learned to reckon with me, I've given them hell on several occasions; it's not for nothing that they're afraid of my unsettling articles. And it's not a reputation of the past of which I speak. That's where my abilities are. My talent. My flair. That isn't going to desert me. When I do something, it's going to work. Simply because it is *I* who is doing it. As I've told Dr. Heinrich: I'm just waiting for the right moment, I'm waiting for the propitious occasion. I'll attack as soon as I've found my battleground. Perhaps I'll go abroad. I'm not miserable.

KRISTINA: I'm not saying you're miserable.

MARTIN [*Screams*]: I—am—not—miserable!

KRISTINA: What's wrong with you? I want only what's good for you.

MARTIN: I could kill you. But it probably would be easier if I left you.

KRISTINA: Why don't you try. The house is open . . . everything's free. You can go wherever you want to. Just see how far you'll get. You're sitting in my prison exactly the way I'm sitting in yours. You won't get out of this story that easily.

MARTIN: You're little. You're pretty little. It appears that you might be teachable. [*He grabs* KRISTINA *by the scruff of the neck*] I want you to be teachable. I'm taking you! So that you'll follow my tracks. I am taking you and I'll push your face into my tracks!

KRISTINA: You're hurting me! You're going crazy!

MARTIN: Nothing keeps me from being reasonable and raving mad at the same time! Back to the elements! To the elements we'll return! You hear? Take that book there from the windowsill!

KRISTINA: Which window?

MARTIN: Look around.

KRISTINA: When I'm with you, I'm looking at you. I didn't come here to look around.

MARTIN: I see I'm having no influence on you.

KRISTINA: I am with you. I am all around you. Right through you. You're going through me. I'm speaking like you. I don't meet anyone else. You are my coming and my going. You are my voice. You are my perennial slamming of doors. My in and out, my out and in. I have come to you so I'll become nobody. I don't know anymore who I am. What I do. What I've done. I, nothing. You, everything.

MARTIN [*In defense*]: Odeon. School of memory. Ideal school. Asylum. Place of rest to experience the terror . . . Clinging, clinging, is that your strongest emotion? Stronger than love?

KRISTINA: Yes. It is much stronger. But it's also selective. It didn't want anyone yet as much as you.

MARTIN: Only so you're not alone . . . [*He sits down in the doorway*]

KRISTINA: Where are you going?

MARTIN: I'm listening. I'm watching. Eventually it will fall upon us. I hear if something is gathering out there. The only thing I can trust now is my sense of danger.

KRISTINA: I don't hear anything anymore. I believe we are the last of them all. The last couple in the whole world.

MARTIN: The couple! First element of human order . . . What a chaos, little person, what a chaos.

KRISTINA: What do you think: Will our story have a good ending?

MARTIN: What would that be, a good ending?

KRISTINA: That there wouldn't be one!

[*Signal of time, light break*]

5

KRISTINA *steps from the small room in elegant attire. Black, knee-length skirt, cobalt blue jacket. She sits on the chair at the window. Puts sleeping mask and fan on the windowsill. Looks at herself in the shard of a mirror.* MARTIN *comes crawling from the small room.*

MARTIN: To drink, to drink . . .

KRISTINA: The tank is empty. All the water has been drunk.

MARTIN: Thirst . . . when you'll go shopping . . . when you went shopping the last time . . . when you'll come back from shopping . . .

KRISTINA: What are you trying to say? What?

MARTIN: Thirst . . .

KRISTINA [*Turns toward* MARTIN, *opens her knees*]: Teacher, see me!

MARTIN: I want to get up . . . I want to come to you . . . I want to . . .

KRISTINA: You're seeing me and still don't forget yourself? What's going to become of our old game, my friend, my master? What happened to your looking-at-me, your clear-cut will, your intrepid courage?

MARTIN: I've used up most of it, when I looked at you and always only at you.

KRISTINA: Do you think now it's my turn to return all your gifts? Then come! I want to give it to you. Come, there will only be giving, giving until the bottom is empty.

MARTIN: I mustn't lose my responsibility . . . It's my duty to be clear-headed . . . I want to help you find your way . . . I've lived longer than you. God hasn't made me to run blind in circles!

KRISTINA: There's no water left. Shall we go out?

MARTIN: Yes. We'll go out.

KRISTINA: You know what you're talking of? Are you giving up, teacher?

MARTIN: No . . . no.

KRISTINA: Hold me!

MARTIN: Hold me.

KRISTINA: Take me!

MARTIN: Take me.

KRISTINA: Listen to me!

MARTIN: Listen to me.

KRISTINA: Don't give up!

MARTIN: Don't give up.

KRISTINA: You don't recognize me. Even though I'm quite distinct.

MARTIN: You haven't recognized me. You have never seen me.

KRISTINA: From now on, you'll know that I'll always be the *woman*, something that never will cease, as everything else, to be the opposite of you.

MARTIN: You'll always know that we are the covenant, not the story anymore.

KRISTINA: Shall we go now?

MARTIN: Yes. We'll go.

[A *Pan figure appears in the window.* KRISTINA *jumps up and she and the figure immediately begin to thrash each other, she with her fan, the figure with a jester's bat. After she has beaten off the intruder, Kristina glides, back against the wall, down to the floor.*]

KRISTINA [*Softly*]: Help . . . Help . . . Who was that?

MARTIN: I.

[*Signal of time, light break*]

6

MARTIN *and* KRISTINA. *In same positions.*

KRISTINA: What are you thinking of?

MARTIN: I'm thinking of aquatic plants as big as elephant ears. I'm thinking of fresh figs after a refreshing thunderstorm. I'm thinking of something as heartfelt as washing my hands.

KRISTINA: I must go . . . I'm going now . . . I still have to polish my shoes . . . The archaeologists are waiting for me . . . Thank God I'm in disguise. It's much easier for me, you know, after all that time . . . I think no one should be forced to see herself as the dim little light she really is . . . I've taken my sleeping mask and cut out two eye holes . . . don't you at all want to know what's going on outside?!

MARTIN: Oh, well.

KRISTINA: The archaeologists are giving a feast. Just before they go home to their institutes. They're playing and dancing. They're roasting a ram on a spit . . . If I'm not mistaken, it's the crazy twentieth of October today, isn't it?—Yes, yes. I feel it. I'm not fooling myself. [*Pause*] Teacher? Teacher?

MARTIN: Yes?

KRISTINA: Am I still beautiful?

MARTIN: Yes. Very.

KRISTINA: But the radiance—the radiance has been switched off.

MARTIN: No. That isn't true. Little figure.

KRISTINA: I'm trembling when I face the big road that's racing toward me . . .

MARTIN: Now go. Go for me. [KRISTINA *begins to walk slowly back and forth*] Try to leave the house. Go, little figure. Faster. Try to go out. Run! Yes, run now! Now you're big! How grown-up you are! How beautiful! On high heels! Faster! Lighter! Yes, my sweet bitch! Run, run! Now show it to me! Show it to me! Oh . . . Big, big! [KRISTINA *collapses on the threshold*]

KRISTINA: I can't, I can't!

MARTIN: It's all right, my little one. Well done. You've run quite well. It was a wonderful try.

KRISTINA: Make that: I'm quiet inside, quiet.

MARTIN: But yes, my heart. My beloved. Let's try it again, right away.

KRISTINA: Later, later!

[*Signal of time, light break*]

7

The empty room. KRISTINA *enters the house.*

KRISTINA: Teacher? Are you here? [*She walks through the room and into the smaller room. We hear a stifled scream. She comes back. Behind her* MARTIN *steps into the doorway. He looks a complete mess.*]

MARTIN: Where have you been?

KRISTINA: I'm back again. Isn't that enough?

MARTIN: Water!

[KRISTINA *takes a bag with water from her old shoulder bag and throws it at his feet*]

KRISTINA: The tank is filled again. You've got enough water.

MARTIN [*After he has drunk*]: Where have you been all this time? Let me have a look at you . . .

KRISTINA: Don't. You're dirty.

MARTIN: Dirty? What have you done? With whom have you been? Touch me, Kristina. I say: you should touch me . . . [KRISTINA *puts her hand against his cheek*] More gently!

KRISTINA: I can't do it more gently.

MARTIN [*Softly*]: My love, touch me gently. I'll kill you. I'll squash you.

KRISTINA: Stop it. Lay down on the floor again, where you belong.

MARTIN: Stand straight! Look into my face!

KRISTINA: No—don't! You're going to hurt me!

MARTIN: You yellow bitch! Are you afraid I'll throw acid into your pretty little face? Are you? You wouldn't be able to flirt with anyone then! You . . . what are you doing to me? I love you, don't I . . . I only want to kiss you.

KRISTINA: Let me live, teacher, let me live. I've come to get my things. He's here.

MARTIN: He's dead.

KRISTINA: He's here. That's the way it is. That's the way it's been ordained.

MARTIN: You know he's dead.

KRISTINA: Who is?

MARTIN: Your . . . Vassily.

KRISTINA: It's someone else.

MARTIN: You're lying! It's Vassily!

KRISTINA: You're mad. Completely mad.

MARTIN: And what's his name?

KRISTINA: I don't know yet.

MARTIN: You see. You're lying. It's all nonsense.

KRISTINA: Look out the window. Back there you can see him. There he's standing quite visibly, and is waiting for me. He'll carry my bag down the mountain. Below, at the roadside, is his car. We'll be driving to Athens. What else do you want to hear?

MARTIN: You won't get out of here anymore. Or as a bride. Or dead.

KRISTINA: I've been your bride for a long time.

MARTIN: You never were my bride. Never joined with me.

KRISTINA: Ha! What do you think we've been doing here, all that time?

MARTIN: That was no wedding. Not by far.

KRISTINA: Please, let me get my things.

MARTIN: Be careful! Beware! Beware! You've led us both far out, now lead us home again.

KRISTINA: But it was good with you. I can't recall anything that wasn't good between you and me. Not one day. Not one minute.

MARTIN: You won't get out of here anymore. Or as a bride. Or dead.

KRISTINA: I know, teacher.

MARTIN: Kristin?

KRISTINA: Yes!

MARTIN: Why are you lying to me?

KRISTINA [*Embraces him*]: Oh my beloved! My love, my love! Do believe me, it's over!

[*Signal of time, light break*]

8

MARTIN *on the chair.* KRISTINA *is walking up and down.*

KRISTINA: We've made quite some progress. Called those damned things by their rightful name. Counted all our sins. No one is shouldering more guilt than the other. For days on end, nights on end, explained, talked, cried, confessed, accused, and again explained, talked, cried, discussed everything to the very end, explained . . . made quite some progress. Cried. [MARTIN *sits with hunched shoulders and speaks inaudibly.* KRISTINA *bends down to hear him.*] What? What did you say? I can't understand you. Speak up.

MARTIN: But it can't be that all this is true.

KRISTINA: Oh no! Don't! Please! Not again!

MARTIN: You are my wife. I've got no one else.

KRISTINA [*Tries to drown his voice*]: Tatata. Tatata. Tatata . . .

MARTIN: Be quiet. It's unthinkable.

KRISTINA [*Like an echo, nearly babbling*]: Unthinkable, unthinkable. I can't even imagine it. Inconceivable. Without precedent.

MARTIN: All the time we've talked about nothing else. But what we talked about doesn't exist at all. A mere invention. It was only a discussion.

KRISTINA: Discussion. Everything discussed. Made quite some progress. Cussed, cussed, cussed.

MARTIN: Don't fall asleep.

KRISTINA: I don't. Just can't keep my head straight anymore.

[MARTIN *gets up, goes to the window.* KRISTINA sits down in the chair.]

MARTIN: I could have killed you—
KRISTINA: I know. Too late.
MARTIN: But I haven't hurt you. I've never hurt you, have I?
KRISTINA: No. You haven't.
MARTIN: But you said just now that I made so many mistakes. What mistakes have I made?
KRISTINA: Nothing, love. Nothing at all.
MARTIN: It's all a mistake, a fundamental mistake. From the very beginning—
KRISTINA: Be quiet. That isn't true.
MARTIN: True? Is there anything left that's true? Are you listening to me?
KRISTINA: I can't go on.
MARTIN: I can't go on.

[KRISTINA *sits with hunched shoulders on the chair.* MARTIN *steps behind her, lifts his hands to grab her neck. Kristina suddenly jumps up, dances and skips, her arms folded behind her head.*]

KRISTINA: Help! . . . help! . . . help!

[*A hoofed foot knocks sharply and wickedly against the house wall. Light break.*]

9

MARTIN *sits stage right, next to the doorway to the other room, half asleep. Across from him,* KRISTINA *sits on her traveling bag next to the exit door.*

MARTIN: Are you back, Kristin?
KRISTINA: No. I'm just about to go. Are you, too, going to leave? Are you going back to your school?
MARTIN: No.
KRISTINA: What are you going to do?
MARTIN: I'll wait. You'll come back. Every time, you've come back.
KRISTINA [*Shakes her head no. She gets up, picks up her bag.*]: Good luck, teacher.

MARTIN: Good luck . . . [KRISTINA *walks out the door*] One day, one day—
we! [*He slowly gets up, walks to the window, takes the book from the sill.
He sits on the chair. Noon passes. He reads aloud.*] "The way Pan who
already believed he had captured Syrinx, held in his hands only reeds
instead of a nymph's body. The way, then, the wind, while the god was
sighing, played on the reeds creating a tender and moaning sound, and
the way the god, enchanted by this new art and its voice's sweetness,
called out: 'This conversation with you I'll cherish forever!' and pro-
ceeded to join together reeds of various length with wax, and the way he
preserved the name of the girl in the name of the flute.—All this, Mercury
still wanted to tell, but he saw that all eyelids had drooped and sleep had
covered all of their eyes."

[*Darkness*]

Mein Kampf

GEORGE TABORI

•

Must you forever be playing and jesting?
You must, oh my friends, which sickens my soul
For only the desperate must.
—*Friedrich Hölderlin*

Editor's Note

•

Mein Kampf had its premiere in George Tabori's own staging at the Vienna Burg Theater's second house, the Akademie Theater, on May 6, 1987.* (Due to the sudden illness of an actor, the author himself played the role of Lobkowitz.) Of the more than twenty plays by Tabori that have been produced between 1952 and the present, *Mein Kampf* is probably his most widely performed work. It is the adaptation of a short story by the same title, which the author published in 1986.

The quotation from the German early nineteenth-century poet Friedrich Hölderlin, with which Tabori prefaced both texts, points to the author's intention: only jest and play will enable us to bear the unbearable and help us to live with the despair inflicted on humankind during this dark century of unceasing violence. As the critic Wend Kaessens has stated, "Jest has been incorporated in Tabori's school of purification, it makes us laugh when we feel like crying and has its models in Groucho Marx, Charlie Chaplin, and Buster Keaton. . . . Jokes and anecdotes touch upon taboos and thus expose a much larger context." The context exposed in *Mein Kampf* is the project of Hitler and his fellow anti-Semites to exterminate the Jewish race and is the fruit of a tradition with deep and ancient roots in the collective subconscious of Christian Central Europe.

The play's title is, of course, that of Hitler's infamous book that expounded his political agenda and proclaimed that the Jewish race, being the root cause of Germany's woes, ought to be eradicated from German society. Tabori's plot is based on the fact that, in 1910–12, the young Adolf Hitler was living in a Vienna flophouse, where he eked out a meager living by painting watercolors, which a Jewish roommate, who had befriended him, peddled for him in the streets. At the same time, as Hitler wrote twelve years later in *Mein Kampf*, he began to loathe the Eastern European Jews he encountered in the streets of the Hapsburg capital.

These facts, however, are merely the starting point for the play's wild flight of fantasy, which merges fragments of factual history with biblical legend, talmudic argument, the folklore of Vienna, elements of silent movie

---

*Tabori wrote the play in English; the German translation for the Vienna premiere is by Ursula Grützmacher-Tabori.

farce, and many allusions to persons whose deeds shaped the course of the twentieth century. For instance, the character of Himmlisch (the word means heavenly, in German) obviously stands for the boss of the SS and its concentration camps, Heinrich Himmler; on the other hand, the Jewish peddler Shlomo's last name, Herzl (little heart, in Viennese dialect) cannot but make us think of Theodor Herzl, founder of the Zionist movement who, at the turn of the century, lived and worked in Vienna as a journalist. The play presents us with a theme that recurs in Tabori's texts, namely, that victim and victimizer become inseparable partners in an unholy symbiosis, making them engender and need each other.

George Tabori was born in 1914, son of a well-known journalist in Budapest. In 1932, he went to Berlin to learn the hotel business; it was at this time he began to write. Tabori returned to Hungary in 1935 but emigrated a year later to England, where he took up journalism as a career. During the war he worked for British intelligence and the BBC in the Middle East and, from 1943, in London, where his early novels were written. His father and other members of his family died in Auschwitz; his mother, by sheer accident, escaped deportation to Poland and survived. In 1947, Tabori moved to the United States and settled as a screenwriter in Hollywood, where he met—among other exiles—Bertolt Brecht, who was to become a major influence. Tabori wrote screenplays for directors such as Hitchcock, Losey, Asquith, and Litvak. A number of his stage texts were presented in New York, on Broadway and off, among them Elia Kazan's 1952 production of *Flight into Egypt,* the well-known *Brecht on Brecht* adaptation (1962), *The Cannibals* (1968), and *Pinkville* (1970).

With his own staging of *Pinkville* in Berlin, in 1971, Tabori began his German theater career. He has lived and worked in Austria and Germany ever since. He has directed more than sixty plays, many of them his own; he also has published numerous essays as well as several volumes of prose. Among his more recent stage texts are *Whiteman and Redface* (1990), *Goldberg Variations* (1991), and *Requiem for a Spy* (1993). A highly acclaimed and productive playwright/director, Tabori has become a grand old man of the German theater. His work combines aspects of Brecht's theater with the method of Strasberg's Actors Studio, Gestalt therapy, and a collective practice of rehearsal that, though quite different in its motivation, is in its intensity and physical demands reminiscent of Grotowski's former Theater Lab in Vroclav.

Carl Weber

Mein Kampf

CHARACTERS

Herzl
Lobkowitz
Hitler
Gretchen
Mitzi (a chicken)
Frau Death
Leopold (a servant)
Himmlisch
The Day Bums
Seven Tyrolean Leather Freaks
Two Gendarmes

●

Vienna. Winter 19—. A flophouse on Blood Street.

Act I

Dawn. Thursday. It is snowing. LOBKOWITZ *prays. A cock crows. The* DAY BUMS *stir out of their beds to scurry into the city.* HERZL *arrives balancing a pile of unsold books on his unnaturally strong right arm.*

LOBKOWITZ: So there you are.

HERZL: Am I?

LOBKOWITZ [*Hits him*]: Trying to sneak past me?

HERZL: Oh no, my Lord.

LOBKOWITZ: I called out in the dark, from behind the burning bush, where art thou, Shlomo Herzl, to receive the glad tidings that I reduced the Ten Commandments to three, but adultery is still in; plus the good old evergreens: (A) One God Is Enough and That's Me. (B) If You Cannot Honor Your Parents, Call Them at Least Once a Week. (C) Before You Covet Your Neighbor's Wife, Make Sure He's Smaller Than You. How is business?

HERZL: Terrible, my Lord.

LOBKOWITZ: Trouble makes a man wise.

HERZL: So how come I've stayed stupid?

LOBKOWITZ: You're stupid because you worry too much. [*Hits him*] He who worries has little or no faith, and faith withers without works, so remember what is in the sky above and you shall not fall into sin.

HERZL: Faith cannot be commanded, my Lord.

LOBKOWITZ [*Hits him*]: Learned fools are the worst fools.

HERZL: In an argument, it is always the loser who wins.

LOBKOWITZ: Who says?

HERZL: You says.

LOBKOWITZ: Can't remember saying that.

HERZL: By the Red Sea, when the waters retreated.

LOBKOWITZ: Not a bad trick, eh? Thirty thousand Egyptians drowned.

HERZL: Twenty thousand.

LOBKOWITZ: Twenty five?

HERZL: Twenty.

LOBKOWITZ [*Hits him*]: You doubt my omniscience, you worm.

HERZL: If I do not doubt, what am I?

LOBKOWITZ: If you only doubt, what are you?

HERZL: Not a theologian.

LOBKOWITZ: Nor am I.

HERZL: Be as it may, my Lord, a broken heart such as mine, a bleeding heart, you would not despise.

LOBKOWITZ: Did I say I despised you?

HERZL: You called me a worm, my Lord.

LOBKOWITZ: What d'you have against worms?

HERZL: If you are against me, who is for me? Mine enemies press close upon me. Only last night, a waiter in the Café Central told me, no dogs and no Jews.

LOBKOWITZ: No dogs? Outrageous! If you learn to fear me, you need not fear anyone in the cafés.

[HITLER *appears*]

LOBKOWITZ: Once I saw a skull bobbing on the waters of Vienna, and I spoke to it: "Since you drowned someone, they drowned you. But even those that drowned you, shall be drowned, for I am just." By the way, how many Bibles did you sell tonight?

HERZL: Five, my Lord.

LOBKOWITZ [*Hits him*]: You're lying.

HERZL: Three.

LOBKOWITZ: Which version?

HERZL: Luther's.

LOBKOWITZ: You call that a Bible?

HERZL: I don't, my Lord. He did.

LOBKOWITZ: Fornicating renegade! Forgetting my finest command—that I chose you not because you are special, far from it; I chose you, worm, as my helpmate to establish a kingdom in this snow, in this dread hour before daybreak, an hour that may decide your eternity, so repent and return to my patient bosom before it is too late. Between you and me, Shlomo, what are you waiting for? [*Hits him*]

HERZL [*Hits him back*]: Lobkowitz, I'm writing a book.

[*Thunder and lightning*]

LOBKOWITZ: "Lobkowitz"? Did I hear you say "Lobkowitz" instead of "my Lord"?

HERZL: Yes, Lobkowitz, I said "Lobkowitz" instead of "my Lord."

[LOBKOWITZ *collapses*]

HERZL [*To audience*]: I don't quite know what gave me the chutzpah to call him "Lobkowitz" instead of "my Lord," but my nose was freezing and my back hurt. I was sick and tired of our game. For three years now, we have been playing the same game.

LOBKOWITZ: Four years!

HERZL: What made me submit in the first place? Perhaps I felt sorry for this God who, being omnipresent, was invariably present in Vienna, for He loves His Jews so much that He won't let them out of sight. But in that dawn, in that snow, I'd had it, and unmasked this God as a cook. This God was of course not God. You know who I mean. There is, after all, only one, His name be praised, but Lobkowitz the Loon, a kookie kosher cook, defrocked some years ago by his boss Moskowitz for mixing cream cheese with boiled beef, an insult to Mosaic Law. Why? "I'll tell you why," said Lobkowitz to Moskowitz. "Because I'm mad at Moses for wandering for forty years in the wilderness—"

LOBKOWITZ: Thirty-nine!

HERZL: —instead of settling down in Vienna. Be that as it may, Moskowitz retorted, "You are fired." "May all your teeth fall out except for one, and may that hurt till the end of your days," said Lobkowitz, and he tore off his cook's apron and threw it into the borscht!

LOBKOWITZ: Mulligatawny!

HERZL: Then he fell into a coma, came out of it ten days later, a classic case of mistaken identity, which he explained to Dr. S. Freud as follows:

LOBKOWITZ [*Upstaging* HERZL]: "I think I am God. You think you are S. Freud. Both of us may be wrong."

HERZL: Sorry, Lobkowitz, to have called you "Lobkowitz" instead of "the Holy One," His name be praised, but I'm writing a book.

LOBKOWITZ: For me?

HERZL: No!

LOBKOWITZ: About me?

HERZL: Not quite.

LOBKOWITZ: Back to Babylon, and weep!

HERZL: Lobkowitz, wouldn't you like to know what my book is about?

LOBKOWITZ: Not at all!

HERZL: I don't know myself. I haven't written it yet. Perhaps that's what it's about. In these past three years, I have tried to get past the beginning. Care to hear the beginning I can't get past?

LOBKOWITZ: By no means.

HERZL: A scorpion bites me to start again each morning. My disgust chokes me each morning. I wish this book were a daily prayer. What holds me back is a pagan giggle, cascading inside my head as I scribble His name, unmentionable in Vienna, fading into blasphemy; it may only be mentioned in vain as a sigh or a curse or a conjuration, "Goddamm it" or "fuck God" or . . .

HITLER: Good God!

[HERZL *and* LOBKOWITZ *take no notice of* HITLER, *who stands rather impatiently in the doorway*]

HERZL: Besides, what's the point of writing yet another book. There is only one book, and it has already been written, and this one book, that has already been written, says everything about everything, including your tears, yet I must write my own, so as to put the wickedness out of my heart, this shadow falling across my threshold, so I ask you, Lobkowitz, tell me as Lobkowitz, what to do.

LOBKOWITZ [*Happily*]: You? Ask? Me? As Lobkowitz, am to tell you what to do? Well, I tell you as Lobkowitz, if you cannot get past the beginning, you should begin before the beginning. What is the title, what do you call your book?

HERZL: "My Life," I call it.

LOBKOWITZ [*Shaking his head*]: "My Life"? You call that a title? You call that a possible title for an important commentary? Shlomo, I am disappointed.

HERZL: How about "My Memoirs"?

LOBKOWITZ [*He and* HITLER *shake their heads*]: That's terrible! "My Memoirs"! Ask yourself, Shlomo, would your mother want to buy a book called "My Memoirs"?

HERZL: No!

LOBKOWITZ: Try again!

HERZL: "Shlomo in Wonderland!" "The Seven Shlomos of Wisdom." "Shlomo and Juliet." "Lady Chatterly's Shlomo." "The Merry Shlomos of Windsor." "Waiting for Shlomo." "Ecce Shlomo." "The Concise Oxford Shlomo." [LOBKOWITZ *keeps shaking his head*] How about "Mein Kampf"?

LOBKOWITZ: That's it!

HITLER: You've got it!

[HERZL *and* LOBKOWITZ *finally take notice of* HITLER]

HERZL: Who asked you?

HITLER: What does it mean?

HERZL: "My Struggle."

HITLER: Is this Frau Merschmeyer's flophouse below her butchery?

LOBKOWITZ: No.

HERZL: Didn't your mother teach you manners?

HITLER [*In one breath*]: Yes, indeed, she did. Lately deceased, may she rest in peace, after a hard life ministering to our poor but honest household, a blessed hausfrau, she has never failed to admonish me not to place my elbow on the dinner table, to yield my seat to old ladies on the tram, to tip my hat when meeting my elders in the street, to wash my hands before and after passing water, admonitions that I have dutifully observed in spite of my ingrained reluctance to obey authority, which has finally crystallized itself into an unshakable resolve not to follow in my blessed father's footsteps as a state employee, he too was felled by destiny's axe into a premature grave, but to seek my fortune in the City of the Waltz as an artist, a vocation predestined by my considerable graphic talent. [EV-ERYBODY *takes a deep breath*] However, I must first signal my utmost amazement, no, no, no, my disgust at your having dragged my sainted mother's memory into a casual conversation, whose motivation frankly escapes me, instead of offering a word of welcome to this unsuspecting country youth, who, having suffered the discomforts of all-night travel in a crowded third-class carriage all the way from Braunau-on-the-Inn to Vienna-on-the-Danube, tramped all morning through the snow-swept avenues in search of Frau Merschmeyer's home for the homeless, and, however overawed by the glorious examples of imperial architecture, is chilled to the core and longing for the well-deserved haven of a warm bed in this dreary dungeon, which is all that I, in my impecunious state, can afford until Dame Destiny will reward my not-yet-recognized genius with fame and fortune.

HERZL: I have asked you a simple question, I expect a simple answer, not the Nibelungen saga.

HITLER: If you fail to appreciate my exhaustive manner of speaking, which my beloved history teacher in Linz, Dr. Leopold Pörtsch—

LOBKOWITZ: Pötsch!

HITLER: —has recognized as expressive of a natural rhetorical talent—Why Pötsch?

LOBKOWITZ: Sounds better!

HITLER: What I find appalling, no, no, no, disgusting from a foreigner, is your attempt to reduce my intuitive mastery of verbal felicities to a ridiculous yes-and-no game worthy of the Inquisition.

HERZL: Foreigner? Did I hear you say foreigner? In this place, you are the foreigner, boy. Besides, even if you were one of one billion Chinese, remember that the majority of mankind are, from any point of view, including the Chinese, foreigners. So let us start again, shall we? Didn't your mother teach you manners?

HITLER: I'd be glad to accept your challenge to a bout of racial discussions some other time, when I'm less chilled or constipated, a family weakness aggravated by all-night travel, meanwhile, permit me to be the sole judge of what I consider to be foreign, your accent, for example, your entire demeanor, and especially your nose, not to mention your twisted tongue, which turns into a question what you obviously intend as a statement; for, as I suspect, instead of wishing to ask me if my mother taught me manners, you are actually telling me that, in your estimation, she did not, which puzzles me, for I am not aware of having broken any rules of civilized conduct.

HERZL: You barge in here like a bison into a china store. This is not your house. You're a stranger here, yourself—at best, a guest. I might have been sleeping. I could have been entertaining a friend. It so happens, I was working on a book until God interrupted me.

HITLER: Who?

HERZL: G-O-D.

HITLER: Is dead.

LOBKOWITZ: That's what you think.

HERZL: You bust in like a yokel, offending my privacy. You're not in some Brown-Ouch-on-the-Inn. You are in the city of Schiele, Schnitzler, and Schubert—

LOBKOWITZ [*Hums "An Einem Bächlein helle"*]

HERZL: That's enough!—and Shlomo Herzl. In other words, your mother must have neglected to teach you to knock before entering.

HITLER: Clever, clever! I could tear your un-German arguments to shreds, but I decline, and to demonstrate my inborn generosity, I shall submit. [*He picks up his gear, goes outside, closes the door, knocks, opens the door, and enters*] Satisfied?

HERZL: No, You knocked *and* entered. That's wrong. The rule of yore runs like this: You knock, wait for the one inside to say, "Come in," you enter. Try again.

[HITLER, *a blush reddening his ruddy cheeks, picks up his gear again, goes outside, closes the door, knocks*]

LOBKOWITZ: Entréz.

[HITLER *comes in, closes the door, puts his gear down*]

HERZL: Want some coffee?

HITLER: No.

HERZL: Milk and sugar?

HITLER: Both.

HERZL: The only free bed is by the window. Wrap up your head, or the draft will kill you. You can leave your junk under the bed. Nobody steals around here, at least not from each other. The toilet is over there, get your own paper, the *Observer* is kindest to your ass. Your roommates are the Day Bums of Vienna: thieves, beggars, students, revolutionaries, a schlattenschames, and the fag who sweeps the laurel in front of the opera house. Their feet are not roses of Sharon, so learn to breathe through your mouth. I sleep by day and work at night. I sell books. I could give you a special rate on the Bible or *Fanny Hill,* not necessarily in that order. Speaking of *Fanny Hill,* we are here in spitting distance of the modest abode where the composer W. A. Mozart composed some of the filthiest letters ever composed, suggesting for instance, that his cousin blew into his behind.

HITLER: He did not.

HERZL: Yes, he did.

HITLER: What an extraordinary suggestion.

HERZL: Why don't you try it?

HITLER: I have no cousin.

HERZL: Vienna is not the place for libertinage, sexual or political, but once a week I get a sweet visitation. I'd appreciate it if, in that case, you took a walk.

HITLER: A cousin?

HERZL: I suspect a misunderstanding. Fräulein Gretchen Maria Globuschek-Bornemissza-Eszterfalvy is not only the last virgin over fourteen in Vienna but a being between the species, free of the evolutionary gap between the frog and the Homo sapiens. She is part of nature; when she quacks, the ducks reply, the elephants in the zoo greet her with a primal bellow, and migrant birds are known to have followed her into the Viennese woods instead of flying as scheduled to Africa. Don't you have a winter coat?

HITLER: No.

HERZL: It's cold.

HITLER: Yes.

HERZL [*Offers his coat; it hangs between his finger rotating like a hanged man*]: You can have it while I sleep. The left pocket is torn; don't put any coins into it, they'll slip down to the bottom of the lining—you'd have to scrabble around till you're blue in the face. What's your name?

HITLER: Hitler.

HERZL: Funny, you don't look Jewish.

HITLER: Well, you don't look Chinese, either.

HERZL: Clever, clever. Pleasant shrewdness, but I'm not doing you the favor of falling for it. You want me to say, "Well, but I'm not Chinese," so you may retort, "Well, but then I'm not Jewish, either." I know what I know. You must be a Lemberg one.

LOBKOWITZ: Odessa?

HERZL: A Löw-Pinsker on the mother's side. Why Odessa?

LOBKOWITZ: Sounds better!

HERZL: In that case, a distant cousin. What a happy coincidence! Welcome to Vienna!

HITLER [*Eyes bulging, moustache quivering and drooping, specks of foam bubbling in the corner of his mouth*]: Lemberg?

LOBKOWITZ: Odessa!

HITLER [*Foaming*]: Odessa? Löw? Pinsker? Coincidence? Cousin? You must have water on the brain. My blood is pure as driven snow, issue of a stock that is hard as flint, fast as a whippet. By a happy dispensation, Destiny has assigned Braunau-on-the-Inn as my birthplace, that bucolic little town, bordering two Germanic states, whose reunion by all available means is the towering task of all true patriots. Ploughs into swords! Out of the tear ducts of war grows daily bread for posterity!

HERZL: Whatever the case may be, calm yourself and stop mixing metaphors. Drink your coffee before it gets cold. What's in a name, boy? Let me tell you what in a name may be. Herz, or heart, rhymes with Scherz, or jest. On the other hand Herzl, or little heart, rhymes with Scherzl, or the little round rump of a loaf of bread. Each deserves the name he gets. If you think you are the only Hitler in this vale of tears, you're in for a sobering surprise. There are, I estimate, twenty-three Hitlers in the Viennese telephone directory, all of them, I suspect, scions of a twin tribe, one of Odessa, the other of Munkacevo, nestling in the Carpathian foothills. The Odessa gang was, some two hundred years ago, bullwhipped out of town and settled in Lower Bavaria. Zwi ben Avraham Löw, our grandsire, was the Little Drummer, so-called, in Holzhausen. A kind of living newspaper, he'd drum the villagers together once a week to tell them the news, which was mostly bad. His youngest son, the unforgettable dwarf Benjamin, was in charge of garbage—*Schütt* as the natives called it—in the Starnberg area and was jovially nicknamed Ben the Schüttler; but due to a bureaucratic error in City Hall, the *ü* was replaced by an *i*, one of the *t*s got misplaced during the Seven Years War, while the *c* was lost in the aftermath of a pogrom, which his English-speaking wife, Rebecca, not surprisingly, resented. When the Shitlers retired in Ambach, smoking trout for a hobby, and the glad news of the emancipation reached them, she dispatched Benjamin to the Department of Germanizing Names so that he might purchase something suitably euphonious. She would have liked Hohenzollern or Beethoven, but they were not in the public domain. Rosenduft or Rosenkranz were too expensive. How much money you got? the clerk asked Ben. Tuppence, he replied. For tuppence, said the clerk, an anti-Semite, I can do only one thing for you, cut the *S*, that's all.

HITLER: So this is Vienna.

HERZL: No, but it's Talmud.

HITLER: Another cousin?

LOBKOWITZ: A book.

HITLER: In German?

LOBKOWITZ: As well.

HITLER: Do you like Karl May?

LOBKOWITZ: In small doses.

HERZL: You see, we do have something in common.

HITLER: I doubt it, considering your nose. How did it get to be that way?

HERZL: "Common," A Talmudic word, is contradictory, like God, meaning "mean" as well as "typical." When "vicious," it divides, when "ordinary," it unites. Let me give you an example.

HITLER: I was afraid of that.

HERZL: Twins fall through a chimney, one comes out dirty, the other clean. Which one will clean himself?

HITLER: The dirty one.

HERZL: Wrong. Looking at the clean one, he thinks he is clean, too. Shall we try again? Twins fall through a chimney, one comes out dirty, the other one clean. Which one cleans himself?

HITLER: The clean one. Looking at the dirty one, he thinks himself unclean and cleans himself.

HERZL: Wrong again. If twins fall through a chimney, how come one comes out clean, the other dirty?

HITLER: You speak with a forked tongue, you caught me off balance. But not for long. My father warned me not to believe everything I am told in Vienna.

HERZL: I advise you not to believe everything your father told you.

HITLER: I'll take no instructions from you in filial piety. Nor in rebellion against paternal authority. I loved my late father, but I won't deny our heroic generational conflicts. "You, son, a painter?" "Me, dad, a painter!" "Never, you shall!" "Nevertheless, I will!"—I must now go to sleep, so as to refresh myself for tomorrow, when, with a carefully selected pack of paintings, I will keep my appointment at the Academy of Fine Arts to pass my entrance exam, which I undoubtedly will with flying colors.

HERZL: Let's see. [*He sits next to* HITLER, who unlaces a folder]

HITLER: They may be too advanced for your taste. The Jews, after all, never had a culture of their own. Here, a kind of radical realism, a still life, called *Corn in the Twilight*.

HERZL: Astonishing.

HITLER: One day, I left it on the windowsill and a crow came to pick on the cob.

LOBKOWITZ: Makes my mouth water.

HITLER: You like corn?

LOBKOWITZ: Grilled, preferably.

HERZL: With melted butter.

HITLER: Right on the nose!

HERZL: See, another area of agreement, cousin.

HITLER: Here, an aquarelle. Do you know what aquarelle is?

HERZL and LOBKOWITZ: We heard of it.

HERZL [*To* LOBKOWITZ]: You heard of aquarelle?

LOBKOWITZ: I heard of aquarelle.

HITLER: I call it *My Dog in the Twilight*. That, down there, is my dog.

LOBKOWITZ: I thought so.

HITLER: Observe the perfect perspective with which his loyal gaze is drawn to the church spire.

HERZL: You do like twilights, cousin, don't you?

HITLER: A challenge, yes, to catch the Weltschmerz of fading light, and if you call me cousin one more time, I'll break your back. Used to dabble in sunsets. Sometimes they came out like fried eggs, sunny side up, so I moved on to attempt the impossible greys. Here, a reverent sketch, charcoal, *My Mother Shelling Peas in the Twilight*.

HERZL: Very touching.

HITLER: Your mother still alive?

HERZL: Skewered in a pogrom by a Cossack sword.

HITLER: What was she like?

HERZL: Fat. Her legs wouldn't carry her fast enough, she stumbled into a ditch, the sword quivering between her buttocks.

HITLER: My mother thought I ought to be a master builder. True enough, this morning, passing the Burg Theater, I immediately saw that it could be improved, needs more columns. I like columns, don't you?

HERZL: In small doses. D'you know what Michelangelo asked the pope before starting on the Sistine Chapel?

HITLER: No, what?

HERZL [*In an Italian accent*]: What-a color-a you want-a, boss?

HITLER: That was a joke, I take it?

HERZL: Yes, Hitler, that was a joke.

HITLER: I can't stand jokes. I keep forgetting the punch line. But then, I must admit I prefer profundities, the earnest poise. Life, after all, is a very serious matter.

HERZL: No kidding.

[HERZL, LOBKOWITZ, *and* HITLER *go to bed*]

HITLER: Actually, my first love is music. A baritone at fifteen. Sang in the first row of the choir. To be honest, there was only one row in the choir, and my music teacher in Linz, a Frau Przemyshl, thought my deep tones weren't deep enough for Tannhäuser. I don't suppose you know Tannhäuser?

HERZL: Which Tannhäuser d'you mean? Otto Tannhäuser? Bernie Tannhäuser? Itzig Tannhäuser?

[HITLER *launches into* "My Fair Evening Star." HERZL *and* LOBKOWITZ *chime in, trying to harmonize. They sing themselves to sleep.*]

Act II

Dawn. Friday. The DAY BUMS *are already on their way.* HITLER *is wallowing in his suitcase, throwing things about, a sock lands in the coffeepot, a pair of long johns is dangling from the ceiling light. He starts shining his shoes.* HERZL *returns, with books. Hitler throws a fit.*

HERZL: Anything wrong?

HITLER: Everything! The Bard of Bayreuth was right, it's all the fault of the Jews and the bicyclists.

HERZL: What do you have against the bicyclists?

HITLER: Look at these shoes!

HERZL: What do you have against these shoes?

HITLER: Everything!

HERZL: Everything?

HITLER: Almost everything. [*Roars, eyes almost popping out of his head*] Tried to shine them but, due to the dimness of this hellhole, smeared by mistake brown paste over them, and they happen to be black, and now they are the color of chickenshit.

HERZL: Hitler, calm yourself.

HITLER: Go to hell!

HERZL: Take a deep breath, cover the brown paste with black, and black being darker than brown, the shoes will shine as good as new.

HITLER: I will take no instructions in shoe shining from a Mosaic bookworm.

HERZL: D'you know how to shine shoes?

HITLER: Shlomo, how does one shine shoes?

HERZL: I'll show you how to shine shoes.

HITLER: Look at my hands!

HERZL: What d'you have against your hands?

HITLER: Everything.

HERZL: Everything?

HITLER: Almost everything. What are you trying to do, knife me in the back?

HERZL: Yes.

HITLER: Undermine my future?

HERZL: Yes.

HITLER [*Wipes his hands and face on someone else's bedsheet*]: Why oh why did I ever leave Braunau-on-the-Inn?

HERZL: Why, actually?

HITLER: Everywhere, filth, stench, disorder. I should have listened to Dr. Pörtsch—

LOBKOWITZ: Pötsch!

HITLER: Why Pötsch? Do you know him?

LOBKOWITZ: A little fat bimbo with a bow tie.

HERZL: Had a beautiful daughter, Roswitha, with a "*th*."

LOBKOWITZ: Roswitha!

HITLER: Vienna, Vienna, thou multiracial Sodom, thou unmelting pot of scum. Where are my trousers? [*He grabs his trousers, kicks his feet into them, buttons up his fly, a button pops and lands at* HERZL's *feet. Hitler looks at it, his eyebrows leaning to the middle of his brow, and throws a tantrum, flinging himself onto someone else's bed, drumming with his fists on the pillow, gargling abuse.*]

HERZL: I suggest you drink your coffee and relax by counting to one hundred, as my grandmother would whenever someone was dying or getting born. [HITLER *counts*] Then you should wash yourself, but kindly use your own towel. Meanwhile, I'll take care of your shoes and the button, so you don't have to appear at the Academy with your shlitz open. And, incidentally, look around the room. I know you must have been a spoiled child, mother's little darling, I'm not blaming you for your uncouth manners, but consider the sock in the coffeepot. We are here an underprivileged but civilized community. I'll clean up for you this one and only time. From tomorrow on, you'll have to grow up and do it yourself.

HITLER: Your critique leaves me cold. I'm an artist, not a petit-bourgeois peddler.

HERZL: Richard Wagner was also an artist, but I dare say he didn't leave his socks inside the coffeepot.

LOBKOWITZ: He did. [HITLER *slams the toilet door behind himself.* HERZL *sews a button on the trousers.*] The way you are mothering that peasant borders on masochism.

HERZL: In the eyes of the High One, hospitality weighs as heavily as divine service.

LOBKOWITZ: The law is my love, but I must say this shoeshiner manqué makes it hard to obey it. He sleeps all day, his mouth open. He either snores, a terrible buzz saw snore or talks in his dreams, snorting shreds of maledictions. Also, he is a champion snot flinger: a snort, a scrabbling excavation, producing a caterpillar-sized piece of desiccated slime, contemplates upon it with the curiosity of an archeologist, rolls it into a neat ball, flicks it across space. One lands, bang, on the windowpane, another, in a wide arc, splash, between my eyes.

HITLER [*Returns half dressed: winged collar, an old school tie, starched white panties*]: How do I look?

HERZL: Dashing.

HITLER: I know I'm not beautiful, but my features, I've been told, radiate iron character.

HERZL: Do you insist on that iron moustache?

HITLER: What is your objection?

HERZL: It makes you look like a Hun, and they do not fancy Huns hereabouts. I do like Huns, but the Academy of Fine Arts is notoriously patriotic.

HITLER: I let it grow, and it grew.

HERZL: I'd better prune it.

HITLER: I don't give a fig, turn me into a grocer.

[HERZL *combs up* HITLER's *moustache, it drops, he clips one end, then the other, they won't stay even, lopsiding the face, until Herzl gets the bush down to a respectable toothbrush nestling in the nose. Then he brushes Hitler's hair, it won't stay up, a lock keeps falling onto his forehead. Herzl rubs a bit of schmaltz into it, finds the parting. Hitler looks in the mirror, still sulky. After Herzl has helped him into his winter coat, he picks up his folder. Herzl buttons him up and picks a piece of lint off the lapel.*]

HITLER: Jew, I appreciate your assistance. When my time has come I shall reward you suitably. I'll buy you an oven, so you'll be warm, and when you get old I'll find you a solution, some comfortable old folk's home in the hills, with old folk dances Saturday nights.

HERZL: Go now, or you'll be late. Expect nothing and you won't be disappointed. Van Gogh painted several thousand pictures and sold only one, to his brother.

HITLER: I have no brother.

[HITLER *leaves.* HERZL *works on his book.*]

HERZL: Alone at last.

LOBKOWITZ: Man is never alone.

HERZL: Well, here we go again, provided I can read my own writing.

LOBKOWITZ: Try it!

HERZL [*Reads*]: "In a cold night greying into dawn, the coldest in memory . . . " How do you like that as a beginning?

LOBKOWITZ: It sure ain't *The Brothers Karamazov*.

HERZL: What's as good as *The Brothers Karamazov*?

LOBKOWITZ: *The Brothers Karamazov,* for instance, is as good as *The Brothers Karamazov.*

HERZL: "The cock crows, the clock ticks; 'time, gentlemen, please,' as the bartender might warn the drunks, the hounds of hell are breathing down my neck, eager to snatch this book, this paper baby, my only child, a last chance to remember what I had forgotten in my youth, namely the Holy One, His name be praised."

LOBKOWITZ: There is something wrong with that sentence.

HERZL: Shall I cut it?

LOBKOWITZ: Whatever is cut, gleams in silence, footprints of a thief in the night.

HERZL: Well, how shall I start? "By night on my bed, I sought Him whom my soul loveth"?

LOBKOWITZ: It is easy to purloin the Bible and to pervert the prophets. I am going.

HERZL: You're leaving me?

LOBKOWITZ: God needs man. And man needs man as well. But you've lost part of your humanity since you've been mothering that Braunau bastard, and you know what happens to mothers, they die with swords in their asses. I am worried about you, but I am going to leave you and go back to Moskowitz to teach him the difference between eating and gobbling. Ask me about the difference.

HERZL: Tell me the difference.

LOBKOWITZ: When we were young, at the time of the big famine, Moskowitz and I cooked potato soup in huge pots, and five thousand Viennese turned up and ate. Since they were hungry, it tasted like manna, and this was good. Later, in a time of affluence, full of ulcers and satiety, we stuffed ourselves until we puked. Tonight I had a dream, I was taking a vacation at the hotel Two Seasons, more I could not afford. You came by. I sat in my room and cried bitter tears. "What's the matter," you asked, "Is the room too small?" "No." "The service impertinent?" "No." "So what is it, Lobkowitz?" And I said, "At 6 o'clock they wake you with tea, schmaltz, and crackers. Then breakfast, four courses, with cream puff. Then brunch, cold cuts, cereal. Then lunch, eight courses, with cream puff. Then siesta with seven seven-layer cakes. At 5 o'clock, sandwiches and cream puffs. Dinner, ten courses, more cream puffs. Supper at ten, Beluga caviar, lobster American-style; for a nightcap, hot milk with lox and bagel." "So what are you griping about, Lobkowitz?" "They don't give you a chance to shit."—You're waiting for Hitler?

HERZL: I know a suicidal type when I see one. I already have a vision of him floating in the Danube, not to mention my winter coat.

LOBKOWITZ: Watch out, Shlomo. Love is a deadly danger to life and limb.

[LOBKOWITZ *leaves.* HERZL *cleans up, sits down. Night falls. The* DAY BUMS *return, exhausted, and go to bed.* HITLER *staggers drunkenly through the door.*]

HITLER: To quote Shakespeare, "Where have you been?"

HERZL: "Here," to quote Shakespeare.

HITLER: Unfeeling swine!

HERZL: For the first time since my pleurisy in nineteen-oh-five, I interrupted my nightly rounds, which I can ill afford—the rent is due Monday.

HITLER [*Grabs* HERZL's *nose between bent knuckles and pulls him closer*]: I meet my Waterloo, and you go gallivanting.

HERZL: Next to policemen and horses, what I dislike most are drunks. [*Extricates his nose*] If you do that again, I'll break your neck.

HITLER: You? Break? My? Neck?

HERZL [*Kicks* HITLER *in the shinbone. Hitler lets out a yell, Herzl yells too.*]: Shut up, you'll wake the others. So how did it go?

HITLER: It didn't go, it slithered like greased lightning, singeing my youthful confidence. As I presented myself to the rector, requesting an explanation for the reason of my nonacceptance, the gentleman informed me that a cursory survey of my fine-arts samples had convinced the professional committee of my hopeless nonability as a painter. This pigdog expressed it more rudely. Young man, he said, the only thing you should be allowed to paint is a kitchen wall. I rose and left with a withering remark.

HERZL: Namely?

HITLER: Good-bye. What else could I have said to this Baron von Kropf . . . or Tropf?

HERZL: Topf.

HITLER: Why Topf?

HERZL: Sounds better.

HITLER: Do you know him?

HERZL: Everybody in Vienna knows him.

HITLER: Undulating hairdo, perfumed handkerchief in his breastpocket, a pearl stuck into a silk bow tie, dove-grey spats, this baronial rec-tor-rectum, exuding decadence, dared to suggest that I become a house-painter.

HERZL: Alcohol kills, stupefies, and miserifies. I have warned you, haven't I? Now, if you care to listen to an older man, I'd advise you to forgo an academic education. Leonardo was also self-taught.

HITLER: He was not.

HERZL: Depends which Leonardo you mean. Leonardo Ellenbogen, for instance, was self-taught. He sat next to me in kindergarten. On the other hand, what's wrong with being a housepainter? My second cousin Joshua started by whitewashing the synagogue and ended as a royal purveyor of wallpaper by appointment to the Hannoverian dynasty at Herrenhausen.

HITLER [*Chokes* HERZL]: Me a housepainter? Kiss my ass!

HERZL: Better be choked, than a choker, says the Eleventh Commandment.

HITLER: Traitor! Dagger in my back! A worldwide conspiracy by the Elders of Zion! I suspected as much! You're in cahoots with von Kropf, plotting to hinder my ascent to the pinnacles of fame! Who sent me away without trousers this morning?

HERZL: Nobody is perfect.

HITLER: I should have known better, but these are my years of learning; after I had goose-stepped out of Kropf's office and betook myself to a nearby café, a smoke-filled den of iniquity, my innocent eyes opened wide and I saw them: these Shylocks, these black birds of pestilence, with their furry hats, their greasy kaftans, no water lovers, I could tell, a stench of steamy lust emanating from their armpits, while they were wolfing a Christian baby schnitzel.

HERZL: No salad?

HITLER: Chips.

HERZL: Ketchup?

HITLER: No. They offered a devilish drink, some Maltese concoction, and Heaven, Arse, and Twirn! a woman with breasts like watermelons holding up her chin. She nibbled at my earlobe. No one has ever dared to nibble at my earlobe. I will not tolerate anyone nibbling at my earlobe! Say, Shlomo, between us, this intercoursing, is this a fact?

HERZL: How d'you mean, a fact?

HITLER: The Reverend Basedow warned me that it is.

HERZL: What is?

HITLER: He said, watch out, in a big city like Vienna, they are in fact doing it.

HERZL: Doing what?

HITLER: Well, shit, you know what I mean, men and women, together, like dogs.

HERZL: Not necessarily like dogs, not in Vienna.

HITLER: But they are doing it, a fact?

HERZL: Well, the population grows, Adolf.

HITLER: Call me "Adolf" one more time, and I'll wring your neck! Is it nice?

HERZL: Can be.

HITLER: Is it sinful?

HERZL [*Places a rabbinical hand upon* HITLER's *skull*]: Man's delight does delight God, in small doses.

HITLER [*Whispers wetly*]: One summer's day, in Braunau-on-the Inn, I saw a woman lying by the river Inn. She was drying her naked backside, her udders swinging in the breeze. She lifted a leg and I saw her center, and it was dark like the night. What's your opinion of the night?

HERZL: The night, one of two possibilities. It comes and goes, the night. A sting in the side is God's finger in the night, which is God's time, a time to love, a time to die. When you are old, you prefer the day.

HITLER: I get my best ideas at night. I'll tell you something. If you betray me, I'll have you burnt like a breakfast roll. I don't really want to be a painter. I don't want to paint the twilight. That's only a tactical device to fool the fools. I want something else.

HERZL: Like what?

HITLER: The world.

HERZL: Oh, well! All of it?

HITLER: Yes.

HERZL: Including New Zealand?

HITLER: Especially New Zealand.

HERZL: What's so hot about New Zealand?

HITLER: I don't know, but I want it.

HERZL: Adolf, be reasonable. Consider what comes with the territory. Like millions of muzhiks in Russia.

HITLER: They'll be shaved.

HERZL: And the fags in England? The sands of Araby? And all those blacks with the night in their behind?

HITLER: They'll be scrubbed white. Don't bother me with trivialities! I have it all worked out, not all the details though. Heinrich's here to help me, a schoolmate, a fly-leg plucker, a scientific genius. He specializes in skulls, he knows how to shrink them down to the size of ping-pong balls. He is now working on the process of shrinking the rest. People are on the whole too tall or too fat, they're jamming up the streets; by shrinking them, one would gain lebensraum. I want shrunk people about me, to keep them in line and, if necessary, to push them off the edge. One thing that has always worried me about the world is its roundness, I don't care for roundness, round things, they are too chummy, remind me of . . . you know what I mean.

HERZL: No.

HITLER: This round world keeps rotating without a chance to fall off it. Frankly, it doesn't make sense, so another thing we'll have to take care of is gravity. I've never thought much of gravity, have you?

HERZL: It doesn't bother me one way or another.

HITLER: Keeps you stuck in the mud and nose in the ground, stops you from pushing the little people off the edge. Confidentially, I am enamored of the idea that one should be able, on a rainy day for instance, or at night with the fledermice flying about, to line up all those shrunken people along the edge, and phew! blow them off, so they fall like fallen angels into nothing. It might be necessary to restructure the roundness of the world into a square—like, say, dice—so the people won't be able to crawl around the roundness but hang from the edge until you step on their fingers, and whee! they fall, shrieking. How do you feel about it?

HERZL: It's an innovation.

HITLER: Got you! [*Spits in* HERZL's *eye*] You fell for my ruse, you pisspot, you garlic gobbler! Your evil stand's exposed. Your triumph would be a dance of death, this poor planet rolling emptily about the ether. But beware! Nature is eternal and will inexorably revenge the transgressing of its commands. By unmasking you, I have acted to the glory of the Almighty. Immortality, be mine; Judah, kick the bucket, amen. If you breathe one word into your book about our confidential conversation, I'll strew your ashes to the four winds and never talk to you again.—I'm going to bed.

HERZL: Golden dreams.

[HITLER *crawls into bed and falls asleep.* LOBKOWITZ *returns, wounded.*]

HERZL: Who hit you?

LOBKOWITZ: I was surrounded.

HERZL: How many?

LOBKOWITZ: One.

HERZL: Better be hunted than a hunter.

LOBKOWITZ [*Yells*]: That's what the fucking hunters say!

HERZL [*Cleans* LOBKOWITZ's *face*]: Love thy enemies as thyself, which is not asking much, since you do not consider yourself so great either.

LOBKOWITZ: I do not *consider* myself great. I *am* great!

HERZL [*Offers* LOBKOWITZ *a sip of Maltese*]: Drink and remember, next year in Jerusalem.

LOBKOWITZ: Yes, but what about this year?

Act III

Saturday. HITLER *asleep, his terrible feet hanging overboard.* HERZL *shakes him to awaken him.*

HERZL: Morning, Hitler! Get up, get up, Hitler! Early to bed, early to rise, makes a man healthy, wealthy, and wise.

[HITLER *does not stir.* HERZL *knocks on Hitler's head as if it were a door. Hitler creaks as if he were a door, digs himself deeper into the pillow. Herzl fetches cold water and pours it into Hitler's left ear.*]

HITLER [*Cries*]: Who are you? Where am I? Help! [*He sits up like a prairie dog*] What are you trying to do, give me a heart attack?

HERZL: It's eleven o'clock in Vienna. [*Dressing* HITLER] The sun is shining, it's holy Shabbes. I've worked out a varied cultural program for you, so let your heart rejoice. Take first a leisurely walk down the Ring to admire the architectural wonders. A tram ride to Schönbrunn Palace can't do you any harm. Arm yourself with hot chestnuts. If you do not suffer from vertigo, brave a ride on the Prater Wheel, enjoy the bird's eye view. In the afternoon, there is Charlie Chaplin chased by the Cheystone Chops in several movie houses. You may be back by sundown. I'll have apple strudel for your reward.

HITLER: I shit on your apple strudel! I'm staying in bed. I don't feel well. It's probably the Spanish flue, which has already decimated Europe.

HERZL: I don't care what you have, bubonic plague or housemaid's knee, you get out of here and pronto. I'm expecting a visitation, which calls for privacy.

HITLER: Uh-huh! You don't want me to meet your friends, you're embarrassed by my provincial bluntness. And this is what you call comradeship?

HERZL: I call it chutzpah. Can't you take a hint, Hitler? I want to be alone with my visitor.

HITLER: Uh-huh! Intercoursing, what?

HERZL: One day, when you are less of a bore, I might explain the purity of this romance. Now get your ass moving, or I'll call Frau Merschmeyer and her axe.

HITLER: Is the Danube still frozen? If anything should happen to me, break it gently to my mother.

HERZL: I thought she was dead.

HITLER: I'm in no mood for sophistries. I don't suppose you'll feel sorry, but most probably you'll never see me again. [*His chin quivers*] You may keep your winter coat. [*He drops it on the floor*] I want no favors from a sex maniac.

HERZL: Enjoy yourself! [HITLER *leaves*, HERZL *prays*] Let us wait, Shlomo. Waiting is the true time. Waiting for the Messiah is what matters, not the coming. So sit down, Shlomo, meet your maker with praise and a prayer, stop the clock and enjoy, enjoy the voice of the turtle, which sounds sweet in the land. It is already late, the death bell tolls, each of our days may be the last. [GRETCHEN MARIA GLOBUSCHEK *skips in, a big hen under her arm. She undresses; unnoticed by* HERZL.] All your deeds have turned to dust, Shlomo. How very much you would have liked to start the Russian

Revolution, but the goddamm Russians beat you to it. How lovingly you hoped to elope with Sarah Bernhardt, but no, she grew a wooden leg. What would you not have given—your right arm!—to win the Dreyfus case, but the captain told you, "Go away, it's already won." O Lord, you great and merciful God, keeping the covenant and mercy to them that keep your commands, which I don't, for even while I am consumed by prayer, I imagine the child Gretchen Marie Globuschek touching me where I am not exactly untouchable. My wicked fingers itch and uncurl at the vision of her sweet globes. I sit by the stove like by the waters of Babylon, waiting for the Messiah, all right, but I am not sure I want to be around when he comes. O Lord, frankly I would rather the Globuschek came, though I know I shall be punished for my transgression. Besides, what really bothers me, O Lord, here I sit and wait, instead of going to the synagogue or at least worrying, say, about the poor Hindus dropping dead like flies from starvation, while I am hoarding gumdrops as bait. Instead of worrying, I sit here and worry about the Globuschek and how it will be when she slips out of her slip, her marble body ablush with freckles, and parts her knees, a revelation of the night. Shlomo, you are not only wicked, you are—and this is worse—unserious. You don't read the papers, the news is terrible, have you forgotten the Lord's commandment, Weep in the night, but weep for others, not yourself. And what Anton Pavlovich Chekhov said: "Only the serious can be truly beautiful." Fuck Anton Pavlovich Chekhov. Let my beloved come into my garden and eat my pleasant fruits.

GRETCHEN: Good morning, dear Shlomo!

HERZL: Good morning, Gretchen!

GRETCHEN: Got any gumdrops?

HERZL: Yes.

GRETCHEN: How are you, Shlomo?

HERZL: Cold.

GRETCHEN: Let me warm you.

HERZL: On holy Shabbes?

GRETCHEN: You don't have to do anything, just sit there. And I'll cut your toenails, too.

HERZL: O, my Lord, hear me. What next?

GRETCHEN: What's the matter with you, Shlomo? Today is Saturday, and on Saturdays, when you are alone, I always come to you and rub you all over to thaw out your frightened heart and whatever else. Don't be afraid, Shlomo. I will stay with you the whole day and protect you from horses, the police, and God. And today, surprise, surprise! you may even fondle my hymen.

HERZL: My dear adorable Miss Globuschek: but for my chalk-infested joints, I would go down on my knees and charge ye that ye stir not up, nor awake my love. What, may I ask, do you see in me? I am old, poor, ugly, and no Chinese. Besides, Vienna is lousy with dashing guardsmen, lecherous schoolboys, heroic tenors, master waltzers, profound thinkers, champion melancholics, most of them blond and with enormous Viennese willies. If you want to act out the Beauty and Beast legend, why don't you pick on someone beastly, instead of putting me in the mortal danger of being punished by the Morality Police as a dirty old lecher? A river of fire divides us in age and belief and appetite. I am too weak to mount your balcony, and even if I did once or twice a month, wheezing in panic, what would you get out of it but a feeble fondle, and I'd be faint from fear that the entire police force would break down the door and boil me in oil. So let it be, get out of my frozen life, Miss Globuschek, the joints of thy thighs are most probably like jewels, thy navel is like a round goblet, which wanteth no liquor, thy two breasts are like two young roes that are twins, end quote. Solomon, with all his flair for ill-disguised pornography, knew what he was singing about. But my darling child, here is a pound of gumdrops for a farewell present.

GRETCHEN: I'm staying!

HERZL: Explain yourself.

GRETCHEN: My parents, he a guardsman, she a born Baroness Bornemissza, committed suicide one summer evening by drowning one another in a bubble bath, which my father excused in a scented farewell note: "My dearest Gretchen, your mother and I are young, rich, beautiful, in the pink of health, very much in love, and devoted to you, our only beloved daughter. What shall we do? Forgive us, if you can, we shall see you in heaven or in the other place." I brought you a present. Mitzi, the hen. Housebroken. She'll keep you warm in all the Viennese winters.

HERZL: Thanks a lot.

GRETCHEN: How ugly you are, Shlomo. Especially today. I could cuddle you all over.

HERZL [*Praying*]: Out of the depths, my voice cries out for help. Is cuddling permissible? [*As God*] "Cuddling is permissible."

GRETCHEN [*Cuddles him*]: What is ugliness, Shlomo? Animals are beautiful, especially hens. The face of a hen makes sense. But people's faces, do they make sense? I could nibble at those hideous little hairs in your nose. But that nose, that incredible nose, Shlomo, does it make sense? It is as mysterious as the North Pole. When I look at a human face, it makes no sense to me: an irregular ball, bush on top, two holes for eyes, two for the ears, one for the mouth. Try to look at a human face upside down, and it is absolutely illogical. But your face, my dearest, however mysterious, makes sense to me, and your crippled little body, too. You look like an animal. Perhaps you are, my dearest. With you, I feel at home, like with hens. If only you could give up your mysterious guilts, you could be my household pet. I could feed you and comb you and delouse you and take you for walks and let you sleep in my bed, and we'd live happily ever after. Shall we get married?

HERZL: They wouldn't allow it.

GRETCHEN: God would allow it.

HERZL: Which one?

GRETCHEN: There is only one.

HERZL: Unfortunately, that is open to controversy. Only one, yes, but which one? There is one for you and one for me. Could they be the same? Besides, they are grooming you to be a bride of Christ.

GRETCHEN: Thanks, but no. I have decided not to become a nun. It is monotonous, and no pets are allowed. Besides, how many brides can Christ have? I would want to be the only one. Also, Grandpa left me his estate on the Schwaitlalm near Salzburg. In four years I'll be of age. We could retire in the hills and breed ducks, weasels, dogs, cats, hens, cocks, and butterflies. And one day, we'll have children. Oh, Shlomo, can you visualize all those carrot-colored babies, with your nose, crawling about the hills of Salzburg?

HERZL: I say, aren't you going to catch cold?

GRETCHEN: I'm warm. Look at me. There is no evil in my flesh. Whenever I look at myself in the mirror, I say to myself, "Pity that Shlomo cannot see you. Show yourself to Shlomo, his eyes are as pure as a rock pool in the Alps." Let your gaze wander like a deer. [*She takes a locket off her gold chain*] I brought you my hymen. I lost it last night.

HERZL: How very kind. [*Takes the locket*] What happened?

GRETCHEN: In the shower, last night, I slipped and did a split like a ballet dancer, and I heard a little squeak. Now I am a woman, but still immaculate, and I'll wait another four years for our wedding night. Meanwhile, take your shoes off, so I may cut your toenails while you tell me a story.

HERZL: Ah yes, a story. Perhaps that is, after all, the purpose of poetry, to sit with a naked child and tell a story to this naked rose of a child. Good thing I washed my feet this morning. What kind of story?

GRETCHEN: Your story, when you were small. Anything but a Bible story! Forgive me, dear Shlomo, but what is the matter with you Jews? All those curses and lamentations, those rules and regrets! Even as King Solomon cries out, "Awake, O North Wind, and come thou South, blow upon my garden that the spices thereof may flow out," he is awakening not some fair maid. It is Christ who awaketh the church. What, by the way, do you think of Christ?

HERZL: What do I think of Christ? Oh, my fair lady, I could tell you stories that would make your hair stand up. Well, it depends. Which Christ do you have in mind? Arthur Christ? Hugo von Christ? Fjodor Christ?

GRETCHEN: Jesus.

HERZL: Oh him. Him I love.

GRETCHEN: Then why did you kill him?

HERZL: Who, me? Kill Jesus Christ? Whatever gave you such a wild idea?

GRETCHEN: The Evangelists, for instance.

HERZL: Gossip-gobblers, what do they know? Nothing, that's what they know, dreaming out their own dreams, not his. They can't agree on the slightest detail. Why? They weren't there, that's why. But I was there, I know what I know. I would know if I killed him. I didn't. I was all day in the crowds on the Via Dolorosa, ask his mother, right next to her in the crowd, when he came tottering by under the cross and collapsed. I told the mother, ask her if you don't believe me, I told her: "Go on, do something, he'll never make it up the hill, the poor kid can hardly stand on his feet." So she pushed her way out front to help him with the goddamm cross, but he stopped her, hissing between clenched teeth, "Let me do it my way, mother!"

GRETCHEN: Go on. Even if you're lying.

HERZL: Of course I'm lying. Even as a child, I was the master liar of Pest, because that which was in Pest was wicked, so I turned it into that which it should be, the good. Got it from Grandma Fanny, who lied me to sleep every night with lies from Shakespeare, and no matter how many corpses littered the end of the tale, Grandma would always add, "And they lived happily ever after." No wonder that at the age of six I was the antiprophet of Pest, I came out of the whirlwind in a sackcloth, honey on my tongue, locusts in my hair, and I told them in kindergarten and in the palaces and in no uncertain terms that that which is, is grey with lies, and that which ought to be is the rainbow truth. So they beat my mouth with dead fish until my teeth fell out, pearls before swine, like my father. I don't like the word. I'd rather call him the Organ-grinder, and my most famous lie, the one that saved his soul, I call the "Organ-grinder's Truth." I see him in a heap, curled up in the corner of the police room, covering his broken spectacles against the blow of rubber truncheons that rained upon his bald head. With each blow there sprang a blob of blood out of his bald head and streaked down his face, so that when they had finished with him, his shielding hands, each knuckle smashed, rolled down into his lap, and his face was striped red. Booksellers are not supposed to cry.

[HERZL *gasps for air. The naked* GRETCHEN *rocks and fondles his feet as though they were bawling babies.*]

HERZL: While my fat mother was sliced by the Cossack sword, the Organ-grinder was hiding in the shed, instead of picking the Cossack off his feet and swinging him around by his feet and dashing his brains out against a stone wall. That's how it began. To me, he wasn't hiding in the shed. To me, he came roaring out of the shed to smash the Cossack's head, and the stone wall shone with all the colors of the rainbow. Whenever I had doubts about the lie, I said to my doubting self, "Doubt not; he missed his chance in Lodz, but one day, here, in Pest, he will come roaring out of the shed, one of the just, to do justice to the memory of a fat woman who lies, sliced in two like a watermelon, moldering in a mass grave." To tell you the grey truth, he did nothing of the sort. He simply sang in the synagogue, the lousiest cantor ever. My God, was he lousy, never hit the right note, couldn't keep in tune. In the grey truth, got the psalms mixed up. They fired him. He bought this organ and ground it on street corners, grinding out godless tunes, "Wien, Wien, Nur Du Allein" and other syrupy songs. Now it came to pass that the kids in the neighborhood asked me, "Tell us, Shlomo, why does thy father grind that awful organ?" And I spoke to them, "My brethren, the organ is a lie to fool the police. The truth is, my father is about to storm the Winter Palace in St. Petersburg and go roaring through the marble halls to find the Tsar and smash his wicked head against the marble walls." And my brethren believed me and told the police, and the police came, two gendarmes, cockfeathers in the bowlers strapped under their chins, swords drawn with white gloves, and they took me to their room and gave me hot chocolate and turned the light into my eyes, and I told them the truth: how Danton came to tea, how Bakunin slept on the kitchen floor, how the copper coins dropping with a clink into the Organ-grinder's hat were all sent to London to help the Schnorrer Marx pay his rent and buy one tulip for his darling Jenny. And the gendarmes believed my truth and fetched my father and made him sit under the light, facing me, and they asked him about smashing the Tsar's head against the marble walls, like I told them. In the silence he looked at me over the rim of his spectacles, considering whether to say, "This child is sick with lying." But he did not say such a thing, for the ceiling had opened, and I looked, and behold, there stood the Angel Michael on this side of the bank of the river clothed in linen, and I asked him, "How long shall it be to the end of these wonders?" And he said, "Go thy way, Shlomo, for the words are closed up and sealed till the time of the end; many shall be purified and made white, but the wicked shall do wickedly; and none of the wicked shall understand, but the wise shall understand." And I heard but understood not. But my father spoke to the gendarmes. "Yes, this boobele has spoken the truth, and since the Tsar is not hereabouts, I will now smash your heads against the wall." And he did, until a host of gendarmes came swarming into the room. And before my eyes, they beat him until his soul left him with a childish squeak. And so it came to pass that, for a change, the father died for the son.

[HERZL's *tears, several thousand years old, come spurting through his eyes and nose and mouth, with a bellow out of his bowels. The naked* GRETCHEN *pulls his face to hers and wipes his face in her bosom.*]

GRETCHEN: Cry, my beloved, so that I may finally know what the matter is with you Jews.

[HERZL *and* GRETCHEN *sit on the floor, until* HITLER *bursts in, careening across the room*]

HITLER: Don't let me interrupt. [*Clutches his breast*] But if you can spare a moment, would you be so kind as to call an ambulance with oxygen? [*Wheezing, he trips*] Do you happen to know a good brain surgeon?
HERZL: No. I'm a stranger here myself.
HITLER [*Croaks*]: Never mind. It's probably too late anyway. What are the symptoms of galloping TB?
GRETCHEN: Spitting blood.
HITLER: That's it! [*He spits, though anything but blood*]
HERZL: Let me put you to bed.
HITLER: I want no favors from a corrupter of youth. [MITZI *struts a few steps toward him*] The rage of the vulture! Not yet, death-bird. Get thyself out of sight!

[HERZL *and* GRETCHEN *try to help* HITLER *up. Hitler makes himself deliberately heavy but lets them lift him by the armpits, the whites of his eyes showing. He mumbles all the way, as if in fever, while they drag him to his bed.*]

HITLER: Walked the white streets . . . imperial splendor . . . radiant with beauty . . . but inside . . . the marble precincts . . . this kaftaned death-bird . . . slimy side-whiskers . . . trafficking in pure Austrian pussies . . . all sorts of pussies . . . mainly blond and round . . . little ones, big ones, medium-sized, silken, wiry, balding, wet and figlike . . . "step closer, folks, and pick your heart's desire . . . two for the price of one."

GRETCHEN: Sir, if you have something new to say about pussies, please say it loud and clear.

HITLER [*Loud and clear*]: I'm delirious. Don't you see I'm delirious?

HERZL: You should have worn my winter coat on a day like this.

HITLER: I want no favors from a debaucher of innocence.

[HERZL *touches* HITLER's *forehead and sticks an old thermometer up between his buttocks.* GRETCHEN *warms up the chicken soup.*]

HERZL: Thirty-six, five.

HITLER: Thirty-six, nine.

HERZL: Thirty-six, six. You're a terrible actor. [*Pulls off* HITLER's *boots*] You should go into politics.

HITLER: D'you really think so?

HERZL: Yes, I really think so. Nothing to it. Of course, you should brush up your grammar. Study St. Mark in matters of grammar. "He came into Galilee and his fame spread abroad and he preached in the synagogues." Mark improved the grammar by adding "their" synagogues and thus invented the ghetto. It's as simple as that. Forget Shlomo, a Jew; remember only *them* Jews, and you'll be a king walking on a carpet of bones, and they'll follow you in the snows and the desert to the burning temple.

HITLER: Thanks.

HERZL: Don't mention it.

HITLER: You wept. I watched you weeping, a repulsive habit in grown men. But I cannot help admitting a sneaking admiration for your having wept. Obviously, you are a talented weeper. Where did you acquire the skill?

HERZL [*Shrugs*]: Practice makes the master.

HITLER: You must have been weeping for years.

HERZL: Five thousand, give or take a couple of weeks.

HITLER: As long as that?

HERZL: Since the Second Destruction of the Temple.

HITLER: Oh, I didn't even know about the first one.

HERZL: You must be reading the wrong papers. But, anyway, I sat down by the waters of Babylon, or was it Pest, and wept.

HITLER: I'm afraid I'm not very good at it.

HERZL: Well, you can't have everything.

HITLER: At my mother's funeral, for instance, I pressed and pressed. No tears, only a wet fart.

HERZL: Pressing's no good when it comes to tears. No muse comes with a kiss, when pressed.

HITLER: Well, is there a particular technique you would recommend?

HERZL: You have certainly picked the right town. The Viennese School of Weepers is nonpareil in the world. Technically, they weep more wetly than the Jews. No wonder, they carry their own Wailing Wall within. Nomen est omen. If you switch the vowels around, "Wien" becomes "Wein," not so much "wine" as "whine." There is even a song about it. [*Sings with tremolo*] "Wie-hin uhund deher Weihein." Nevertheless, I must caution you about the Vienna weeping. They are, on the whole, day weepers; and they that weep by day, weep on the whole for themselves only, turning grief into schmaltz, which, incidentally, rhymes with "waltz." True tears, beloved by God, are wept at night, and those who weep by night are heard from afar; if you weep at night, everyone who hears your lament will weep with you; even the stars and the planets will weep with you, if you weep at night, until their eyelashes fall out.

HITLER: Very touching. Could you teach me how to cry?

HERZL: Haven't you ever?

HITLER: Not that I remember.

HERZL: Can't you think of something sad?

HITLER: Frankly, no.

HERZL: Give it a try.

HITLER [*Closes his eyes*]: Sunset among cypresses? Twilight in an Alpine glade? All I see is myself creeping unwillingly to school.

HERZL: Forget about yourself. That only leads to day weeping. How about your late mother?

HITLER: Shlomo, you wouldn't want me to fart again, would you?

HERZL: Close your eyes, Hitler, and see her dead in her coffin.

HITLER [*Obeys. A small giggle struggles inside his puffed cheeks*]: Very well, I see her dead in her coffin.

HERZL: What exactly do you see?

HITLER: I see her dead in her coffin.

HERZL: What is she wearing?

HITLER: A dirndl.

HERZL: Stop giggling and describe the dirndl.

HITLER: Vast pleated skirt with red and blue flowers.

HERZL: What about her face?

HITLER: Like cheese.

HERZL: What else?

HITLER: Smell of cancer.

HERZL: What's that like?

HITLER: Rot.

HERZL: Rot like what?

HITLER: Smelly feet.

HERZL: Can you smell her now?

HITLER: Yes.

HERZL: Say something to her.

HITLER: Good-bye, mother.

HERZL: Say something to her you always meant to say to her but didn't.

HITLER: You never noticed when I lied.

HERZL [*Acting the mother*]: "No."

HITLER: You never realized that I had stolen money from your handbag.

HERZL: "No."

HITLER: You didn't know that I watched you taking a bath through the keyhole.

HERZL: "No."

HITLER: You didn't catch me under the appletree in the unsuccessful act of self-abuse.

HERZL: "Yes, I did."

HITLER: You're counting on my stupidity. You think yourself superior to me, an exceedingly honest Aryan. Out of the haze of your motherliness rises grinning the grimace of Jewishness.

HERZL: End quote.

HITLER: Besides, you don't love me. Nobody loves me.

HERZL: I love you.

HITLER: Oh really? Prove it!

HERZL: Hitler, how do you want me to prove such a thing? You are not exactly lovable. Nevertheless, at this moment, as you sit there with wet eyes, I love you.

HITLER: Then kiss me.

HERZL: Oh my God, policemen and horses I can somewhat reticently abide, but get me out of the clutches of this Tyrolean faggola!—No Hitler, I'm not going to kiss you, but instead of pursuing this embarrassing flirtation, allow me to tell you a story about true love.

HITLER: Stories, always these insane stories!

HERZL: That, after all, is the purpose of poetry, to tell stories to loveless children until the shiver runs down their spine. Now it is related of the great Rabbi Elieser that he had lovingly brought up the daughter of his dead sister and let her sleep in his bed, until she was sweet thirteen and showed unmistakable signs of womanhood, front and back. And the great rabbi spoke to her, "Go from my house and become wife to a man." She replied, "No, I am your maid and wish to stay, so I may wash your feet and those of your disciples." And he said, "No, little daughter, I am an old man, it is better that you go from my house and choose a youth that fits your own youth, one with feet that need not be washed." But she answered, "I am telling you for the second time, let me stay as your maid, so that I may wash your feet and those of your disciples." And he blessed the stubbornness of her love and let her stay in sanctity.

HITLER: Very well, then, wash my feet.

HERZL [*Washes* HITLER's *feet.* GRETCHEN *fondles Hitler.*]: Serves me right, telling tales of love to the loveless with stinking feet.

Act IV

Sunday. HERZL *shaves* HITLER. *Hitler reads the Bible and* Fanny Hill *at the same time.*

HITLER: Have you cleaned the oven?

HERZL: No.

HITLER: Swept the floor?

HERZL: No.

HITLER: Brushed the crumbs off my sheet?

HERZL: No.

HITLER: Mended my socks?

HERZL: No.

HITLER: Pressed my trousers?

HERZL: No.

HITLER: Made coffee?

HERZL: No.

HITLER: Warmed up the chicken soup?

HERZL: No.

HITLER [*Reads*]: What's fellatio?

HERZL: A kind of spaghetti.

HITLER: Damn Jews turn every sheep's fart into a sermon! [MITZI *walks by,* HITLER *flings the Bible at her*] Watch out, or I order you for dinner.

HERZL: Hitler, you have been abusing my humanism. I am not your butler or nurse. You mend your ways or you're fired! This last week you have been developing some of the worst habits of both Germans and Jews. You think too much, mostly rubbish. You whine and wheedle, you speculate, you theorize, you prophesize, you onanize, you polarize, it's always either/or with you, forgetting that the tossed coin may fall not only head or tail but stay in midair. And furthermore you hide hideously inside your hypochondria. If you believe that art and pathology have a particularly productive relationship, you must have fatally misread *Beowulf*. Why don't you go out and get yourself a job, if only to reduce the alarming rate of unemployment? At least you could paint a few watercolors that I might try to sell, some luminous still life, for instance. *Pig Knuckles in the Twilight.* Or, if the muses refuse to kiss your extremely low brow, at least try to improve your household skills. Learn, for example, to screw the cap back on the toothpaste tube. Learn, for example, to tie your shoelaces properly by crossing the loops anticlockwise. Learn, for example, the proper way of wiping your ass, a skill your sainted mother apparently neglected to teach you. And finally, Hitler, if you dare throw the Holy Bible at my beloved bird again, I'll cut your heathen throat!

HITLER: Suit yourself. At least we know where we stand. I thought we were friends. I may have expected too much. My old weakness, the unshakable trust in comrades who will stand by me not only on the sunny side of the street but in stormy weather as well. As for my hypochondria, so-called, I admit my pleurisy has improved, though there are a couple of moist spots left in my left lung; on the other hand, my duodenal ulcer, caused by too much chicken soup, has reached the pre-bleeding state of terminal constipation. I shall now go and try the impossible. You may pack my pitiful belongings, and I'll take the first train back to Braunau-on-the-Inn. [*Gets up, takes a few uncertain steps, then spins around and kicks* HERZL *in the groins. A deadly duel follows, Hitler grabs* MITZI, *holding her like a hostage in front of himself.*] One more step, and I'll wring her neck.

HERZL [*Disarmed*]: You win.

HITLER: Down on your knees, Jew, and cry forgiveness!

[MITZI *shits into* HITLER*'s hand. He throws her away with a Hellenic howl, bolts for the toilet, banging the door behind him.*]

HERZL [*To* MITZI]: Relax. This will never happen again, I promise. The ogre will be out of here in a jiffy.

[FRAU DEATH *enters, accompanied by* LEOPOLD, *a servant*]

HERZL: No peddling.
FRAU DEATH: Oh, goodness me, no! Is that what I look like?
HERZL: No.

[FRAU DEATH*'s fingers fish many bits of paper out of her purse. Finally, she finds the right one.*]

FRAU DEATH: I'm looking for a Herr Hotler, or Hutler—no, Hitler.
HERZL [*In a butler's voice*]: Who should I say is calling?
FRAU DEATH: Death.
HERZL: Do you have an appointment?
FRAU DEATH: Yes, I suppose so. [*She looks for more bits of paper*]
HERZL: I have no record of it. Are you sure it's the right Herr Hitler you are looking for?
FRAU DEATH [*Sighs*]: Oh dear, where is the list? Ah yes, here. I suppose it is. Adolf Hitler.
HERZL: Yes, but which Adolf Hitler? The ritual butcher? The candlestick maker? The mermaid?
FRAU DEATH: That's him.
HERZL: You've got the wrong one.
FRAU DEATH: How embarrassing. [*She looks at the list again*] Born Braunau-on-the-Inn?
HERZL: That proves nothing. There are so many Braunaus, you know, on the Inn, by the Inn, for the Inn. Besides, this is a most inconvenient moment.
FRAU DEATH: It usually is.
HERZL: I'm not at all sure he is in. And if he is, he is in a meeting, affairs of state, vital decisions. Couldn't you come back some other time?
FRAU DEATH: Yes, I suppose I could. I have other errands in the neighborhood. But I ought to proceed according to the list. Though I must confess it's not easy to keep to the schedule. I do admire Vienna, a magical city, even if not quite as moribund as Venice. But I must say, their sloppiness is beyond endurance. Nothing tallies. You can't dot the *i*s. I'm

wearing my feet out on wild goose chases. May I stay and rest for a moment?

HERZL: Frightfully sorry, madam. This is hardly the moment for resting. Some other time, perhaps.

FRAU DEATH: What time? There is a time for walking, and there is a time for sitting down. I regret the intrusion, my good man, but try and see the problem from my point of view. Parking is so difficult nowadays, the city wasn't built for heavy traffic. Leopold finally found a place for his hearse where he can leave it without undue interference from the police. I know I'm being rather a nuisance, but let me at least talk to Herr Hitler and arrange another appointment. Do try to understand—I've been up and about since dawn, rush, rush, and still lagging behind schedule. Mrs. Organdi was stiff as a stovepipe when I got there, and the day is by no means over yet.

HERZL: Please wait here. I'll see what I can do. [*He rushes to the toilet.* HITLER *is groaning inside, taking, apparently, the hardest shit since Luther saw the devil in the privy.*] Hitler, you've got a visitor.

HITLER: Not now.

HERZL: It seems urgent.

HITLER: Visitor? What visitor?

HERZL: Death.

HITLER: What's he want?

HERZL: It's a she. And she wants you.

HITLER: Now?

HERZL: Yes, now.

HITLER: Can't you see I'm busy? The least interruption may have fatal results. Tell her to go away.

HERZL: What d'you think I've been doing? She is quite insistent.

HITLER: Tell her to be insistent with someone else. I can't be bothered now. I want to be alone!

HERZL: Not so loud! I'll chat her up and stall. You stay quiet in here, no groaning. If you hear her coming this way, get out through the window, and hide above among Frau Merschmeyer's pig knuckles. [*To* FRAU DEATH, *who has sat down*] Consider yourself at home. How about a nice hot cuppa tea?

FRAU DEATH: Oh, yes! You took the words right out of my mouth.

HERZL: How fascinating. I mean, from a specialist, as it were, like yourself, I'd have thought tea was a major mortality factor, quite fatal if taken daily.

FRAU DEATH: Oh, absolutely fatal. Like everything else. Life, on the whole, is a hazard to health, an incurable disease so to speak. As for tea, it tightens the blood vessels until they're ready to pop, not mentioning the tannic acid that nibbles through the intestinal walls.

HERZL: Would you rather have coffee?

FRAU DEATH: Coffee's even worse. Decimates your brain cells, spreads carcinomic little bumps up and down the epidermis, and gives you, at best, varicose veins, an occupational disease. Comes from walking up the bloody stairs, down the bloody stairs, all night long.

HERZL: Yes, I am very busy. I suppose, you must be very busy too.

FRAU DEATH: A woman's work is never done. I hate to complain, but the stress is beyond decent limits. In the old days—I'd rather not indulge in nostalgia but, good grief—in the old days one had skilled help, chaps with the scythe, you know, strangulating angels, the lot. And people popped off singly, so to speak. A case of syphilis here, a touch of TB here, epidemics a rarity, thanks to Dr. Koch and Company, but all this newfangled violence nowadays, this modern impatience. Why can't they wait for their natural appointment? D'you mind if I smoke?

HERZL: I must say I do admire your courage.

FRAU DEATH: Chronic bronchitis. Hacking cough at night, grey blobs of phlegm in the morning. Wheezing even when descending a flight of stairs. Nevertheless, what I do like about Vienna is the nicotine nebulosity, a mackerel sky, hanging in salons and cafés, complementing the highest suicide rate in Europe. Smoking, like swallowing pills or jumping into the Danube, is a sort of premature antioptimism, isn't it? . . . What cowards call Viennese necrophilia is in fact a brave new world of realists who have realized that nobody lives forever.

HERZL: Are you sure?

FRAU DEATH: Oh, quite sure.

HERZL: Yes, everybody says so. The evidence is overwhelming. The cemeteries are crowded. Cremation, though a sacrilege, is becoming the fashion. I used to work for a while in a morgue, washing corpses. I can't deny the evidence. But even so, forgive my naïveté, I find it difficult that I, for example, should die.

FRAU DEATH: You will. Take my word for it.

HERZL: I do, I do. And yet, as I sit here in this little world of mine, which includes you, dear lady, and this cup of tea, and the pigs hanging overhead in the butchery, and Herr Hitler in there, trying, next to affairs of state, to move his bowels, I believe that all of it exists only insofar as I perceive it. And if I were no longer here to perceive it, this little world of mine, with you, dear lady, and the pigs, and Herr Hitler's bowels would cease to exist.

FRAU DEATH: So?

HERZL: What's it like?

FRAU DEATH: What's what like?

HERZL: Dying.

FRAU DEATH: As if you didn't know! People are so peculiar with their pretended ignorance. You start dying the day you are born. Each slice of skin flaking off, each fall of a hair, each forgotten name is a daily death. The big one is not so different, if done properly. Children die best. The old can be difficult, hanging onto a pain or two, until they get bored with hanging. If I may offer a piece of advice, give in, don't fight it.

HERZL: Does it hurt?

FRAU DEATH [*Shrugs*]: It's up to you. It's rather like birth. If you don't resist, it's easy; you simply wiggle into another time.

HERZL: And then?

FRAU DEATH: And then what?

HERZL: I don't mean to pry into professional secrets, but what is it like? A something? A nothing? A heaven? A hell? I would appreciate some inside information, about Judgment Day for instance, a thought which has given me headaches. And about God. Forgive my indiscretion, but what is he like? I mean, is he nice?

FRAU DEATH: Oh dear, so many questions! And only one answer: like everything else, it's up to you.

HERZL: Some answer.

FRAU DEATH: Sorry. Freedom is a frightful thing. Pushing the rock up the steep slope, it keeps sliding back, a full-time job. But that's the way the cookie crumbles. It's up to you, always. Don't pass the buck on to someone else like God. What can I say about him? If you're nice to him, he'll be nice to you. The rest is commentary. You know the Commandments, don't you?

HERZL: Vaguely. Secondhand only.

FRAU DEATH: Do you keep them?

HERZL: All of them?

FRAU DEATH: There are only ten.

HERZL: With a lot of footnotes.

FRAU DEATH: What did you say your name was?

HERZL: Zoff.

FRAU DEATH [*Shakes her head*]: I don't work alphabetically. Today I've had one Warlicka and one Baruch, for instance. You're being less than candid. [*Scrabbles around for another bit of paper*] Herzl? Herzl? Got no Herzl today, so let's drop denials. How would you like to die?

HERZL: Frankly, I wouldn't want to die at all, but I'm open to compromise. What this poor body wants is another tomorrow, so he may finish his book. Is that asking too much?

FRAU DEATH: Yes. So you're writing a book?

HERZL: Trying to.

FRAU DEATH: What is it about?

HERZL: You.

FRAU DEATH: How far have you got?

HERZL: Approaching the end.

FRAU DEATH: Approach it, Herzl! Don't delay too long, or the pen will drop out of your hand in the middle of a word. And less lying, Herzl. [*Rises and pats* HERZL's *cheek*] Stick to what is, not what ought to be, all right? Your friend has just crawled past the window in his repulsive underwear into the hereafter. You saved his wretched life for another day. Are you sure that is what you wanted?

HERZL [*Humbly*]: Yes, madam. That might be the purpose of poetry. To chat up death and stall.

FRAU DEATH: I'm not interested in your friend as a corpse. As a corpse, as a victim, he is absolutely mediocre. But as a criminal, as a mass murderer, as an exterminating angel, a natural talent. I enjoyed our conversation. See you again.

HERZL: This crazy town is full of people who are not what they are.

FRAU DEATH: Who is? [*Leaves with* LEOPOLD]

Act V

Day of repentance. HERZL *dreaming. Seven* TYROLEAN LEATHER FREAKS *brownwash the walls. Hitler's bosom buddy,* HIMMLISCH, *prepares break-fast.* HITLER *has turned* GRETCHEN *into a Hitler Girl. Everybody wears white smocks.*

HITLER: Good morning, Shlomo!

HIMMLISCH: Having golden dreams?

GRETCHEN: You laughed in your sleep.

HIMMLISCH: A crescent roll, hot from the oven, with butter and marmalade, lime-blossom honey, fresh orange juice, two fried eggs, café au lait.

HERZL [*Happy as a child*]: What's going on?

HITLER: The master has finished his piece. A masterpiece no doubt. Anyway, a book is born.

GRETCHEN: We decided to surprise you!

HERZL: How do you want to surprise me?

HITLER: By turning this dungeon into an abode of refreshing clarity.

HIMMLISCH: Where is it?

HERZL: Where is what?

GRETCHEN: The masterpiece.

HITLER: "Mein Kampf."

HERZL: Wherever it may be, it isn't really finished. It has an ending, but it isn't what you might call finished. I'm a slow burner when it comes to what one might call finishing, just like the Frenchman Gustave Flaubert. But if all goes well, which I doubt, in a couple of months I might offer something legible, if not readable.

GRETCHEN [*Coolly*]: Herzl, where is it?

[*Silence*]

HERZL: "The joints of thy thighs are most probably like jewels, thy belly is like a round goblet, which wanteth not liquor, and thy two breasts are like two young roes that are twins."

GRETCHEN: Herzl, where is it?

HERZL: End quote.

[GRETCHEN *hits* HERZL]

HITLER: Take it easy, Gretchen. The little one is impatient. Let me explain, Shlomo—

GRETCHEN: You do like explanations. All Jews do.

[HERZL *spits coffee in her face*]

HITLER: It would be more convenient if you told us first where the masterpiece may be hidden.

HIMMLISCH: We have been looking for it all morning.

HITLER: Our curiosity is overwhelming. You may take that as a compliment. How many masters could boast of eight strapping Tyrolean patriots—

GRETCHEN: Ten.

HITLER: —looking for their book all morning?

[HERZL *is silent*]

HITLER: Your modesty, Shlomo, typical of a true master, is very touching, but our need is sore, we should dearly like to peruse your masterpiece before it is presented to posterity. You see, I have taken your advice, Shlomo, I have gone into politics. It is my granite destination to save the world—the lot—including New Zealand. And if I am to dedicate my life to public service, I must be concerned with my reputation, so as to avoid false impressions, diabolical legends, misconstrued mythologies, and so forth. Now, in your book, a diary so-called, you could not help dropping a hint or two—

GRETCHEN: Three!

HITLER: —about my humble person, describing in your inimitable prose my rather touching incompetence. Such historical Tratsch, or gossip, is a legitimate device. But in my case, at the start of a new career, it may lead to all sorts of tiresome misunderstandings by the morons who make up the masses, whose cooperation I would unfortunately need for saving the world, including New Zealand. Shlomo, don't get me wrong, it isn't a question of censoring your masterpiece, heaven forbid. But if you'd be kind enough to let us study the manuscript, we might perhaps feel moved to make a few editorial suggestions to correct, if it proves necessary, a false impression or two—

GRETCHEN: Eleven!

[*Silence*]

HITLER: —suggestions that you yourself might find useful for achieving the final, the perfect, shall we say, authorized, version. Now where is that fucking book?

[HERZL *throws the breakfast tray at them.* HITLER *and* HIMMLISCH *drag him by his feet across the room to the wall, where they begin to frisk him with such ticklish fingers that Herzl can't help squeaking with laughter. Meanwhile,* GRETCHEN *ravages the bed, ripping mattress and pillow, horsehair and goose feathers flying all over. She finds a first-grade exercise book.*]

HITLER: Silence!

[EVERYONE *stands still, except* HERZL, *who crawls into a corner, and* HITLER, *who turns pages with fanatic fingers. A goosefeather floats into the silence.*]

HITLER: Shlomo, I see only one sentence here. The last one: "And they lived happily ever after."

HERZL: I told you, didn't I? It isn't quite finished yet.

HITLER: Where is the rest?

HERZL: Inside my head.

HIMMLISCH: Oh, well, in that case, let us turn that inside out.

HERZL: Now just a minute! Surely you don't expect me to tell you all that may be floating around in my head?

HITLER: That, exactly, is what we expect you to do.

HERZL: Now?

HIMMLISCH: Now.

HERZL: All of it?

HIMMLISCH: All of it.

HERZL: It may take, like, forever.

HITLER: We have time.

[*Silence*]

HITLER: This pause is too long, Heinrich!

[HIMMLISCH *moves swiftly, the others move with him, they corner* MITZI *in a corner, feathers fly, a last cackle, and Himmlisch emerges, the plucked bird, a strangled corpse, dangling from his hands.* GRETCHEN, *who has tried to prevent Mitzi's death, is being dragged away by the* TYROLEAN FREAKS. HITLER *empties a pot of brown paint over her head. Himmlisch plops Mitzi into a frying pan on the stove, produces salt, pepper, butter and breadcrumbs. Soon, Mitzi begins to sizzle.*]

HIMMLISCH: I'm serving tonight chicken cutlets, a Mitzi Schnitzel, in a delicious blood sauce. To prepare the breast, turn the chicken on its back, cut the joints in two, grab the wing and, with half of the breast, tear it off. Do the same on the other side, strip the meat, chop off the lower wing, pound it, fry it, chopped with bacon and marjoram. What's the final solution for a chicken? Stab it, seize it by both wings, bend its head, and cut so deep that blood flows. Blood, much blood, it should be a flood! Pluck and singe! Remove throat through the incision at the neck, loosen the entrails by placing a finger inside, wobble it left to right, turn the chicken around, cut tail upward, cut out heart, liver, gall bladder, gizzard through a hole. Take care not to break the gall. If the gall should break, it is a mistake! Sever the gall from the liver, cut out all the green stuff, cut the gizzard open, turn inside out, strip off the inside skin. Chop off the feet at the knee! Gouge out the eyes. Tear off the beak. Then prepare the carcass. Give it a firmness and fine appearance. Turn it on its back. Push the legs down. With a long needle threaded with thin white twine, pierce the point at the right side, pushing needle through the body in such a way that it will pop out at the left joint. Then shove the left wing through to the right wing, up to the tail. How do you collect blood without thickening? Hold up the carcass by its feet so that the blood runs out through the wound, collect the blood in a dish, stir in vinegar, so it won't thicken. Then fry our chicken! With bacon, onions, anchovies, juniper berries, pepper, thyme, thyme! Mix the blood with red wine, pour it over the chicken, and serve with a pancake. I only obey orders. When chicks are young, pour pitch and scald. Old birds should be hung up till they cry "mercy"!

HERZL: If you start burning birds, you'll end up burning people.

HITLER: Need more persuasion?

HERZL: No.

HITLER: Then start.

HERZL: Ah well, the purpose of poetry may after all be the entertainment of the wicked, provided you keep them awake. The most helpful thing would be to tell you to kiss my ass and let you proceed by crucifying me. But the idea of a wicked tongue upon my flesh is quite unpleasant. As for the crucifixion, martyrdom might be attractive, of course. Who would not want the world to shed a tear or two? [*To* GRETCHEN] If the ending cannot be happy, let it at least be laughable. I begin. [HITLER *nods, hugely pleased, slapping his thighs*] In the beginning was not the word, but the flight.

[*Music.* EVERYBODY *waltzes.* HERZL *flees. A chase á la Mack Sennett. Herzl is saved by* GRECHEN. FRAU DEATH *enters, followed by two dashing* GEN-DARMES.]

FRAU DEATH: Finita la commedia.—Follow me inconspicuously.

HITLER [*To his followers*]: Follow me inconspicuously.

TYROLEAN FREAKS and HIMMLISCH: No, thanks. [*They vanish into the air. The* GENDARMES *grab* HITLER.]

HITLER: May I get my toothbrush?

FRAU DEATH: Yes, of course. There are plenty of teeth, hair, and gold fillings in the place we're going.

[*The* GENDARMES *escort* HITLER *into the toilet. He stops at the door.*]

HITLER [*To* HERZL]: Pack my things.

[FRAU DEATH *sits down and smokes.* HERZL *begins to pack.*]

FRAU DEATH: Have you finished your book at last?

HERZL: It refuses to end.

FRAU DEATH: All good stories end with death.

HERZL: You are not exactly modest.

FRAU DEATH: Do you still want to live forever?

HERZL: Oh, well, the possibility is not without charm. "Nearer My God, to Thee," but not too near.

FRAU DEATH: My poor Shlomo. If you knew what is to come!

HERZL: Keep it to yourself, please.

FRAU DEATH: Fire will be set onto you. It will eat up every green and dry tree. Every face, from south to north, will be singed. Fire, fire. And you will envy the broiled bodies that will have been lighted by your roommate.

HERZL: Serves him right. Conquering the world, a goyish pleasure. [*His face sags as he rolls up a pair of stinking socks*] A Sock in the Twilight. I was too dumb to know that some people can't take love.

[HITLER *returns with toothbrush and* GENDARMES. HERZL *goes to him, buttons him up, picks lint from his lapel, wipes toothpaste off his chin.*]

HITLER: To quote Shakespeare: "Are you content, Jew?"

HERZL: To quote Shakespeare: "Yes."

HITLER: Is that all you have to quote?

HERZL: No. You have stolen my coat.

HITLER: I thought you had given it to me.

HERZL: Let's not get bogged down in details. Give my regards to the worms.

FRAU DEATH [*To* HITLER]: The beginning of a wonderful friendship.

HITLER: Madam, I shall not disappoint you.

[HITLER *leaves conspicuously with* FRAU DEATH *and* GENDARMES. HERZL *takes the remains of* MITZI *out of the pan, washes them, lays them out on a pillowcase.*]

HERZL: Does a chicken have a soul?

GRETCHEN: Oh yes. Look. There she lies, a burnt child, by time aborted. Our child.

HERZL: Let us pray.

GRETCHEN: I feel unclean, drenched in shit. You should have scrubbed me, too.

HERZL: Prayer does more than water.

[HERZL *teaches* GRETCHEN *the Kaddish.* LOBKOWITZ *appears from a dark corner.*]

HERZL: Some God. Where have you been?

LOBKOWITZ: I was here. I'm always here. Only you forgot to look. [*Sniffs at the pan*] Smells good. Eat, my son, not in hunger, but in the hope to ingest the martyr's strength you will need in all the years to come. You will need it.

[HERZL *eats, chokes, retches, stops*]

LOBKOWITZ: Wanna hear a joke?

HERZL: No.

LOBKOWITZ: Grief ain't enough, Boobele. In the heart of each joke hides a little holocaust. Like for instance, thief on the cross, hanging, groans. Second thief asks, "Does it hurt?" First thief says, "Only when I laugh."

[*All three laugh*]

THE END

Carmen Kittel

GEORG SEIDEL

•

**Translated by Frank Heibert,
in collaboration with Seven Stages**

Editor's Note

•

The premiere of *Carmen Kittel* was at the Mecklenburg State Theater in Schwerin, October 28, 1987. A revised version was staged at the Berliner Ensemble in 1989; this translation is based on that version and was performed at Seven Stages in Atlanta, Georgia, in 1991.

Seidel began writing the play in an effort to paraphrase the plot of the German naturalist Gerhart Hauptmann's drama *The Rats* (1911), in which a woman's desperate desire to have a child leads to betrayal and murder. The title also invokes the proudly independent heroine/victim of Mérimée's novel and Bizet's opera. Seidel tells the story of an eighteen-year-old woman in the former East Germany during the 1980s. On the surface, the narrative proceeds in linear fashion; however, by inserting brief interludes and songs in non sequitur fashion, the author creates a mosaiclike structure that adds up to a devastating indictment of the human toll the so-called building of socialism exacted in the German Democratic Republic.

The protagonist grew up in an orphanage. She has just moved into a small apartment of her own and works at a menial job in a potato-processing factory. She is pregnant but is forced by her boyfriend to abort the baby. Meanwhile her co-workers in the factory shower her with encouragement, advice, and presents for the child, so she goes on pretending she is pregnant. Eventually, the baby's father leaves her. Under increasing pressure from her female colleagues at work, who eagerly anticipate the little one's birth, she steals a baby; but, helpless in face of its being sick, she chokes the child to death.

This young working-class woman lives in a country where the working class is proclaimed the "ruling class," where everyone's well-being is supposedly guaranteed, since everyone is part of the "great collective," where the people are constantly encouraged to believe in a better socialist future. Seidel shows us a vastly different reality, as critic Martin Linzer explains: "*Carmen Kittel* starts from a state of increasing social alienation, a growing isolation of the individual and the disintegration of all collectives or, rather, their perversion into enforced pseudo-communities that are manipulated by slogans. In such a society someone like Carmen Kittel has no chance, in spite of the seemingly well-functioning social net (i.e., work, housing, a TV, etc.) and the pretended safety in the womb of a socialist work-team." One of the play's characters, the journalist Stein, coins a succinct metaphor for society's sorry state of affairs: "We wanted to build a paradise on earth, and when we were boring shafts for the foundations, we came across brown coal, and that's how the trouble began," referring to the vast lignite industry that was the main cause of the GDR's massive environmental pollution.

Carmen, the working-class East German, is about the same age as the happy-go-lucky drifter Kristina, from West Germany, in *The Tour Guide*. The two young women may be seen as emblematic of the two systems that shaped them. With numerous references to Greek mythology and classic culture, Strauss ties his protagonists to the education any West German received who attended a gymnasium (a high school where ancient Greek is taught). Seidel has his characters quote or paraphrase the literature, slogans, and folklore with which most East Germans were thoroughly familiar: the "International," the anthem of the Communist movement; Mayakovski's "Left March"; and Brecht's poetry (represented by lines from his "Fatzer" fragment), as well as folk songs, fairy tales, pop tunes, and so forth. He loads his text with references and metaphors. Seidel once stated about his and his peers' writing in the former GDR: "All of us inevitably worked our way ever more into metaphor, or, should I say, a heightened 'slave language,' to be able to write at all."

However, the power of his language, the strength of his imagery, the dry wit so characteristic of GDR citizens as a way to live with the fossilized state of things—all these made Seidel's play a success with audiences in Atlanta, who hardly were familiar with life in East Germany. The alienation and frustration of Seidel's blue- and white-collar characters, their anger and despair in the face of seemingly unalterable forces controlling their lives, and the grim sense of humor they developed to survive in dismal times are aspects of the play contemporary audiences anywhere can appreciate.

Georg Seidel was born the year World War II ended, 1945, in the East German city of Dessau. He was trained as a toolmaker and, after military service, became a stagehand/electrician at the Dessau Theater. Later, he worked at DEFA movie studios and, eventually, at Berlin's Deutsches Theater, the state theater of the GDR. In 1980, he submitted his first play, *Evaporated Milk Panorama*, to one of the theater's dramaturgs and was soon invited to join the dramaturgy department. Of his six completed plays, four were staged in the GDR, but not without official misgivings: beginning with *Jochen Schanotta* in 1985, the cultural watchdogs of party and state either insisted on textual changes or orchestrated a barrage of negative reviews. Seidel lived under the surveillance of the security service until the

GDR's disintegration began with the opening of the Berlin Wall in November 1989.

Seidel died of cancer on June 3, 1990. He did not live to see Germany's unification four months later, an event he would not necessarily have welcomed, since he hoped for a reformed GDR that would avoid the pitfalls of both Eastern socialism and Western capitalism, as he explained when interviewed in early 1990.

Carl Weber

Carmen Kittel

CHARACTERS

Carmen Kittel
Frau Schaller
Sonja
Frau Tschirch
Kraatz
Stein
Frau Wolf
Leps
Harald
Frau Schubert
Achim
Mourners
Gravediggers

●

Act I

1

Foyer of a dance hall. CARMEN, FRAU SCHALLER.

FRAU SCHALLER: Carmen, paint your lips red! This is nice!

[*Exit* FRAU SCHALLER. *Enter* SONJA.]

SONJA: Hey, you wanna go after the rich old goats? I know this girl, she picks up a guy 'round here, fat and greasy dude, disgusting. They go up to his place, everything really plush, gross. Next thing, he wants to marry her. And whaddayaknow, that's what they're doin'. Three days later, the fat ass kicks off. She rode him to death. But then he left her everything, the house, the money. Went to see her once, she smokes only with a cigarette holder and is bored to death.

[*Enter* FRAU TSCHIRCH *from the dance floor*]

FRAU TSCHIRCH: You coming, Carmen?

[*Exit* FRAU TSCHIRCH]

SONJA: And who's she?
CARMEN: We're here from work.
SONJA: Still doing potatoes? [CARMEN *nods*] Potatoes, what a dull vegetable! I'm outta here. Girl, you *are* wobbling.
CARMEN: My shoes are too big.
SONJA: You're smashed. I'm smashed all the time. Why are you staring like that? Whaddayou already have somebody, or what?
CARMEN: We're just celebrating.
SONJA: Let me tell you, you won't find nothing but shit here. Know that joke? Man is sitting in a bar saying: "I'll be back right away, just gotta go home and beat up my old lady." That's the kinda guys round here. All horny shit.

[*Enter* FRAU SCHALLER]

FRAU SCHALLER: Come on, Carmen, it's time to groove to the music now.

SONJA [*Tries to hold* CARMEN *back*]: Don't go, your tits are gonna be black and blue. That is music! Up, down, down, up, down, down. They make each other kings.

FRAU SCHALLER: Carmen, you must come now. [*Exits*]

SONJA: Go on! Look, your ball gown is getting old. [*Exit* CARMEN] Warbling everywhere: "Liberty and justice for all. Let freedom warble." Why don't you play the left wing march without the goose step for once. This is *square* dancing.

Wake up Earth damned this
Wake up Earth damned this
Wake up Earth damned this

[*Exit* SONJA. *Enter* KRAATZ, STEIN.]

KRAATZ: Blood-red night, but howling everywhere.

STEIN: You've got to understand, when there was still a God, people knew that paradise would be happening in heaven, and you had a future well beyond death. But now, what with God gone and heaven, you know, and paradise having to happen here and now, everybody struggling, then it's always nothing but better refrigerators and cars, you see. Hence the disillusion.

KRAATZ: That's poetry, man! You're a newspaper writer!

STEIN: Don't yell at me. So when people read that stuff, what's their conscience, what's their mood, what's their motive, after all? I want to know, can you plan history? Am I dependent? And on what? Look, yesterday, at national guard training, I'm clearing the scaling wall, and in no time, I'm a different person. Do they hope we'll remember the fighter in ourselves? We gotta be idiots. I have fathered three children, and none of them calls me "Father," imagine that. "Jack," they call me. "Jack," "Jack!" Why not "Jack in the Box!" So what's my place in this world? Last night I dreamt of an elephant without a head. Only when you see him like that, without a head, you start to realize what a colossus an elephant is.

[*Enter* THE WOMEN]

CARMEN: That's how you dance the waltz!

FRAU SCHALLER: Three glasses of liqueur, and already drunk!

FRAU WOLF: It will knock her legs out from under her in no time.

KRAATZ: Why don't you write about the women?

STEIN: What do you want me to write? "In some big bomb shelter of a place, women are shoveling Sprout-Stop on potatoes, and all of a sudden I spot a girl from our building. That girl—how she was shoveling. I felt sorry for her, but what can she do with my pity?"

KRAATZ: But that's a moral question, and we have to see that in a positive way. These are the last slaves. Everyone has a roof over their heads, though, central heating and hot water. One day, there'll be beer from the faucet, I wouldn't oppose that, life isn't that hard anymore, and the price will be we'll only have psychotics around. You either go under or you become an artist. In that sense, you can already say that each city is an artists' colony, where the sicklied masses paint their white bread. But we'll find a remedy for that, as well. You can't fool Mother Nature.

FRAU SCHALLER: We're getting mock turtle soup now, come on.

2

Carmen's room. CARMEN. *She's tired. Enter* LEPS.

LEPS: You need any bolts in them walls? [CARMEN *shrugs*] I'll shoot 'em in, right here! [*Shows his bolt gun*] One-fifty a bolt. What do you say? [CARMEN *nods*] How big you want the bolts? [CARMEN *shrugs*] What are you gonna hang on them? Pictures? [CARMEN *nods*] Cat got your tongue? [CARMEN *shakes her head*] Where you want the pictures?

CARMEN [*Pointing to scribblings on the wall*]: There and there.

LEPS: A bolt gun is expensive, too. Push the button, pow, the bolt's in—and wham, the next one's in too. [*Sets the gun to the wall*] Here? [CARMEN *nods*] Nails don't go in, they bend. Steel pins might, but they break off. A bolt holds for eternity. [*Looks around searching*] Where else?

CARMEN [*Pointing arbitrarily to the walls*]: There, there, and there.

LEPS [*Shooting bolts*]: Just tell me. It doesn't matter to me.

CARMEN: Vodka?

LEPS: Yes, just one. [CARMEN *pours vodka*] That's too full.

CARMEN: That's not too full. Cheers.

[BOTH *drink. Silence.*]

LEPS: That cracking sound is the heating pipes.

CARMEN [*Nods, holds up bottle*]: Another one?

LEPS [*Shaking his head*]: I don't like to drink.

CARMEN [*Pointing to the wall*]: Put another one in there.

LEPS: I could plaster your whole wall with bolts.

CARMEN [*Nods*]: I'll drink some more.

LEPS: The apartment's nice.

CARMEN: Brand new!

LEPS: Where'd you live before?

CARMEN: A home.

LEPS: A home! How long were you in?

CARMEN: Always!

LEPS: But now you got the apartment.

CARMEN [*Nods*]: The TV doesn't work.

LEPS: Broken?

CARMEN: Just now.

LEPS: Got to take it somewhere. [*Lifts TV*] Thing's heavy. Want some more bolts?

CARMEN: Don't know.

LEPS: Well, I can come back. Six bolts, that's nine marks.

CARMEN [*Hands him a bill*]: Keep the change.

LEPS: Thanks.

CARMEN: You live in the building?

LEPS [*Wants to leave*]: No, I don't live here.

CARMEN [*Clings to* LEPS *who accepts it, bewildered, then clumsily tries to kiss her*]: No kiss, just hold tight, hold tight.

LEPS: But you're crying.

CARMEN [*Shaking her head childishly*]: I never cry!

[*Enter* FRAU SCHALLER]

FRAU SCHALLER: Why's the door wide open?

CARMEN [*Points to a bucket full of water*]: The stairs, I wanted to mop them.

FRAU SCHALLER: The stairs! Stop smoking so much. And you've been drinking too. Your head, how do you keep your head straight? [*To* LEPS] Who are you? Go away, Mister, go away.

LEPS: Everything is shifting. [*Exits*]

FRAU SCHALLER: Who was that?

CARMEN [*Proud*]: Oh him, I've known him a long time!

FRAU SCHALLER: That's why you left work early? Him? Now you got everything, now you seem to think you don't need to work anymore. Why did you leave early?

CARMEN: Tired!

FRAU SCHALLER: Tired? That's no reason, everybody is tired! What more do you want. Didn't we go out eating, didn't we go out dancing together? All you think about is having fun.

CARMEN: Fun is work too.

FRAU SCHALLER: Oh, child, child.

CARMEN: Don't call me "child" all the time.

FRAU SCHALLER: Then show us you're a big girl. Show us. You'll show us! Or do I have to talk down to you? What about the vodka? Let's get the water drunk. Yes, we'll get the water drunk. [*Pours vodka into the bucket*] Put something on, we'll go for a walk around the block. You sleep better with fresh air in the lungs.

3

Street. Night. HARALD.

HARALD: On the upswing! Look at my pay stub! Are these numbers? These are numbers! The top, I'm at the top. On the upswing! [*Smoking a cigar*] The lungs can take it. [*Touching arms and legs*] Everything okay. [*Thumping his chest*] I'm loaded all right. Nineteen, that's seven and eight. [*Waving the pay stub*] I'm whipping the air, I'm whipping the air. Upswing.

4a

Potato-peeling bunker. FRAU TSCHIRCH, FRAU SCHUBERT, FRAU WOLF.

FRAU TSCHIRCH: Cold.

FRAU SCHUBERT: The potatoes smell like shit again. [*Throws potato against the wall*]

FRAU TSCHIRCH: The potatoes always smell like shit.

[*Enter* FRAU SCHALLER]

FRAU SCHALLER: Shut up! Where is Carmen?

FRAU TSCHIRCH: Where else? Sleeping on the john.

FRAU SCHALLER: Hold it, you're not doing her work.

[*Exit* FRAU SCHALLER. THE WOMEN *stop working; only* FRAU SCHUBERT *goes on with her work.*]

FRAU WOLF: My sister has a very nice job, now. In the morning, she goes there, that's the first thing. She has to take everything off and goes stark naked into this air lock. She can't take anything with her, no money, nothing, not even a comb. Then she has to wash her hair and shower. And then she's blown dry by warm air. And then, that's still in this air lock, they give her clean clothes, shirt, pants, smock, kerchief. All is white and washed every day. When she comes out of that air lock, she has to go to her work station very slowly.

FRAU TSCHIRCH: Why so slow?

FRAU WOLF: So that the air doesn't move. The air must not move! Then my sister looks into a microscope. She isn't allowed to move either. Those women from the women's prison also work there.

FRAU TSCHIRCH: Do they get clean clothes too?

FRAU WOLF: Yes, everybody gets clean clothes!

[*Enter* FRAU SCHALLER, CARMEN]

FRAU SCHALLER: Don't get on the bad side of all us women! Come on now, cut the eyes out of these potatoes! No, first haul away those sacks! What?

CARMEN [*Hauling the sacks*]: I didn't say anything. I'm doing it.

FRAU SCHALLER: If you think the work's too tough, go sell cotton candy, yeah, cotton candy.

CARMEN [*Hauling the sacks*]: I didn't say anything, I'm doing it.

FRAU SCHALLER: She doesn't even listen. Are you daydreaming? What are you daydreaming about?

FRAU WOLF: She needs a man.

FRAU TSCHIRCH: Take mine.

FRAU SCHALLER: Mine too. He would knock her up against the wall. That's what he'd do. You bet. [*Stamping her foot on the floor*] There, that's the world, and there, that's you. You are that, you, you, you. Cut out the eyes.

[CARMEN *cuts eyes out of potatoes*]

FRAU WOLF: She's gonna end up ramming that knife into her chest.

[*Enter* KRAATZ]

KRAATZ: May I?

FRAU SCHALLER: That person from the paper. [*Shakes hands with* KRAATZ] I am Frau Schaller, that is Frau Wolf, that is Carmen Kittel, Frau Tschirch.

FRAU SCHUBERT: Schubert.

KRAATZ: Kraatz.

FRAU SCHALLER [*To* THE WOMEN]: Comb your hair.

KRAATZ: No, stay like that, stay like that—and just stand over there. [THE WOMEN *take their positions*] But don't square your shoulders, you're standing like you're about to be shot. Would the lady move one step forward?

FRAU SCHALLER: Me?

KRAATZ [*Pointing to* CARMEN]: I meant you.

CARMEN: Me?

FRAU SCHALLER: Yes, you.

[CARMEN *moves one step forward*]

FRAU TSCHIRCH: How much of us will show in the picture.

KRAATZ: Head to toe.

FRAU SCHALLER: Smile.

[THE WOMEN *smile, except for* CARMEN]

KRAATZ: Don't smile. Look like the young one does.

FRAU WOLF [*Turning* CARMEN'S *head*]: How *do* you look.

CARMEN: I don't look.

FRAU SCHALLER [*Serious face*]: Is this right now.

KRAATZ: Look like you're important people.

FRAU SCHALLER: Ready?

KRAATZ: This is not gonna work. Let's go outside in the sun.

FRAU SCHALLER: Is it too dark?

KRAATZ: The light's too vertical. Your noses throw far too much shadow. Let's go.

CARMEN: Did you hear that? Our noses throw far too much shadow! Our noses throw far too much shadow!

FRAU SCHALLER [*Angry*]: Shadow, that's what you like, shadow.

FRAU WOLF [*Pulling* CARMEN'S *hair*]: Look at this! Doesn't wash her hair either.

FRAU SCHUBERT [*To* FRAU WOLF]: Lye, Sprout-Stop, all these poisons around us, till we are poison ourselves, full of venom!

4b

SONJA:

The muck from last winter still
lies around everywhere.
When springtime comes,
the weeds will grow over it.
Prussian blue is gray on gray,
and rain washes my hair.
The earth comes, the earth comes
into her strongest time.
Who dreams about love,
what counts is luck,
upright gait decreed by the State!
Prussian blue, prussian blue
are my frozen hands,
and when springtime comes,
red radishes again.
This here [*Points to the potatoes*]
is not for me.

4c

THE WOMEN

FRAU SCHUBERT [*Hauling sacks*]: You work yourself to death, and your own kids just grab the money right out of your hands. "Gimme ten marks, gimme ten marks," as if ten marks were nothing.

FRAU TSCHIRCH: That business with the picture in the paper was no good. "That's you," my daughter said. Makes you feel ashamed. Yech! And then she started to cry.

[*Enter* CARMEN]

CARMEN: Good morning.

FRAU SCHUBERT [*Pushing* CARMEN *offstage*]: Get lost, girl, I can't stand any more of this! There she comes, she picks up a potato, yawns, cuts one eye out of it, yawns again, stares at the potato, cuts out another eye, and then eventually another one, yawns again, then drops the potato, it goes bump, then she yawns again, picks up the next potato, stares at it, but doesn't cut out any eyes, she drops the potato, and then her eyelids drop shut as well.

FRAU WOLF: Where'd she go.

FRAU SCHUBERT: Who knows, off and gone.

FRAU WOLF: Did you see that movie last night? This man and this girl. The girl reminded me of Carmen the whole time.

FRAU SCHALLER: Why did the girl remind you of Carmen?

FRAU WOLF: She was supposed to dance, but she would keep dropping her arms all the time. They kept saying: "Arms up, arms up." She would put them up, but then she would drop them right away.

[*Enter* CARMEN *with flowers*]

CARMEN: There.

FRAU SCHALLER: What is it now?

CARMEN: Flowers! For all of you.

FRAU SCHALLER: Who are they from?

CARMEN: Me.

FRAU SCHALLER: For us?

CARMEN: I have some candy too.

FRAU SCHALLER: You wanna get in good with us again. No way, child, no way. You're on our shit list. Forever.

5

Carmen's room. CARMEN *and* LEPS. *Carmen is entering her room backward, staring at Leps, who's following her.*

LEPS [*Hesitantly*]: It's me. I've memorized the number of the building and the floor. But I'm not really from here. I just work on the construction site. I'm a driver. I drive earth. I shoot bolts on the side. Where I live, everybody but me is in the booze all the time, and if you wanna go out, all you can do is get drunk. I don't like to drink with men. I prefer working. Last time, I charged you for six bolts, but you only got five. You get some money back. Here it is. [*Hands* CARMEN *money*]

CARMEN: Thanks!

LEPS: I didn't mean to, but I added wrong last time—afterward, I remembered everything. Are you glad I'm here?

CARMEN: Sure.

LEPS [*Taking a bottle out of his pocket*]: This is good brandy. If you want to. I would have come earlier, but I had an accident. A cement mixer skidded right smack into me on some ice. They had to cut me out of my old hunk of junk. I was in the hospital twelve whole weeks. Fracture of the pelvis and lacerations, but only a few scars. I would have written to you, but I didn't know your name. Now I know, it's on the door: Carmen Kittel. [CARMEN *nods*] Last time, nothing was on the door. When I rang the bell just now, I was thinking, maybe another woman lives here now.

CARMEN: And me, where am I supposed to live?

LEPS: You still peeling potatoes?

CARMEN: Yeah, but you can't call that peeling. The machine does the peeling. We just cut off the really bad parts.

LEPS: First I was a tractor driver, now I'm a regular driver. What I used to like most was potato harvesting. [*Points to the bottle*] Do we want to drink something?

CARMEN: No! He drives earth over the earth, drives earth over the earth. I've had a boyfriend for a long time now!

LEPS: Stupid, this is stupid.

CARMEN: Yeah, too bad. Out!

LEPS: I'd have treated you good, really.

[*Exit* LEPS. CARMEN *alone. She stares at the brandy bottle, takes the top off, puts it back on, takes it off again.*]

CARMEN: Drives earth over the earth, drives earth over the earth . . .

HARALD [*Offstage*]: Just throw your jacket somewhere.

[CARMEN *hides the bottle offstage. Enter* ACHIM, HARALD.]

HARALD: Well? [*Caresses* CARMEN] This is Achim. This is his hat. Me with a hat! Crazy. Get going, fry some meat.

CARMEN: I don't have much meat.

HARALD: Then we gotta eat bread. Anything to drink?

CARMEN: I have nothing to drink.

HARALD: Then give me money, Achim will go get something. We're both broke.

CARMEN: I've got no money either.

HARALD: Don't lie.

ACHIM: We don't have to drink. I'll leave.

HARALD: She's got money. You stay. I bet I'll find some. Where should I look? [*Searches, opens* CARMEN's *handbag*] Nothing but candy wrappers. I'll find something in the kitchen. [*Exits*]

ACHIM: He's drunk.

CARMEN: I can see that.

[*Enter* HARALD *with brandy bottle*]

HARALD: No money, but booze. Why are you lying to me. [*Yells*] Nobody lies to me, you hear me? [*Shaking her*] They don't dare. When do you get paid again?

CARMEN: Monday.

HARALD: Great weekend. But what do we need money for? We have French brandy. Where did you get it, anyway? Don't buy this expensive shit. The main thing is, the stuff spins, it's gotta spin in your head, the RPM's gotta be right. Or what? [*Opens the bottle, sniffs*] But you're right. Why should the ruling class always drink cheap booze? We workers are the ruling class, long live brandy. [*Drinks, then to* CARMEN] Get going, fry some meat.

CARMEN: Give me the bottle.

HARALD: "Give me the bottle, give me the bottle." Don't talk to me like that. We had a hard day, too. One of us bought it. Fell off the eighth floor at the site. One minute you were talking to him, you turn around, and the next thing you know he's dead, dead. It's not like in the movies, somebody dead like that. See, when he lays there, spread out and all bloody, it makes you weak in the knees, you're shaking, shaking, and all you can do is puke your guts out! I had just talked to him, and ten seconds later, he doesn't exist anymore. But anybody can go just like that, any one of us. I covered the body with my jacket, but the blood even soaked through the fabric. Go and fry some meat.

[*Exit* CARMEN]

ACHIM: The way you're treating her!

HARALD: She lied to me. But she knows a good thing when she sees it. Come on, have a drink.

ACHIM: But if she doesn't want us to.

HARALD: "Doesn't want!" What does that mean? She bought it for me. Gotta take what you can get, or else you go to the dogs. That's how life is, always has been. You're probably too soft. Hesitate, always hesitate, and then you die, and what do you have to show for your life? To freedom!

ACHIM: Freedom! You know what freedom is? When a guy has the freedom to shoot a sea eagle, and he shoots it and brings it to me, at the museum, so that I stuff it. That is freedom, the sea eagle is freedom. And then a guy comes along and he's allowed to, he shoots freedom dead, shoots the sea eagle dead, because he has the freedom, you understand, he shoots freedom dead. [*Raises his glass*] To the freedom of the sea eagles. And I was supposed to stuff him, to stuff freedom!

HARALD: Forget it. Now you're at a construction site.

[*Enter* CARMEN]

CARMEN: Sucked it all down, huh?

HARALD: If you're not here. There wasn't that much in the bottle anyway. Achim, go home.

ACHIM: Man's cage.

HARALD: Man's cage. You're staggering, man. You know how it goes after work sometimes. The table is full of liquor bottles, and then the fun starts. And the first one to puke pays. He pays for everything, everything!

ACHIM: 'Bye. Or do you want me to say a poem before I leave?

Above all know
the point of the map at which we
crawled out of the blood-smeared, vague,
damned crust of the earth
What they feed on here
What kind of people and how many
are still there. 'Cause here,
I can feel it,
we'll stay longer.

[*Exit* ACHIM]

HARALD: You wouldn't think he was able to do something like that. But you gotta watch out for him, he doesn't have the elbows for a crowd, no elbows and no backbone. It always looks like you're about to cry. I know why you said you didn't have anything to drink. You wanted to save the booze for me and you, right? But I'll buy us a new bottle. Nice bottle. [*Blows into the bottle. Whistling sound.*] I'm a locomotive. [*Whistling sound*] Locomotive. [*Whistling sound*] No sense of humor, huh. Want to be a swan, huh, a white swan.

CARMEN: I passed out today.

HARALD: Where did you pass out?

CARMEN: I passed out at the factory.

HARALD: Worn out.

CARMEN: I'm gonna have a baby. When I was lying there, the women were all saying the same thing: "You're gonna have a baby." They're happy about it.

HARALD: You're gonna have a baby? You don't need one.

CARMEN: Would be nice, though, if I had one.

HARALD: Don't you dare have a baby! I don't want one, you hear me? I'm no father, I can't be a father, not me. Look at me. No, you're no good for anything either. You know what you are? Anemic, that's what you are, yeah, anemic, I didn't say that, my father did. He doesn't like you, but I come around anyway. If you like, I won't go home, but you gotta get rid of the baby. Done it already?

CARMEN [*Shakes her head*]: No.

HARALD: Everybody has abortions, no big deal. If you don't do it, I'll never come back. There's your keys. You can get rid of it, right?

CARMEN: I don't want to.

HARALD: Nobody needs to have a baby at eighteen, only when you're older, maybe in five years. It's much better then. For your health it's much better, too. Give me your hand. Promise me you'll do it. [CARMEN *shakes her head and steps away*] Give me your hand. How do you think you can start a family? You don't even know what that is. Do you know what it is, a family? I've been through it: It's shit. Shit. Are you gonna get rid of it?

CARMEN: Yes.

HARALD: Shake on it, come on. [*Takes* CARMEN's *hand*] That settles it. See how easy it is?

CARMEN: But what will I tell my women?

HARALD: You tell them you were wrong. No, tell the truth, nowadays, no one has to lie. Tell them you had it taken out. Your women, they'll understand, see. Too bad there's no more brandy. Did you buy it because you're pregnant and you're happy?

CARMEN: No.

HARALD: How come you have it?

CARMEN: I'm not telling you.

HARALD: You don't have to say anything, it's gone anyway. But I'll buy you another bottle of this. Because you didn't get any of it. Just for you alone.

[*Embraces* CARMEN] You have to like me a little too. My father acts ugly with my mother, and so she's ugly to him too. I don't want to be like that. Love does exist.

CARMEN: No.

HARALD: Yes it does, really, you just got to believe in it, and each time things get hard, now, I stand by you. [CARMEN *shakes her head*] You don't need to shake your head. When it's gone, the baby, we'll have a big party.

[*Music. Curtain.*]

6

A coffin is being lowered into the earth. GRAVEDIGGERS *stand with shovels full of dirt.* MOURNERS *throw handfuls of earth on the coffin, then exit. Exit gravediggers, dragging the shovels behind them.* HARALD *and* ACHIM *play the Jew's harp.*

HARALD: Those dirt clods on the coffin, when they were falling down, what pounding, boom, did you hear that too, boom. But being dead, if we were in his place, being dead now, not much to show for it.

ACHIM: You have somebody.

HARALD: If that were possible, to lift yourself up into a better life and then pull along that other person. But as it is, I don't know, we are the hygienic species, because a living corpse doesn't smell rotten. What are you doing, praying?

ACHIM: I can't pray at all.

HARALD: Recite something for him. [ACHIM *plays Jew's harp*] We should break the coffin to pieces with these fists, maybe he'd wake up again. [ACHIM *plays Jew's harp*] He doesn't hear a thing.

ACHIM:

We will chop off the lion's claws,
because the lion devours the innocent lamb.
We will slaughter the lamb,
because the lamb eats the green grass.
We will rip out the grass,
because the grass exhausts the earth.
We will scatter the earth
to the four winds,
because the earth covers the stones.

And when we have ground
all stone and the pebbles to dust
everybody will get a glass house.

[*Enter* KRAATZ, STEIN]

KRAATZ: Trying to swipe flowers? Get out!
HARALD: Assholes!

[*Exit* HARALD *and* ACHIM]

STEIN: One should write about cemeteries, as well; everything so straight
and precise. It's in cemeteries that the future begins.
KRAATZ: That is a daring prognostication, very daring!

7

Carmen's room. HARALD *sitting, smoking, waiting. Enter* CARMEN *with a suitcase. She seems tired and exhausted.*

CARMEN [*Happy*]: I could tell from the street that you were here.
HARALD: 'Cause the light's on.
CARMEN: Yes. Why do you look so glassy-eyed?
HARALD: I'm still tired from yesterday.
CARMEN: What was yesterday?
HARALD: The funeral. Maybe a human being only counts when he's dead.
But the living are drunk, and the dead are gone. There are these holes that
we fall into, Achim said. At first he was shit-faced.
CARMEN: I know a poem by heart too:

I want to sneak to every door, still
and demure I want to stand;
pious hand will give us food, still
I'll walk on to another land.
Everyone will feel so happy,
when my image appears to him.
He will weep a single tear, still
why he cries I won't understand.

HARALD: Where did you get that from?

CARMEN: From the tear-off calendar. Goethe.

HARALD: Did you have it taken out? The baby.

CARMEN: Yeah, it's out now.

HARALD: So it worked, or was it hard? [CARMEN *stays silent*] It's like they cut off a wart. Or so I've heard. But it doesn't really hurt, anyway. Here's your brandy back. [*Hands* CARMEN *the brandy bottle*] Just be glad you don't have a child. And men! Take a good look around! You have a nice home! You don't need a man yet. [*Tosses the keys to* CARMEN] There's your keys. I won't come around any more.

CARMEN: Sit down.

HARALD: I don't love you. It wouldn't have worked between us anyway, I'm not a good person.

CARMEN: You can still keep the keys.

HARALD: I don't want you to love me, do you hear me, I don't want you to love me, it's me that should have been aborted, yes. [*Hits* CARMEN] There, there, like that it's easier for you to forget me: Hate me, I want you to hate me so I can get out of here, hate me.

CARMEN: You still owe me one-fifty.

HARALD: Oh yes, of course, there you are. [*Hands* CARMEN *money*] Anything else, was there anything else?

CARMEN: No. In the end I might be the winner.

HARALD: What do you want to win, we can't win anything. Stop biting your fingernails.

CARMEN: You can go. I said you can go.

HARALD: Better times will come now, better times.

[*Exit* HARALD]

CARMEN: That pig. What a pig. [CARMEN *opens suitcase, looks for something, takes out mirror, looks at herself, makes faces*] That pig. What a pig.

[*Enter* SONJA. *She carries an accordion over her shoulder.*]

SONJA: I'm out of the orphanage now, too. [*Looks around*] Exactly like mine, to a T!

CARMEN: What?

SONJA: The apartment, everything's the same. Brandy. You're living high on the hog. Good money, huh.

CARMEN: It has to be enough.

SONJA: You look burnt out and blank. [*Points to the TV*] Color?

CARMEN: Yeah. Wanna watch?

SONJA: Naa, gives me headache.

CARMEN: Hot here, and dry.

SONJA: Here, everybody can die away silently without being cold. [*Points to suitcase*] Going somewhere?

CARMEN: Maybe. Are you still playing the squeeze-box?

SONJA: Sure. Shall I? [CARMEN *nods.* SONJA *plays and sings.*]

> Everybody eat your bread,
> everybody eat your bread,
> life is a slow dying;
> the swamps are dying,
> and there's greening everywhere,
> grass is growing and daisies too,
> but the yellow of the egg,
> the essence of the egg,
> the yellow cowslip
> only grows in swamps.
> Is it gonna be or not,
> is it gonna be or not,
> we scream in God's face:
> We see trouble ahead,
> the swamp going dead,
> hey God, shit us new swamps.
> Everybody eat your bread,
> everybody eat your bread,
> life is a slow dying,
> God eats his angels,
> God eats like a beast,

[SONJA *and* CARMEN *together*]

> Hey God, shit us new swamps,
> hey God, shit us new swamps.

SONJA: So you still know it.

CARMEN: Yeah, yeah. Let me play too. [CARMEN *tries to play*]

SONJA: Not bad, not bad at all. Come on, keep on, that's right, keep on. Did somebody beat you?

CARMEN: No. Listen to that, the steam pipes are cracking.

SONJA: Tell your boyfriend to get rid of it.

CARMEN: I don't have a boyfriend.

SONJA: 'Course you have. I was here day before yesterday. He opened the door for me. He was waiting for you in here.

CARMEN: He doesn't come around any more.

SONJA: That's why you're so down. Just be glad you got rid of him. That kinda guy, when they touch you it makes your flesh crawl, uhhh. Girl's hands are much softer. [*Caresses* CARMEN] Can you feel it? Do you remember when I used to come into your bed at night? You touched me and I touched you. You remember. Course somebody beat you.

CARMEN: Well, that's over now.

SONJA: Put the accordion down. I'm not into boys either right now. And when it all starts again, that racket, I'll say, "Don't be afraid. That's just the steam pipes." He *did* beat you.

[*Knocking at the door*]

CARMEN: There he is again, my boyfriend. Go in the kitchen. I'll tell him off.

[*Exit* SONJA. *Enter* FRAU SCHALLER.]

FRAU SCHALLER: Are you sick?

CARMEN: Me? Yeah, I *was* sick.

FRAU SCHALLER: When you didn't come to work, we suspected something right away. [*Wants to touch* CARMEN's *belly*] So, is the little belly getting bigger already?

CARMEN: No, I was in the hospital.

FRAU SCHALLER: Call us if there's another problem. We were worried about you, and we had a surprise for you at the factory. You wanna see the surprise? [*Goes to the door, calls out*] Come in, everything's okay. This is the surprise.

[*Enter* FRAU SCHUBERT, FRAU WOLF, *and* FRAU TSCHIRCH *with sacks, bags, and a baby carriage*]

FRAU SCHUBERT: Carmen, we've rummaged around at home for you, and at our children's places. Open them! You won't need to buy anything!

FRAU SCHALLER: Stack it up neatly now.

[THE WOMEN *empty the sacks and bags, stack baby clothing and diapers, set puppets and baby toys next to them*]

FRAU TSCHIRCH: Carmen, we're so happy for you. You see, even Frau Schaller isn't mad at you any more. [*Whispers*] Say thank you!

CARMEN: Thanks!

FRAU SCHALLER: Now, was that a surprise?

FRAU SCHUBERT: That was a surprise, wasn't it? That was an attack! [*Points to the brandy bottle*] You must have known we were coming. From your boyfriend, huh?

CARMEN [*Nods*]: French Brandy!

FRAU SCHUBERT: He gives you expensive presents! But that's how it should be.

CARMEN: You can drink it.

FRAU WOLF: But the brandy is for you.

CARMEN: Now it's for you too. [*Opens the bottle*] There. [*Pours brandy for* THE WOMEN]

FRAU SCHALLER: Carmen, you don't have a glass yet.

CARMEN: I'd as soon not drink any.

FRAU SCHALLER: That's better for you, too. To the health of mother and child!

FRAU WOLF: Yes, to the health of mother and child!

FRAU SCHALLER: May your belly not be the only thing to grow, but may your love grow also! And don't take any chances with it! Or else I'll smack your face. Cheers! [THE WOMEN *drink*] Well, Carmen, laugh. Or are you just flabbergasted?

FRAU SCHUBERT: My grandmother used to say, "The way it rattles is the way it rides."

FRAU SCHALLER: Let's go. We have things to do at home, too.

FRAU TSCHIRCH: "The way it rattles is the way it rides."

[*Exit* THE WOMEN]

CARMEN: "The way it rattles is the way it rides."

[*Enter* SONJA]

SONJA: You're pregnant?

CARMEN: I got rid of it.

SONJA: Why didn't you tell them anything, scared?

CARMEN: You don't know them. There! Now I'm big. [*Stuffs diapers and baby clothing under her skirt*]

SONJA: The belly suits you, very well! Wait a minute. [*Stuffs more diapers and baby clothing into* CARMEN's *bloomers*] Straighten up! Now you don't have to stand in line at the butcher's any more. Now you'll be king everywhere you go. Mrs. Queen Mother! [*Stuffs baby clothing into her own pants, recites*] "How can you help your people? What is justice? And if there is none, what's the reason? From which burdens do we still have to free you? And once you're free, what for?" [*Sober*] What a nice evening. [*Boxes* CARMEN *in the belly*] Can you feel anything? Can you feel anything?

CARMEN: Nothing. I don't feel a thing.

SONJA [*Rips the baby clothing out of her pants*]: Well, at any rate, you're heading for good times, whenever you don't feel like working, you go"Uh," touch your belly, "Uh, uh, I'm feeling sick, uh," and then you can lie down. "Uh, uh," you gotta moan. Try it out and see if you've got the talent for motherhood. Come on, do it. I've been pregnant three times, but now, no one is pumping me up any more. Come on, do it.

CARMEN: Hah! Hah! Now it's out. [*Sets puppet into baby carriage*] Little kiddy, little kiddy. Car and pooh-pooh. This is a house. This is a tree. This is a bird and this is an auntie. When the light turns green, we cross the street, buy buttermilk, buttermilk.

SONJA: Country-air-dried cotton diapers. Maybe I would have liked to have a baby, too, but the way I am, always drinking and everything, my child would have despised me from the start. I wouldn't know what to teach it, either. Squeeze-box maybe. Be glad you got rid of yours. You wouldn't have been able to teach him anything.

CARMEN: Every man is the architect of his own fortune.

SONJA: Not us! We didn't study architecture.

CARMEN: Car and pooh-pooh.

SONJA [*Pointing to baby clothing*]: Okay, let's get rid of this shit now, and we'll throw the carriage out the window. [CARMEN *doesn't move*] Do it. Can't you tell it stinks in here? It reeks of washing powder. All those shitty diapers reek of washing powder, scented washing powder. [*Rips the baby clothing out of* CARMEN's *panties, kicks the baby carriage*] If you don't throw it out, I will. You want me to. [*Throws baby carriage out the window*] Flies like a stork. [*Looks down*] Come here! It's flat, see? Good and flat. The wheels are doing a split, brrr, from the eleventh floor, brrr, flat. And the scraps you'll take to the ragman.

CARMEN: We could have sold the carriage. It was still good.

110

SONJA: Do you have a sack or a bag to stick all this in? Do you?

CARMEN: No.

SONJA: But you have a pillowcase.

CARMEN [*Picks up her pillow and slips off the pillowcase*]: There.

SONJA: Why'd you use that? You only have one?

CARMEN: Yes, but I'll buy more.

SONJA [*Stuffs baby clothing and diapers into pillowcase*]: Come on, help me, come on. [*She and* CARMEN *stuff baby clothing and diapers into pillowcase.* SONJA *lifts the sack.*] Pretty heavy: You'll get a few marks for that. [*Points to the sack*] Smell that? Really stinks like washing powder. [*Trys to stuff puppet into sack too*]

CARMEN: I'll keep the puppet!

SONJA: Come on, take the accordion. [*A knocking at the door*] If that's those women again, I'll trip them.

[*Enter* ACHIM]

ACHIM: The other day, I forgot my hat. Who plays the accordion?

SONJA: Take a guess!

CARMEN: Here's the hat.

SONJA: Did your Mommy buy that for you? Put it on. [ACHIM *puts hat on*] Real bad! [*Takes the hat and puts it on herself*] Well? Knockout, huh? Suits me better. Can I have it?

ACHIM: If you play something for me on your accordion, it's yours.

SONJA [*Plays one note*]: That enough?

ACHIM: Not enough.

SONJA [*Plays two more notes*]: That enough now?

ACHIM: Still not enough.

SONJA [*Plays one note again*]: Now?

ACHIM: Yeah, I'll give you the hat.

SONJA: Are you very sorry.

ACHIM: I'm not sorry about that. But maybe I can win it back.

It resounds and resounds,
thunders and marches
the cobblestones shoot sparks,
we yellowbellies, yellowbellies
are lying in the grass,
and our presence they can't cloak,
and so we go on living,

man, woman and woman,
loving each other till we croak.

SONJA: Not bad.

CARMEN [*To* ACHIM]: You leave now.

SONJA: Why you wanna send him away? The hat fits you, too. Come on, a left-wing march, but totally without the goose step. [*Plays the accordion*]

CARMEN [*Yells over the music*]: And me? What do I do?

SONJA [*Without interrupting her playing*]: You can drum on the wall with your fists.

[CARMEN *drums on the wall and the floor with her fists*]

ACHIM: And now let's do it on the stairs.

[*Exit* ALL]

8

Outside in a field. Birds screaming. THE WOMEN *and* CARMEN.

FRAU SCHALLER: He who fights and loses has at least fought and thus has already won much!

FRAU WOLF [*Unwrapping food*]: There. Jackdaws.

FRAU SCHUBERT: Those are crows.

FRAU WOLF: Dig in, dig in.

[THE WOMEN *eat*]

FRAU TSCHIRCH: Nice outing.

FRAU SCHUBERT: Nice outing, yeah, but it's no fun without men. Look here, these were once perfectly conditioned legs. I wanted to be a sprinter. Could have played tennis too. Like this! [*Uses umbrella as a tennis racket*] First you hit the soles of your shoes with the racket so the sand falls out of the grooves, then you run the back of your hand across your forehead to wipe the sweat off, then you tug at your soaking-wet shirt to get some air to the skin, then the first serve. Or you take this stance: head forward, butt sticking out and waggling like a polar bear in the zoo, in order to, what'sitcalled, return. [*Eats something*] What's this called?

FRAU WOLF: I don't remember what it's called. I found it in a newspaper. It's tasty. Isn't it?

FRAU TSCHIRCH: I like it.

FRAU WOLF: Carmen, you've gotta eat for two now.

CARMEN: Why?

FRAU WOLF: I keep looking and looking all the time, but I don't see your belly getting bigger.

CARMEN: My belly's none of your business.

FRAU SCHALLER: Why isn't your belly growing? It is growing, right, Carmen, it is growing. I've already reported upstairs you'll be out a while soon. Dig in and don't sit there like a dull knife. I've also pushed through a raise for you. You can't go on living on that small change.

FRAU TSCHIRCH: Say "thank you."

CARMEN: Thanks, Frau Schaller.

FRAU SCHUBERT: She doesn't like the food.

FRAU TSCHIRCH: Whether she eats or not, a baby takes what it needs. And when it gets nothing, it takes from the mother. Then the mother kicks the bucket. That's how it is.

FRAU WOLF: I went to the hairdresser's yesterday. My hairdresser is expecting a baby, too. Her belly is so round already, she could hardly reach my head.

FRAU SCHUBERT: Don't get grease spots on the grass.

FRAU WOLF: What?

FRAU SCHUBERT: Don't get grease spots on the grass.

FRAU SCHALLER: That stuff is melting.

FRAU TSCHIRCH: My stuff is melting too. Anybody got a tissue?

CARMEN: Here.

FRAU TSCHIRCH: That's okay, I can manage. Probably too much butter in it.

[THE WOMEN *wipe their hands in the grass*]

FRAU WOLF: You don't put butter in that. You have to eat it very cold. It's too hot here, let's get in the shade.

[THE WOMEN *pack up*]

FRAU SCHUBERT: You're thinking that stuff will get solid again in the shade?

FRAU SCHALLER: My entire dress is a mess. What *did* you put in it?

FRAU WOLF: I put meat and cheese.

FRAU SCHUBERT: Yeah, the meat was probably too greasy.

FRAU SCHALLER: Into the shade, everybody! Carmen, why don't you help? Into the shade, everybody!

CARMEN: Look there! Dead trees.

FRAU SCHALLER: That's what you see. Dead trees, dead trees. We are a very nice family now.

9

Carmen's room. CARMEN *is pulling baby clothing out of the pillowcase, looks at the pieces, sorts them.*

CARMEN: Good, good, shit, good, bad, shit, good, good . . .

[*Enter* SONJA]

SONJA: Still got all that crap?

CARMEN: Iodine.

SONJA: What does that mean?

CARMEN: Just like it.

SONJA: The word?

CARMEN: Yeah! "Iodine, iodine." What d'you want?

SONJA: Can you lend me some money?

CARMEN: How much you need?

SONJA: A hundred.

CARMEN: Fifty. There. [*Gives* SONJA *money*]

SONJA: Thanks. "Iodine, iodine."

CARMEN: You'll never be a decent person.

[*Exit* SONJA]

CARMEN [*Sorting baby clothing*]: Good, bad, good, bad . . . [*Finds the puppet, stuffs the puppet under her skirt*] They will get their mother cow. [*Sorts baby clothing*] Good, bad . . .

[*Enter* STEIN]

STEIN: What? You're having a baby? Why so serious? You're such a strong person! What shall it be—an athlete or a brainopod? Or a little of both? Something oblong, a philosophizing sprinter, legs over the finish line, head still at the starting block. Excuse me, excuse me, thinking, laughing, finally, the head has a few seconds of freedom. But that's not why I'm here. My john's clogged up. May I? You should listen to music, that's good for the baby. [*Switches on the portable radio. Very loud music plays.*]

CARMEN: No, no, when it goes so fast, it drives you crazy.

STEIN: Gotta take it! Sit down, sit down and just take it.

[*A knocking on the wall*]

CARMEN: That's the neighbors.

STEIN: Chaos! Great, chaos!

Act II

1

Street kiosk. ACHIM, STEIN, KRAATZ.

ACHIM: Text is the same as pretext, and life the same as death. Let's call death a bomb, let's equate the slaughtering of a bird with the smashing of a skull. Or: from positive judgment to the negative horizon, toward which a general is driving his troops. A sigh of relief among the driven: green grass, blue sky. Then a crunch. Four June bugs under the boots. The four June bugs could also be humans. Or ants. Or elephants. The four can be replaced by any other number, 'cause man is a jackass. Or: no animal lives forever.

STEIN: The way you talk, you're risking your neck.

ACHIM: Whenever we talk at all, we stick our necks out, and whenever we stifle, we stick our necks out. Either way it's the same. [*Holds out his hat*] Please!

KRAATZ: What's that for?

ACHIM: In former times, the sighted gave to the blind. Today, it's the other way round. Today, the blind have to give to the sighted. Be generous. It serves the conservation of the species.

KRAATZ: Man, I would say, man overtaxes himself. Take me. When I go to my office in the morning, public transportation kills me. And if I take my own car, the traffic kills me. It doesn't really kill me. But then, when I sit behind my desk, I'm totally wiped out, and I'm supposed to think, the head is supposed to think. And you know what comes to my mind then? Nothing. Nothing.

STEIN: Soon the sea will suppress its own rushing.

KRAATZ: Well, that's low tide.

STEIN: That's right, low tide.

[*Enter* SONJA]

SONJA: Carmen is at home, but she didn't let me in. She was standing behind the door and kept saying "Iodine, iodine" all the time.

ACHIM: Look, there she is, running. Now she's getting on the streetcar.

[*Exit* SONJA, ACHIM]

STEIN: I have to get back to those women. Potatoes, this dull vegetable, able to nourish an entire people. And because that's so, there's never gonna be a decent revolution in this country. The German first has to change his eating habits. The potato, the grayness—and always underground, never seeing the sunlight. And when it does, it turns green, same as we turn red with shame. That's the potato.

KRAATZ: You should see a doctor, get yourself a work release and eat rice, with no meat at all. Meat only makes you aggressive. And you oughta drink vegetable juices.

STEIN: And once I'm healthy again?

KRAATZ: I'm gonna tell you a secret now. Once when I was drunk, I got run over by a streetcar. See, half my leg was chopped off. "My life," I thought, "now it's over. I just can't live with only one leg." But you see, I have this prosthesis. Nobody even notices. You didn't notice anything. Even now that you know. [*Walks a few steps*] You don't notice a thing. Well, I can't run marathons, but that's no big loss. You once told me about a headless elephant. Those are dangerous dreams. I sometimes dream my prosthesis is growing skin and hair.

STEIN: But that's terrible.

KRAATZ: Terrible? My dream? Why terrible? You just don't understand that in the end you suffer anyway. The prosthesis has to become my flesh and blood.

STEIN: But that's not real.

KRAATZ: I wished my dream had a future.

STEIN: You're going to Latin America?

KRAATZ: Yes, I'm going to Latin America.

STEIN: I envy you.

KRAATZ: Envy me? For watching people fight? What am I supposed to tell them about this Europe? I'm afraid to go.

STEIN: Let's go. The night is spooky.

2

Carmen's room. CARMEN *with a very big belly. She stands close to the wall.* HARALD *stares at her.*

CARMEN: What do you think all these idiots are so frantic about. [*Pause*] You go out begging, right? Nobody gives you anything. And now you're here. You eat bread slice by slice, one after the other, like a good boy. You've gotten used to that, haven't you? [*Grins*] What did you expect? The peak of summer, no cracking in the steam pipes. The belly's getting bigger.

HARALD: But you told me you got rid of it.

CARMEN: As you see, I lied.

HARALD: Now you are the winner.

CARMEN: Can't take it, huh? Go away.

HARALD: I'm in the army, I'm on leave, I thought I'd come see you. [*Points out of the window*] They're planting trees down there. You got a new lover?

CARMEN: I don't need a boyfriend.

HARALD: When's it due?

CARMEN: Three more days.

HARALD: You don't have to work any more.

CARMEN: No.

HARALD: What do you do all day?

CARMEN: I cleaned the windows.

HARALD: Maybe I am happy about the child.

CARMEN: No need to be happy.

HARALD: Yes there is. What else does a man have? I don't have a thing. I drive tanks. You know how that is, sitting in such a box in the summertime? These are crummy times, atomic bombs and all. [*Approaches* CARMEN] When I'm gone from there, maybe I'll become an engineer.

CARMEN: What d'you want?

HARALD: I want nothing, I just wanna touch you.

CARMEN: Do, and I scream. [*Takes a knife*] Here! Don't come near me.

HARALD: You're crazy. [*Fights briefly with* CARMEN, *works the knife out of her hand, during which the fake belly drops out of her dress*] Rags! So you wanted to put something over on me! Nearly worked! You knew all along I'd come by one day. You're really something. But now I can touch you. Rags! [*Kicks them away with his foot*] Weren't you hot with that stuff under your skirt? [*Caresses her*] Crazy. [*Takes a large photograph from his pocket*] There, that's me.

CARMEN: Go buy me some flowers.

HARALD: Flowers? What kind?

CARMEN: Yellow ones.

HARALD: Where are there flowers around here?

CARMEN: Gotta look for them.

HARALD: You think I won't do it, huh? Want anything else?

CARMEN: Flowers, I said. Just flowers.

HARALD: Good.

[*Exit* HARALD]

CARMEN: [*Stares at Harald's photo, drops it to the floor, takes the knife and stabs the photo*] You don't stab right, you don't stab right! I want you to stab, stab! That one! Drives tanks! Tanks! Tanks! Moron! Tank moron! Tank moron! [*There is a knocking at the door*] You must think I'll let you in again. I won't let you in again. Fooled you, I've fooled you! [*Stabs with the knife*] Tank moron! I want you to stab! Now it stabs! Stabs! [*More knocking*] Didn't you hear, I fooled you, I fooled all of you, you can knock all you want, go on knocking, sooner or later the neighbors will come, they'll beat you up. Or my real boyfriend will come. You don't believe I've got a real boyfriend? I have got a real boyfriend! Yes, I have got a real boyfriend. You can stand there all day, the world can take it. I could strangle them all, all. Every time someone sits in front of me in the streetcar, that neck, I could wring it. What did you buy, flowers? Strawberries would have been better than flowers. Yellow cowslips.

[*Enter* FRAU SCHALLER]

CARMEN: You? How did you get in?

FRAU SCHALLER: If you won't open the door, I have my keys too. There's your money. Count it. Your belly's gone. [*Touches* CARMEN'*s belly*] What, you've had it already?

CARMEN: Yes. My boyfriend will be coming. You'll have to leave then.

FRAU SCHALLER: Of course, I'll leave then. But where is it.

CARMEN: Me? They kept it. Too thin. It'll probably die.

FRAU SCHALLER: The baby, no, the baby won't die, not today. They always pull through, even yours. But we'll go there.

CARMEN: Maybe I can manage to get it out of there.

FRAU SCHALLER: When?

CARMEN: Tomorrow.

FRAU SCHALLER: You see? What's it called?

CARMEN: "Carmen," too. [*A knocking at the door*] You have to leave, now. That's my boyfriend.

FRAU SCHALLER: Stay here, I'll get it. Good-bye, you. [*Caresses her*] A Carmen. But you'll let me keep her sometimes?

CARMEN: Yes. But don't tell him anything.

[*Exit* FRAU SCHALLER. *Enter* HARALD *with a bunch of asters.*]

HARALD: Was that one of your potato bugs? How she embraced and hugged and caressed me! [*Silence. He's embarassed.*] I don't know how to do it.

CARMEN: What?

HARALD: Present flowers. There. [*Holds the flowers out to her*]

CARMEN: I don't want those.

HARALD: But you said you wanted flowers.

CARMEN: I said yellow ones, yellow.

HARALD: There weren't any yellow ones.

CARMEN: Then you should have kept looking until you found yellow ones.

HARALD: You get flowers a lot, huh?

CARMEN: Give them to me. [*Grabs the flowers from him*]

HARALD: Everything's gonna be okay.

CARMEN: Sure. [*Rips blossoms off the stems*]

HARALD: Why are you tearing the heads off?

CARMEN: Well, they're mine now.

HARALD: Don't do that! You're crazy!

CARMEN: Hands off. Why don't you leave?

HARALD: I'm free till tomorrow morning.

CARMEN: Till tomorrow morning?

HARALD: That's not much time.

CARMEN: I'm going out dancing now. You can come along.

3

A nightclub. LEPS, STEIN.

STEIN: Nothing happening here. Even the Trojan machine's empty.

LEPS: What was that?

STEIN: I've been looking at you for a while. Now I know where I've seen you before. You once shot bolts into my four walls. You were right, you can only do it with that machine, and only those bolts. I've tried with a hammer and nails, no way. It's easier to hammer a splinter of wood into iron. Would you class your machine as a firearm?

LEPS: Firearm? I don't know.

STEIN: But you could shoot pigs with it.

LEPS: Probably.

STEIN: If you can shoot pigs with it, you can also shoot people with it. That thing is a firearm! Compressed air and green lighting. We look like cadavers.

LEPS: A club is a club.

STEIN: My colleague is in Latin America to see how the revolution is doing there. My girlfriend's been making strawberry marmalade. When she finished, she was totally wiped out. Now she's asleep. Well, that's all right. I should be going, too. Tomorrow I have to take a trip to the brown coal country. This is what I'm gonna write. "We wanted to build a paradise on earth, and when we were boring shafts for the foundations, we came across brown coal, and that's how the trouble began." Should we first develop paradise or subdivide the coal? They decided on the coal. But when the brown coal is gone, we'll put paradise right into the empty pit, or we'll play tennis there. And when the pressure on your brain increases, drink, 'cause booze promotes the enlargement of consciousness. But here, nothing doing. The distribution has already taken place, all the dames have been handed out. There was a time when I came here to pick up women. I never got any, and in the end all I was was drunk. Then I came here just to get drunk. But when I was, the dames picked me up. There is no logic. And today, nothing at all. I can't even get drunk right. And there's no one in sight to pick me up. You didn't get any either, huh?

LEPS: Well, what would you do: I'm sitting here, girl shows up, someone I used to know, sits down next to me, says: "If you want to, you can come home with me, all you gotta do is beat somebody up." Would you do it?

STEIN: When you see the couples clinging to each other, you can't help but wonder: Are they tied to their love or to the stake. And I'll tell you something else. You know why there's never gonna be a proper revolution in Germany? It's because of the potato.

LEPS: What do you know about potatoes?

STEIN: Well, what do *you* know?

LEPS: My grandfather was a farmer, my father was a farmer, and I'm gonna be a farmer too.

STEIN: Let's found a farmer's commune.

LEPS: Go and get us fresh drinks.

STEIN: What?

LEPS: Get fresh drinks.

[*Exit* STEIN. *Enter* CARMEN.]

CARMEN: Gonna beat 'em up?

LEPS: But how?

CARMEN: You start an argument, then you beat 'em up.

LEPS: Why d'you want me to beat'em up?

CARMEN: I want you to. It's nice you're here. I saw you once. I was at an intersection and had to wait, and you zoomed past me with your truck. Gonna beat'em up?

LEPS: Right here you want me to beat'em up?

CARMEN: Kiss me. He'll come over here. Then you drag me outside.

[*Enter* HARALD]

HARALD: You pig, keep your hands off her.

[*Exit* LEPS, CARMEN, *and* HARALD. *Enter* STEIN.]

STEIN [*Drinks*]: To the farmer's commune! Took off, took off. To the farmer's commune. Farmer's commune.

4

The street. Dawn. A dead tree. ACHIM *and* SONJA *are painting the tree white. They paint black crosses on the white. Enter* HARALD.

SONJA: Fish lay on the beach. Dead trees pushed up out of the forest floor. The people walked hunched under all the filth in the air. And there was a racket also, injuring the people. This is pestilence. Some were screaming "This is pestilence"; only it leads to a different death. Because—and that's what everybody was so proud about—it was shifted onto the water, the air, the birds, the fish, shifted onto the earth, whose fissures slowly grew wider. They opened up as an abyss directly to hell. Some people had already vanished in the depths.

ACHIM: Hey hard-hat fart, hey hard-hat fart!

HARALD: I'm not any more. Here! [*Makes a movement as if he held an automatic pistol in his hand*] Hands up, hands up! Or else, "ta ta ta ta ta!" That's me now.

ACHIM: What an improvement.

HARALD: Not really. You're right. "Atten-tion!" day in, day out, around and around, and up and down. I'm tired. I'm washed out. I could puke. Sing me something.

SONJA:

Sleeping Beauty lay in the pit,
she really was a beautiful kid.
And soon Knight Valiant came ahead,
ate the last crumb of his bread,
gasped and died. And that's because:
The wall of briars was barbed wire
dripping red with rabbit blood
his heart consumed in dumdum fire
Beauty's mouth was choked with mud.
So she slept for a hundred year
till a new knight came along
left his tank in battle gear
that completes this fairy song.
The sun rose east
and wandered west.
Don't look for rhyme nor reason here,
yelled the prince, that much is clear.
We'll celebrate the wedding night
then you'll go spin and I'll go fight.

HARALD [*To* ACHIM]: Your love of nature coming through again, huh? [*Pointing to the tree*] What's that supposed to be?

ACHIM: Well, there's the monument for the dead soldier, but no monument for the dead eagle.

HARALD:

Eat, drink and be merry,
the slave doesn't starve,
there's bread in his muzzle
and plenty of booze!

ACHIM [*Pointing to* HARALD's *face*]: Is that blood or lipstick?

HARALD: How should I know. When the average Joe hits you, it's nothing to joke about. They can all go to the devil. Nothing to it. [*Desperate*] That was freedom, twenty-four hours of freedom. Air of the barracks! You know how men's sweat stinks from the boots.

ACHIM: Colorful dawn.

HARALD: Fuck dawn. Black crosses and dawn, everything's dead, dawn, dawn.

5

STEIN, KRAATZ

STEIN: Back from Latin America?

KRAATZ: Yes. Notice anything?

STEIN: What should I notice?

KRAATZ: I won't tell you.

STEIN: You're embarassing me.

KRAATZ: Haven't I changed?

STEIN: You're very tanned in your face.

KRAATZ: I have no masks anymore. I told a soldier to shoot off my prosthesis, so the soldiers used it for target practice. You understand, it was a blast! I pulled my pants' leg up, the soldiers got their guns and shot the prosthesis to pieces.

STEIN: But how will you officially present yourself now?

KRAATZ: Me? One day they'll come to Europe, they'll step out of their headless elephant, and they'll shoot off everybody's prostheses, but if none of us shows them where the prosthesis is, because we don't know which part it is, they'll hit the whole man, and that's gonna be our death.

STEIN: Strange images.

6

Carmen's room. LEPS, CARMEN.

LEPS: Why are you shaking like that?

CARMEN: Get lost! I told you to get lost! The way you kicked, full blast against his skull, there's even blood on your shoe!

LEPS: What a big mouth. Guys like him need it right in the kisser.

CARMEN: But just a little, so they don't kick the bucket.

LEPS: Naa, he won't. These flowers were from him? [*Tramples the torn-off flowers*] Hear that crunching? First you're with him, now you want it with me.

CARMEN: I don't want it with you.

LEPS: Sure you want it with me. Dirt! Where's the broom and the dustpan? I—you gotta know that—I prefer things clean, you'll learn that with me. When I was a sergeant, they all learned it. They had to hop to, the dogs. Nice big eyes. I don't usually know the way to a woman's heart, but when I do, I don't let go. Nightclub. Crazy world. But life doesn't have to be crazy. "Take," my mother always said, "take a simple girl." I talked to a guy who wanted more revolution. Idiots! Let them do it. I liked being a soldier. They're gonna shoot those dogs. Come.

CARMEN [*Sharply*]: What?

LEPS: I'll treat you good. There's money. I got a house, too. Not here—in my village. My homegrown potatoes are better than this collective shit. You'll see. City's shit, anyway. You're not going to be a slave anymore.

CARMEN: I have to get my baby now.

LEPS: You got a baby? So a man fights, and that's what he gets? There, I got hit too. You're lying, you don't have a baby, not you.

CARMEN: Wanna see it.

LEPS: I don't wanna see your baby now. And whose is it? That guy again? You did it all with him, huh? Listen, I want it all too. Take off your clothes.

CARMEN: Don't step on those flowers again.

LEPS: Dry mess.

CARMEN: Pick up the flowers. You're gonna bend down and pick up the flowers.

LEPS: We're still the winners.

7

Carmen's room. FRAU WOLF, FRAU SCHUBERT.

FRAU WOLF: There are some women that kill their babies. They give birth in secret, and then they kill them.

[*Enter* FRAU SCHALLER]

FRAU SCHALLER: Hush, she's sleeping in the other room with the baby.

FRAU WOLF: Why doesn't she plant flowers on her balcony?

124

FRAU SCHUBERT: The wind rips them out of the flower boxes. She should plant those little crippled pines.

FRAU WOLF: Crippled pines, crippled pines.

FRAU SCHALLER: But all in all, she's lucky.

FRAU SCHUBERT: Lucky? Why?

FRAU SCHALLER: Everything here, everything.

FRAU WOLF: What's on television?

FRAU SCHALLER: Some variety show. [*Turns on TV*] There, a man is sawing a woman in half.

FRAU SCHUBERT: Why is it always the men in the variety shows that saw the women in half or stick daggers into them. First the men stick the women into a box, and then the women get sawed in half. Why is it never the other way 'round. And the women even enjoy it, when the men do this to them. They smile all the time.

FRAU WOLF: They don't really get sawed in half.

FRAU SCHUBERT: I know that, that they don't really get sawed in half. But probably the men would really like to, you can tell.

FRAU WOLF: If you took everything so seriously, you couldn't go on living, then everything would be somehow wrong. That money they earn for such a little sawing job, I'd take that too. Now he's sawed her in half.

FRAU SCHUBERT: But that's two women. One shows her legs and the other her head.

FRAU WOLF: You have to fold up real small to fit in a box like that.

FRAU SCHALLER: Do you hear? Now Carmen's awake.

[*Enter* CARMEN *with a baby in her arms*]

CARMEN: Oh, you're here already. [*Points to the baby*] Here it is.

FRAU WOLF: It's asleep.

CARMEN: Don't touch it.

FRAU WOLF: I only wanted to hold it.

CARMEN: You've got your own. Go now.

FRAU WOLF: But why?

CARMEN: Mine, it's mine.

FRAU SCHALLER: Let's go. We've seen the baby, that's all we wanted.

[*Exit* THE WOMEN]

CARMEN: That's all they wanted. [*Sings*] Mary, spread your holy mantle and make it shield and shelter for us.

[*Enter* SONJA]

SONJA: Carmen.

CARMEN: The baby's eyes were oozing, and it was coughing all the time.

SONJA: So you played it through! The belly. You did it. The police are everywhere, they're already looking for the baby.

CARMEN: The women kept coming every day, they wanted to see one.

SONJA: You got a fever.

[*A knocking at the door*]

CARMEN: It was coughing all the time. Mine. I choked it.

SONJA: You filthy scum! Quiet, don't open the door now, you gotta breathe. Carmen, gotta breathe. Breathe. Breathe.

THE END

The Beautiful Stranger

KLAUS POHL

•

Translated by Carl Weber

For Franco C.

Also thou shalt not oppress a stranger: for ye know the heart
of a stranger, seeing ye were strangers in the land of Egypt.
—22 *Exodus 21*

Editor's Note

•

The Beautiful Stranger (Die schöne Fremde) was first performed at the Ruhrfestspiele (Ruhr Festival) in Recklinghausen in 1991. It received a decidedly hostile reception by many critics, who objected to the author's treatment of a politically loaded, sensitive topic. Nevertheless, soon after the play was performed at numerous theaters, from Hamburg to Düsseldorf to Zürich, it became a popular success.

Pohl's text was the first effort to explore onstage the hostility and violence against foreigners that had become so notorious in the newly unified Germany. The audience is invited to the town of Bebra, which is revealed as a site where ignorance and unmitigated brutality rule. Bebra happens to be close to Wartburg Castle, where Luther translated the Bible, and to Goethe's Weimar, with nearby Sachsenhausen concentration camp, places that until 1990 were on the other side of the former intra-German border. Bebra, at the geographical center of present-day Germany, might be considered the archetypal provincial town. The Frankfurt School thinker Theodor W. Adorno once observed, "The provincial and the propensity for barbarity dwell close to each other." Pohl's play demonstrates Adorno's point, showing how ignorance and greed foster violence against anyone who represents "the other," anyone who might be perceived as a threat by the narrow provincial mind.

As the author himself puts it, "I hate violence, I hate it from the bottom of my heart, but I am confronted with this brutality every day. I hate it and that's why it fascinates me." It may be his fascination with violence that made Pohl create in his play such a compelling metaphor for the internalized dark urges that have surged to the surface of German society since unification.

The play starts like an especially nasty version of *Married with Children* but escalates quickly into a series of aggressive acts, in which a Polish traveler is brutally slain while a Jewish American tourist, who happens to witness the killing, is sexually insulted and abused. Eventually, the Jewish woman returns to the town of Bebra and exacts her shocking revenge. The text combines elements of a thriller with the dramaturgy of melodrama, while leaving ample room for moments of humor, albeit a very dark humor. Pohl's deft grasp of popular theatrical forms was no doubt one of the reasons the play had such a sweeping success with German audiences; it reflects his comprehensive experience as an actor, director, and playwright.

Klaus Pohl was born in the idyllic old town of Rothenburg in 1952, the child of a resettled family from the former eastern provinces of the German Reich—that is, he was a stranger. After completing his schooling, Pohl was trained as a salesperson. When he refused military service, he served as a hospital nurse instead. At the age of twenty-one Pohl was accepted into the Max Reinhardt Theater Academy of Berlin. In 1975, he began his successful acting career at theaters in Berlin, Hamburg, and Zürich, as well as in film and television.

Pohl's early efforts as a playwright were not well received. However, in 1984, a play that investigated the frictions between indigenous farmers and fugitives from the East who were resettled in the north German countryside after World War II, *The Old Country* (Das Alte Land), was a resounding success at the Vienna Burg Theater and garnered Pohl several awards. He eventually began to direct his own plays. With *The Beautiful Stranger* and the complementary *Karate Willy Returns* (a 1991 play about the ubiquitous presence of former Stasi agents in postunification East Germany), he has become one of the most frequently performed playwrights in the language. Pohl's texts represent a tradition that originated in the Weimar Republic of the 1920s, namely that of the Zeitstück (i.e., plays that speak directly and unabashedly to contemporary social and political issues). It is hardly a surprise that, unlike many of his peers, Pohl never felt embarrassed when labels such as "popular" or "commercial" were applied to his work. One recent play, *Manni Ramm* (1993), has as its protagonist a celebrated soccer player.

Pohl currently lives and writes in New York City. He once said that as an author and actor he wants to investigate "what is doable on stage." And he responded, in 1983, to a theater journal's question about his aesthetics, "I observe. And am wary of quick conclusions."

Carl Weber

The Beautiful Stranger

●

Act I

The Lobby and main room of a run-down small town hotel. An Old-German-style bar, with bar stools. A few tables, a coatrack. A bandstand with a curtain. Wallpaper of a faded flower print, covered with the grime of many decades. Yellow-stained curtains. On the walls, several roebuck antlers and many framed color photographs of prizewinning German shepherds.

1

At one of the tables, the brothers ULRICH *and* CHRISTIAN MAUL *with Christian's wife,* ROSEL. *The brothers Maul are wearing exactly matching checked jackets with black suede elbow patches. While they are stuffing their fat shiny cheeks with food, gulping down red wine between bites, Rosel sits silently before her empty plate. She is digging with a toothpick for particles of food between her teeth, hiding her mouth with her other hand. Behind the bar,* JUTTA MIELKE, *owner of the hotel, is busying herself with all kinds of chores.*

ULRICH: In my book, Wenzel Schuhmacher is the biggest arsehole. That's why he's on the City Council. Let's order another bottle, Christian. And you shut up, Rosel.

CHRISTIAN [*To* ROSEL]: Looks revolting what you're doing!

ULRICH: I was just going to say so!

CHRISTIAN: Digging between her teeth as if she's digging out half a pig stuck in there!

ULRICH: She won't listen!

CHRISTIAN [*Jabs elbow into* ROSEL's *ribs*]: Why don't you listen?!

ROSEL: Ouch!

CHRISTIAN: That looks revolting what you're doing there.

ULRICH: That female makes any man hate women! [*Burps*] Frau Mielke! Hey there! [*Waves an empty red wine bottle above his head*] Reinforcements!

[MIELKE *takes a bottle from the shelf and opens it*]

ROSEL: You're having another one?

CHRISTIAN: Quiet! [*Jabs elbow into* ROSEL's *ribs*]

MIELKE [*Brings the new bottle and puts it on the table*]: Well? How is it? The goose?

ULRICH: It's disgusting! The goose! [*Burps*] The wine's good, though! Tastes of cod-liver oil! [*Laughs*] You! [*To* ROSEL] Did you at least like it?

ROSEL: What was that . . . sorry?

CHRISTIAN: The floor polish! Are you dreaming again about your knight with his black curls?! Rosel!!

ROSEL: What is it you want?

CHRISTIAN: Mousey wants to know if you liked the goose!

ROSEL: Everything, Frau Mielke. Very good. Especially the peas.

ULRICH: Well, you can smell that! [BROTHERS *scream with laughter*] Fill 'em, Frau Mielke. There won't be any wine in heaven. [*Burps*] And it's nine years that I was married to that!

MIELKE [*Fills* BROTHERS' *glasses*]: Then you're getting on with her better than your brother did. Right, Herr Maul?

CHRISTIAN: Better? With her? With that depressing critter? She'd be sitting—God knows where she'd be! But not here, with us at our table! If it wasn't for the income tax! Not one iota of female sexuality. [BROTHERS *laugh raucously.* CHRISTIAN *lifts his glass.*] Cheers! Cheers, Mousey! [MIELKE *walks behind bar*] It warms my heart, sitting here with you!

ULRICH: It warms the heart, doesn't it? [*Clinks glasses with* CHRISTIAN. BROTHERS *empty their glasses with long, greedy gulps.*] Ah!

CHRISTIAN: Ah!

ULRICH: Let's get plastered today! Rosel! [*Burps*] And then we'll fix Wenzel Schuhmacher!

CHRISTIAN: Right!

ULRICH: That ecogreen arsehole! [*Drills his thumb violently into* ROSEL's *hair*] There! Who owns this town?

CHRISTIAN: Those shitheads in the council don't, for sure!

ULRICH: You bet! Who's paying the highest taxes? Who's giving jobs to those shitheads? No, Christian! I want to hear it from Rosel! From our screech owl!

CHRISTIAN [*Jabs* ROSEL *again in the ribs*]: Now you're going to prick up those St. Bernhard ears of yours! Do you hear!

ROSEL: Ouch!

CHRISTIAN: Quiet!

ULRICH: Who's paying the bills in this town? And in the whole Republic?! [*Burps*]

CHRISTIAN: Don't tell me it's the workers. Or the white-collar guys! If you don't know, then say so: "I don't know!"

ULRICH: The business people! You screech owl! Free enterprise! [*Burps*] We paid the subsidies for the border counties with our money, when there was still a Soviet zone! And now we're paying the welfare money for all that illegal immigrant scum! And now that fucking Communism is finished, it's us who're paying our good money so the rotten corpse is made to walk again! I can't stand all that talk of social responsibility any longer. What is it that we've got here? Nothing but rules! Every single little fart's got to be cleared with three government offices! And that's where all those Wenzel Schuhmachers are warming their asses! And bad-mouth free enterprise! It's like the Middle Ages!

CHRISTIAN: But just dare to say it in public!

ULRICH: You've already gone too far!

CHRISTIAN: Makes me puke. I'd love to do nothing but breed my dogs!

ULRICH [*Burps*]: Our paint's toxic! Suddenly they're discovering a toxicant wherever they look! For thirty years we've been working with the same assortment of paints! And not one single bum has ever died from sniffing them!

CHRISTIAN: Yeah, but Wenzel Schuhmacher!

ULRICH: I'll get him caught with his pants down! And then I'm going to paint that arsehole with green enamel, from the top to his toes! Cheers, Christian!

CHRISTIAN: Cheers, Mousey! [BROTHERS *drink*]

ULRICH [*To* ROSEL]: And now you won't hear us!

CHRISTIAN: Do you hear?! Don't hear us! [*Jabs* ROSEL]

ROSEL: Ouch!

CHRISTIAN: Come on! Move! Get up! Sit over there in that nook! My brother's got something to talk over with me. [*Pushes* ROSEL *off the chair. She nearly topples to the ground, goes to the corner he indicates.*]

CHRISTIAN: Quiet! Sit!

[ROSEL *sits down*]

CHRISTIAN [*To* ULRICH]: That's what I hate more than anything about her.

ULRICH: What's that?

CHRISTIAN: That you can do any fucking thing you want to her. You could drive a tank across her foot, she won't resist!

ULRICH: Listen. Wenzel Schuhmacher. You know something?

CHRISTIAN: How we're going to fix him?

ULRICH: Yes. [*Whispers into* CHRISTIAN's *ear*]

CHRISTIAN [*Admiringly*]: You dirty dog!

ULRICH: He's caused too much trouble for our company! Right in the shit, that's where I want to see Wenzel Schuhmacher. Right up to his snoot! And then I'll kick him right in his fucking snoot!

CHRISTIAN [*Admiringly*]: You dirty dog!

2

Enter THE BEAUTIFUL STRANGER *and* THE POLE. *The Pole is carrying The Stranger's suitcase. Through the open door we can see heavy snowfall outside.*

THE STRANGER: You really don't want to? Have a cup of tea with me. No? Well. Then, I'd like to thank you for your kind help. Very, very kind. I wish you good luck with that project of yours. Good-bye. [*Offers her hand.* THE POLE *holds it briefly to his chest without a word and leaves. The Stranger closes the door and walks over to the bar, visibly ill at ease.*]

CHRISTIAN: Look at that chassis, Mousey!

ULRICH: Never seen her!

CHRISTIAN: You've never seen her? [BROTHERS *ogle* THE STRANGER]

THE STRANGER: Good evening.

MIELKE: Good evening. [*Silence*] Well?

THE STRANGER: Oh . . . [*Aware of the* BROTHERS *ogling her. For a moment she is quite irritated.*] You've got a room for me?

MIELKE: Yes, we've got a free room. For one night?

THE STRANGER: Yes. Tomorrow the trains will be running again, I hope.

MIELKE: I don't run the railways. [*Rummages about behind the bar for the pad of registration forms*]

CHRISTIAN: Did you get what she said?

ULRICH: Not everything.

MIELKE: If you'd fill this out. Passport! The passport!

THE STRANGER [*Pulls an American passport from her handbag and hands it to* MIELKE]: Here.

MIELKE [*Scrutinizes passport suspiciously*]: Ah. Now I see. At the bottom, there at the bottom, you've got to [*Slowly*] *write in* the passport number! [*Slowly*] *Numero!*

THE STRANGER: Here?

MIELKE: German? Speak German?

THE STRANGER: I think I speak German quite well.

MIELKE: None of them speak German! [*Takes a room key from its hook*]

THE STRANGER: Is there a phone in the room?

MIELKE: Nix telephone! Nix television! Nix radio! We've got the train station. Here. [*Pushes key toward* THE STRANGER] It's number nine. Breakfast from 6:30 till 8:30. Come along. [THE STRANGER *again looks irritably around the room.* MIELKE *misreads look.*] Third floor. Hop-hop-hop. [*Beckons* THE STRANGER *to follow her upstairs. The Stranger follows Mielke, carrying her suitcase. They exit up the stairs.*]

CHRISTIAN: Did you see that chassis? Mousey! Did you see that chassis! Right, Rosel? You haven't got anything like it, such a chassis! Well—the fancy people staying here! [*Leans over to* ULRICH] Tell me again. The ad! What did it say? Nature's own champagne? Leather? Straps?

ULRICH: Champagne. Leather. Lingerie!

CHRISTIAN: Champagne. Leather, Lingerie! That's the way to get it up.

ULRICH: Yeah. Makes my balls burst.

CHRISTIAN: You dirty dog. Mousey! We're going to send stinkin' Rosel home. And then this angel of yours will teach us fun and games! [*Drinks*] Mine is up already, kissin' my belly button! But first we'll put down another bottle! Jesus H. Christ! Are my pants tight. [*Roars*] Rosel! Heel!

[ROSEL *gets up and comes to their table*]

CHRISTIAN [*Looks at* ROSEL]: Sit down, for heaven's sake! When you're standing up, you look even uglier! [*To* ULRICH] Mielke's got to give us a full report.

ULRICH: Good. Very good. It's time to get screwed, blewed, and tattooed. [*Burps*]

[MIELKE *returns, goes straight behind the bar, starts to examine The Stranger's registration form*]

CHRISTIAN: Frau Mielke!

MIELKE: Herr Maul?

ULRICH: Get us another bottle of your Bull's Blood.

CHRISTIAN: What sort of a person is she? That woman? Frau Mielke!

MIELKE [*Opens a new bottle*]: American.

CHRISTIAN: American?

MIELKE [*Fills their glasses*]: Something fishy about her.

ULRICH: Really?

MIELKE: She put her suitcase on the bed and opened it. I could see her stuff. Lots of dresses, like you see on TV.

CHRISTIAN [*Nudges* ULRICH]: You hear that? That's your angel. The dresses. Lingerie!

ULRICH [*Loud*]: Frau Mielke. She smells of sin. [*Laughs*]

CHRISTIAN: I'd love to smash my piggy bank for that one.

ULRICH: Rent a girl. Rent a girl. Let's get laid. Terrific!

MIELKE: You mean she's that kind?

ULRICH: Haven't you ever seen those ads? You meet 'em at a hotel. A real dirty night. Any desire satisfied.

CHRISTIAN: Straps, champagne, and lingerie! Rosel! If I could wrap you in rubber at least! [*Jabs his elbow into* ROSEL's *ribs*] Quiet!

MIELKE: Well, if she's that kind, I won't have her on the premises.

ULRICH: Don't get yourself all worked up! Just wait a bit! It's a long time that we've had anything like that around here.

CHRISTIAN: First we've got to amuse ourselves with the slut!

ULRICH: *Ameeese* ourselves! That's it! She's a little Ami-mouse, isn't she?

CHRISTIAN: Her whole index of sins. From top to bottom and all the way up again!

MIELKE: I've got to tell Reinhold about this right away. [*Exits, quite agitated*]

CHRISTIAN: You dirty dog!

ULRICH: Now I know how we're going to fix Wenzel Schuhmacher. [*Pulls a business card from his pocket and waves it in front of* CHRISTIAN's *face*]

CHRISTIAN: You filthy dog! But first it's our turn! [*Drinks*] Come on, Mousey. Let's go up to her room. [*Gets up*]

ULRICH: Good night, Rosel! [*Gets up*] Look! [BROTHERS *sit down again*]

[THE STRANGER *comes into the lobby in a fashionable dress that is tightly hugging her body. At the same time,* MIELKE *returns from the kitchen. The appearance of The Stranger confirms in her mind what Ulrich has told her.* CHRISTIAN *and* ULRICH, *who are staring at The Stranger without the slightest inhibition, also see their suspicions confirmed.*]

CHRISTIAN: Dammit! Look at those legs! Mousey! Jesus fuckin' Christ. [*Drinks*] Those legs! When I think of your bent cukes, Rosel, just like Turkish pretzels!

[ULRICH *drinks.* BROTHERS *ogle* THE STRANGER.]

THE STRANGER: Where could I make a phone call, please?

MIELKE: Local? [*Places phone on bar, switches on the meter*]

THE STRANGER [*Interrupts dialing*]: Oh, would you be so kind as to pour me a whisky?

MIELKE: Whisky?

CHRISTIAN: Whisky. Mousey! Whisky.

MIELKE: You want a whisky? What kind of whisky?

THE STRANGER: Bourbon. No ice. Only a bit of soda. [*Continues to dial*]

CHRISTIAN: I can't watch this any longer. Is she calling Australia?

ULRICH [*Stares at* THE STRANGER. *Suddenly a loud burp erupts from his mouth.*]: Schuhmacher!

[MIELKE *pours whisky into a glass and adds soda.* THE STRANGER *finishes dialing and is waiting for a response to her signal. Mielke places the whisky next to The Stranger on the bar and doesn't move an inch away. It is quiet. Everybody is breathless with attention. We can hear clearly the ringing on the line, two or three times. The Stranger picks up the glass while waiting and sips the whisky. Now the other party is picking up the receiver.*]

THE STRANGER: Shorty? It's me, Margrit. Could I talk to Leon? It's terrible. The train got stuck. Yes. The snow's unbelievable. It's been snowing all day. The trains don't get through anymore. It's like Siberia. Yes. Stuck in the snow. Yes, Shorty, thank you. I'll hold.

3

Enter LUTTER. *His hair full of snow. He slams the door behind himself.*

LUTTER: Maul. We've got to take the dogs out of the kennel. They'll be buried by the snow out there. It's very wet snow. It's going to bring down the roof. The two fir trees on Main Street were knocked down by the snow. The Intercity to Hamburg-Copenhagen is stuck three miles from the station. It's total chaos! The way it's coming down. It's brutal! Bebra's going to be wiped out.

THE STRANGER: Leon? Darling, did your brother tell you . . .

CHRISTIAN: Lutter! What about the dogs?

LUTTER: That's what I'm saying. We got to get them out of the kennel. Before the roof caves in.

CHRISTIAN: My God! It isn't still snowing, is it?

LUTTER: It's even worse.

CHRISTIAN: Ulrich! We'll take the jeep. Rosel! Run home right away. Turn the heat up in the basement. Come on, Ulrich. Forget about getting sloshed. [*Pushes* ROSEL *viciously*] Don't dream! Run!

ULRICH: And what about here?

CHRISTIAN: First the dogs! If only the dogs are all right. Why didn't you bring them along in the first place?

LUTTER: They're in a frenzy.

THE STRANGER: Leon. I can't hear you very well . . .

[ROSEL *gets up and quickly throws her coat around her shoulders.* CHRISTIAN *and* ULRICH *rush to the door the way they are. It is obvious now that they all have had quite a bit too much to drink. Their movements are disoriented, and their frantic rushing about makes the alcohol circulate faster so that it is having its full impact. Christian stumbles but is caught by* LUTTER. *Ulrich laughs and knocks a chair over that stands in his way. He, too, is for one moment on the point of tumbling down but manages to take hold of Rosel, who now has difficulty staying on her feet. She gropes for the coatrack, but it isn't stable enough to survive her attack and topples over, and with it Rosel—as well as Ulrich—so that they end up on the floor in a tangle of arms, legs, and coatrack. Lutter helps them back to their feet. Christian has already gone outside.*]

ULRICH [*Slams fist on* ROSEL's *head*]: You're really the worst piece of shit! Good for nothing at all! [*Burps.* LUTTER, ULRICH, *and* ROSEL *exit.*]

4

THE STRANGER [*On the phone*]: You think I'm dreaming this up, do you? Leon. You're crazy. Hey! What's that? I can barely hear you. Yes. Isn't it snowing in Copenhagen? It's very—very bad. You. It's really spooky. No. Why don't you come . . . no, that won't do . . . Darling. I'd love to be with you now . . .

[ULRICH *and* CHRISTIAN *return*]

CHRISTIAN: What a fucking mess! What a pile of shit!

ULRICH: Fucking Polacks!

CHRISTIAN: That ain't possible!

ULRICH: It's unbelievable! A Polack!

CHRISTIAN: Frau Mielke!

[LUTTER *enters with* THE POLE. *He is dragging him by his coat collar toward the bar.*]

LUTTER [*Intimidating* THE POLE]: Shush! Shush!

ULRICH: Frau Mielke, would you maybe have an axe?

CHRISTIAN: Lutter! Go and smash the Polack's piece of junk! I've had it with that scum from the east!

ULRICH: The Polack parked right in front of our car!

CHRISTIAN: Here, in my hometown!

MIELKE [*Comes in with an axe.* LUTTER *takes it from her.*]: You can't get your car out, Herr Maul?

ULRICH: No.

MIELKE: The nerve those bastards got.

LUTTER: Shush. Polack jerk. Lookie, lookie car!

[LUTTER *takes* THE POLE *outside. Sounds of crashing metal and breaking glass can be heard.*]

ULRICH: That can't be helped now.

CHRISTIAN: That's the proper treatment!

THE STRANGER [*On phone*]: Darling. You . . . [*Silent from fear*]

ULRICH: As long as no one is doing anything. [*Pause*]

CHRISTIAN: As long as no one is doing anything. [*Pause*]

LUTTER [*Comes back with* THE POLE, *who is bleeding from the nose*]: Shush. [*Puts axe on the bar*]

THE POLE [*Wiping the blood off his nose with his hands and smearing it clumsily all over his face*]: You make kaput my car.

LUTTER: Shush.

CHRISTIAN: If you don't keep your fucking Polack face shut, our Lutter here is going to make kaput your fucking Polack face too!

LUTTER: Shush.

THE POLE: Why do you do that?

ULRICH [*Hits* THE POLE *on the head*]: What do you want here? Can't you park your car properly?

THE POLE: Colleague. I . . .

ULRICH: Lutter. I'm not a colleague of his. Tell him. That fucking Polack!

CHRISTIAN: Parking in the wrong spot! Gamboling around in our country! Lutter. Rip his fucking Polack snout from his face!

THE POLE: I was only in house . . .

LUTTER: Shush. [*Presses hand brutally in* THE POLE's *face, so that he bleeds even more profusely*]

THE STRANGER: Oh God. Leon? Right away. [*To* LUTTER] Stop that! You're hurting him!

ULRICH: You keep out of it! Hooker! [*Slams the receiver on the cradle and brutally pushes* THE STRANGER *toward the stairs*] Hop in the sack! Move! Move!

CHRISTIAN: Wherever you step! Polacks! Romanians! Gypsies! Nothing but scum!

LUTTER [*Pulls hand from* THE POLE's *face*]: Shush.

CHRISTIAN: We should burn 'em. All of 'em!

LUTTER [*Again presses his hand in* THE POLE's *face, mocking the Pole's accent*]: Here Germany! Here nix Polacky! Your dirty Polack snout in your shitty Polack noodle must keep very still and quickly scram, rrrright? Shush. Rrrright? Scram!

MIELKE [*To* THE STRANGER, *who has stopped on the stairs*]: And you too! Get out of here. [THE STRANGER *exits*]

THE POLE: You Nazi! You German pig.

LUTTER: What's that? Polly? Come on. Say that again. You! I'd like to hear that again. This Polack calls me!—in my own country!—in my Germany!—"Pig! Nazi!" He insults a German! You! We've got to have a word about that. Won't we, you Polish swine? But not here. Shush. This is no place for Polacks. A first-rate hotel like this. [*Leaves with* THE POLE *for the street. Silence.*]

ULRICH [*Walks to the bar*]: A gin. Christian?

CHRISTIAN: Fine with me. But then we've got to . . . [MIELKE *pours two shots of gin*] Wherever you're stepping. Cheers. Those fucking asylum seekers! Germany for Germans! All over town they're panhandling, right in your face. In every underpass they're making their lair. Like rats. [*Chugs down his gin*]

ULRICH: Be quiet, will you! [*Pause. He chugs down his gin and listens again for a noise outside. But it's completely still.*]

[LUTTER *returns with* THE POLE, *who is spattered with blood, his face bloated and bruised*]

LUTTER: He had an accident. Mielke. He hit his head. Crashed his car into the light pole. We've got to get the dogs out of the kennel. [*Slams* THE POLE *into a chair*]

MIELKE: Well, he can't sit here like that.

CHRISTIAN: Right. Messing up the chair. Get up!

ULRICH: When we've taken care of the dogs, Lutter, you'll look after that hooker. She's got to disappear. [*Hands* LUTTER *a business card.* ULRICH, LUTTER, CHRISTIAN *exit.*]

5

THE STRANGER *comes slowly down the stairs*

THE STRANGER: Oh, my God.

MIELKE: He had it coming. Like, we aren't traveling to their country, are we? . . . It's a disaster . . . they should put that wall back again, better today than tomorrow . . . And you watch out and don't get my chair dirty . . . [*Wipes the blood off* THE POLE's *face*] The way he's shaking . . Get a blanket, will you . . . there are two woolen blankets on the shelf when you go to the kitchen, through there . . . [THE STRANGER *runs into the passageway*] Why, man. Don't make trouble for me . . . [*Keeps trying to cool* THE POLE's *forehead with a wet rag.* THE STRANGER *returns with the blankets and carefully wraps them around The Pole.*] I'm calling the doctor. Here. [*Hands her the rag. Runs behind the bar and dials.*]

[THE STRANGER *keeps cooling* THE POLE's *forehead. He is barely able to sit upright. She tenderly holds him in her arms. Suddenly, The Pole's head drops onto his chest. She lifts it up, lets it tentatively go, the head drops down to the chest again. In sheer desperation, she repeats the procedure once more. Again the head drops down. It's only slowly that The Stranger realizes he is dead. Completely motionless, she sits with The Pole's body in her arms. She stares, eyes empty, head stiffly raised, into a void. In the background,* MIELKE *is on the phone. She presses the receiver to her left ear, uttering not a single word. After about twenty seconds, a quick blackout.*]

Act II

A hotel room. Through the window, the yellow fluorescent light of a street lamp. We can sense the railway station outside. It is still snowing.

1

THE STRANGER, *alone. She is standing quite helplessly in the unfamiliar room. She suddenly switches the radio on and immediately switches it off again. She walks to the door. She wants to go down to the lobby and get something to drink. She hesitates. She becomes aware of something. Listens. Then, she suddenly pushes the door open.* LUTTER *stands in the doorway with* GERO, *the dog.*

LUTTER: It's me. The handyman. Don't lock the door. Makes nothing but a racket. They're all asleep. [*Enters, pushes* THE STRANGER *into the room, and slams the door shut with his heel*] Just wanted to look in. Thought you'd still be awake. [*Offers his hand, extending his arm to full length*] Lutter. As in old Luther. Lutter! [THE STRANGER *recoils. Doesn't seem to realize what is happening.* LUTTER *slackens* GERO's *lead a bit. Gero attacks The Stranger. Lutter pulls the dog back.*] Quiet, Gero. The only human being. [*Grins, revealing his rotten teeth*] Heil Hitler! Well? [*Silence*] Well? [*Pause*] He won't bite, only when I tell him. [*Again extends his arm, offering his hand*] So?

THE STRANGER: I . . .

LUTTER: Won't you shake hands?

THE STRANGER: What . . . what are you looking for?

LUTTER: Shush. Don't you give me any ideas. So? Won't you shake my hand? Of course! You're going to offer your paw. Won't you? [*Pause*] No?

THE STRANGER: Yes. Yes. [*Completely at a loss. Offers her hand reluctantly.*]

LUTTER: No. That's no way to shake hands. [*Grins again*] Now I'm getting it. You were expecting someone else. [*Looks at his wristwatch*] Hmm. Late! Well, that's it, I'm afraid. His wife couldn't sleep, maybe. So the green scumbag can't slip from the house! Yeah, yeah. Those big shots. [*Walks around the room in a provocative manner. Comes to a stop at the table.*]

THE STRANGER: What are you looking for! And what are you talking about?

LUTTER: About your business! Ah! What do we have here? A business card! [*Pulls the card out from under her things*] Wenzel Schuhmacher. Just as the Mauls said. Yes, that'll be of interest to them. [*Demonstratively pockets card*] The things those gentlemen leave lying about. Two shapely legs. And right away they lose their head!

THE STRANGER: I don't know what you're talking about.

LUTTER: Of course.

THE STRANGER: I think your behavior is revolting! I think . . .

LUTTER: Absolutely. So do I. Fie, for shame! Gero. Yes. That's my position. [*Fingers* GERO's *muzzle, as if to take it off*] Got it? Yes? I could take it all the way off.

THE STRANGER: No. Please don't.

LUTTER: Strong like a bear. *Gooood boy, Gero.* [*Looks out window*] What weather! [*Turns away from the window and again extends his arm toward her, quite morosely. Pause.*] I can wait. It's on your time. [THE STRANGER *offers her hand hesitantly*] Tomorrow. [*Holds onto her hand*] Tomorrow, and tomorrow, and tomorrow.

THE STRANGER [*Softly*]: What do you want?

LUTTER [*Grins at her, then lets go of her hand*]: I don't know. [*Pause*] I've got to get a decent handshake. How about you?

THE STRANGER: How about me?

LUTTER: Forget it. Are you waiting for someone?

THE STRANGER: I'm a stranger here. Who am I supposed to be waiting for?

LUTTER: 'Cause you didn't lock your door.

THE STRANGER: I was going to get something to drink.

LUTTER: I see, I see. Drinks. I understand. Champagne? [*Pause*] You like dogs?

THE STRANGER: No. I don't like dogs.

LUTTER: And shepherds? German shepherds?

THE STRANGER: Those I hate most of all.

LUTTER: That was a straightforward answer. I like that. Gero. Heel. He can smell it. He can smell you hate him. [*Grins*]

THE STRANGER: Why don't you stop this? Why don't you go away? I want you to leave! [*Pause. LUTTER doesn't budge.*] Go now. Get out of here! Or else—

LUTTER: Or else?

THE STRANGER: Or else I'm going to call the police!

LUTTER [*Laughs loudly*]: The police. I'd be careful. Honestly. In your place. German police. Nix Jewish! Nix Turkish! [*Close to her*] Got your stuff packed?

THE STRANGER: No.

LUTTER: Your . . . those spiffy rags of yours. Shush. Or else I really start getting the wrong idea. By three o'clock I want to be on the Autobahn with you. Well then. Get packing. I'll be watching you. [*Sits down. Talks to GERO.*] Gero. Her! And this weather! Shush. We've got the jeep. We'll get there where we've got to go. Good boy. [*Cleans his fingernails with a match*] You don't want to?

THE STRANGER: Get out of here.

LUTTER: You need to pack! I've got to give you a ride!

THE STRANGER: I am not going to pack! And you're not going to give me a ride! And now you're going to get out of here! It's disgusting, the way you're carrying on. Or do you want me to go down to the lobby? You lout! [*Walks toward the door*]

LUTTER: Gero! Watch out! [GERO *attacks* THE STRANGER]

THE STRANGER: Help! Help! No!

LUTTER: Don't make waves, will you. I'll get you out of the woods. [*Walks up to* THE STRANGER. *Grabs her face and pulls it to his.*] You know something? [*Pause*] No, I won't tell you that. And the soul? Is there such a thing as the soul? Is there a soul?

THE STRANGER: Please.

LUTTER: That's of interest to me. [*Lets go of* THE STRANGER] When I was fourteen I wanted to be a priest. I felt a vocation. The vocation didn't come from up there. [*Pause*] So? What about my question! Does Man have a soul, in your book?

THE STRANGER: Whoever has got a soul.

LUTTER: Good. Very good. You've understood my question. Whoever has got a soul, has a soul. Gero. Why don't you start packing now! [*Pause*] I hate it when I have to get angry.

THE STRANGER: I'm doing it. I'm packing. Please.

LUTTER: Orders are orders. I'll point the Grim Reaper toward you.

THE STRANGER: What? [*Opens the wardrobe, takes out her suitcase, opens it, and puts her lingerie from the drawers into the suitcase. It's all very expensive, white silk lingerie.*]

LUTTER: Nothing. Tomorrow and tomorrow and tomorrow!

THE STRANGER [*Tries to appear calm*]: You're enjoying this.

LUTTER [*Sadly*]: Enjoying it.

THE STRANGER: With the dog around, you're feeling strong.

LUTTER: I don't enjoy anything. Life's too short for that. [*Grins*] One word. When I tell him, "Schildberg," he's going to rip you to shreds. "Schildberg." That's the word. [*Fingers* GERO's *muzzle again*] Come over here. No? Got to tell you something. Right into your ear. Come here! [THE STRANGER *approaches Lutter. She is holding a striking cocktail dress in her hand.* LUTTER *grins and shakes his head.*] Closer. Even closer. Otherwise, it won't get through my lips.

THE STRANGER [*Close to* LUTTER's *face*]: Why don't you stop this?

LUTTER: I am Mephisto. I know why you're here. You. I've been deep down in hell. It's a rare event that anyone ever comes back from down there. Evil is good. I am called upon to liberate evil. That is my mission. [*In a hoarse voice*] Hitler! Stalin! And? What have they done with their mission? They betrayed it with their own vanity. Instead of creating a world ruled by evil. The black souls and hate shall rule! [*Pauses. Grins.*] Are you afraid of me?

THE STRANGER: Who's selling you on that stuff? The two brothers? Your bosses?

LUTTER [*Lets go of* THE STRANGER]: I'm laughing! I've got to laugh! The Mauls! FFFffft. They like to think they're my bosses. Nothing. Not another word. Yes, they are my bosses. [*Darkly*] Tomorrow.

THE STRANGER: What about the Pole?

LUTTER: The things you're wasting your time with!

THE STRANGER: You killed the Pole!

LUTTER: Now you hate me.

THE STRANGER: I've told the press!

LUTTER: So what! The way you hate my Gero, that's the way you hate me.

THE STRANGER: Is that also part of your brutal mission?

LUTTER: That's it! You snake! Poles. Russians. Romanians. Jews! Vietnamese! Niggers! Every day there's more of them. They want to destroy our Germany. They want to take our Germany away from us. If we don't watch out!

THE STRANGER: You're mentally disturbed!

LUTTER: That's it! All the way! The politicians are letting all those foreign scum in. If that's supposed to be normal, then I'm getting a bit more disturbed by the day. Until I'm mad. And then everything's going to burn! Really going to burn. Then all that un-German scum is going to burn.

THE STRANGER: I've got to tell you something.

LUTTER: Nothing!

THE STRANGER: Listen, Lutter.

LUTTER: Prince Lutter!

THE STRANGER: About my family.

LUTTER: Shut your face! Shut your dirty foreigner face! [*Grabs* THE STRANGER *roughly. Rips the cocktail dress from her hand.*] What's that?

THE STRANGER: It's a cocktail dress.

LUTTER: That's a whore's apron. What is that? "It is a whore's apron!" Well!

THE STRANGER: It is a . . . [*Pause. Softly.*] whore's apron.

LUTTER: Put it on! Stranger! You stranger! You'll put it on! Yes?

THE STRANGER: Yes.

LUTTER: Good girl. I'm stepping outside. The dog stays here. And you put that on. Don't make me sad. [*Stretches both his big hands toward her neck*] Gero. [GERO *comes up to him. He whispers something in its ear, then leaves the room. Gero lies down in front of the door.*]

THE STRANGER: God help me. I can't do this.

LUTTER [*Offstage*]: Do it, will you?

[THE STRANGER *suddenly and resolutely takes off her dress and slips into the cocktail dress*]

146

LUTTER [*Offstage*]: Slowly. Much more slowly.

THE STRANGER: No!

LUTTER [*Offstage*]: Shall I tell Gero to get you?

THE STRANGER: No. No.

LUTTER: Then you know what's next. Well, get on with it!

[THE STRANGER *slips the cocktail dress off. She is wearing silk lingerie. (Under no circumstances should she be naked.) For a moment she doesn't know what she is supposed to do. Bends down to pick up her dress.*]

LUTTER [*Offstage*]: Right. You put that on and then take it off again. Slowly! But not too slowly. And show me your back when you're zipping it up.

[THE STRANGER *turns her back toward the door and doesn't notice that* LUTTER *come back into the room. Silence. The Stranger stands with her back to the door. Nothing happens. The key in the lock clicks as Lutter locks the door.*]

THE STRANGER [*Utters a brief scream*]: Why are you locking the door?

LUTTER: I don't want to be disturbed while we're playing games. [*Strokes* GERO] Good boy, Gero. [*Stares at* THE STRANGER] What a beautiful skin. Let's play.

THE STRANGER: Play what?

LUTTER: Not what you're thinking.

THE STRANGER: I'm getting married three days from now!

LUTTER: I know. [*Rummages in the suitcase. Pulls out items of lingerie.*]

THE STRANGER: I'll come back. I'll get you for this.

LUTTER: Yes. We'll play . . . to hate and to be good. [*Holds out a corset*] Your bridegroom. Put it on.

THE STRANGER: Please don't. I won't tell. To no one.

LUTTER: The game goes like this. You sit with your bridegroom on a big cold rock. There. [*Pushes* THE STRANGER *down on the bed*] You kiss him. [*Pulls down a curtain, bunches it up, presses it against* THE STRANGER's *breast*] That's your bridegroom. Kiss him. Make love to him. I sneak up on you from behind. I'm Hagen, and I slay your bridegroom! Oh, do I hate him! [*Takes a coat hanger, goes to the bed behind* THE STRANGER, *and starts clobbering the bunched up curtain*] And you say: "You animal! You traitor! Hagen! You murderer! You brute!" [*Shakes* THE STRANGER *roughly*] Say it! Why don't you say it!

THE STRANGER: You brute.

LUTTER: Dead!

THE STRANGER: Dead.

LUTTER [*Strangely absentminded*]: Yes, dead, all dead. Hagen. Gunther. Siegfried. [*Kneels before* THE STRANGER. *Softly.*] I'll kill you.

THE STRANGER [*Helplessly and softly, almost begging*]: You animal. Your yelping courage . . .

LUTTER: You Jewess! You devil! [*Grins mawkishly and lewdly*] And that you hate me! That's what you hate most of all. [*Laughs*]

THE STRANGER: You ought to be killed and buried like some rabid beast.

LUTTER: Here. [*Pulls a jackknife from his pocket. Lets the blade flick out. Holds the handle toward* THE STRANGER.] Stab it. Kill it, the beast. That Hagen. Why don't you kill him? [*Pause*] As long as my eyes can see you, my blood wants to destroy you.

[THE STRANGER *suddenly holds the knife in her hand. She makes a first attempt to stab* LUTTER, *pressing the point of the knife almost cautiously into the coat Lutter has been wearing throughout the scene. Lutter doesn't resist and stares at The Stranger. Tears well up to her eyes. He pulls her face down and looks into her eyes. From a pocket he pulls a thousand-mark banknote. He spits on it, licks all over it, and sticks it to The Stranger's forehead. Then he kisses her violently. She pulls herself away from his grip. The knife drops to the floor. The Stranger rips the cocktail dress open at her breast, screams.*]

THE STRANGER: O.K.! Do it! Why don't you do it! What's the matter? Can't you?

LUTTER: Shut your face!

THE STRANGER: He can't! Dear me. That's what this is all about.

LUTTER: Shut your face.

THE STRANGER [*Screams*]: Do it! Or get out of here, but fast!

LUTTER: You foreign bitch. [*Pushes* THE STRANGER *roughly across the room*] Get into your rags. We've got to move. It's going to be daylight soon. [*Wipes his mouth*] Damn. I've got to get you out of here!

THE STRANGER: Are you getting hell from your bosses if you don't?

LUTTER: They aren't my real bosses! Move it! The salt must get out of the wound!

THE STRANGER [*Collects her scattered lingerie very slowly*]: What is that?

LUTTER: A thousand signs. Only no one is able to read them. The Maul brothers and my bosses. Hurry up, will you. Lutter doesn't have a boss. Come. Gero.

[*Exit* LUTTER *with* GERO. *The door is left open. From the railway station we hear an announcement over the public-address system: "Express train 438 to Fulda has been canceled. I repeat: Express train 438 to Fulda has been canceled."* THE STRANGER *is alone. She listens for Lutter's steps. She closes the door, bolts it, and pushes the wardrobe against it.*]

THE STRANGER: Oh my God! Oh my God! [*Again and again she wipes her forehead where the banknote had been stuck on with spit*] But you just wait! As soon as it's daylight. You're going to pay for this. You and your dog. So! You and the brothers!

[*Quick blackout*]

Act III

The hotel lobby. MIELKE *is behind the bar. About 10* A.M.

1

Enter FUTTERKNECHT

FUTTERKNECHT: Snow yesterday, and now it's thawing. Good morning, Frau Mielke. My God. What on earth has happened here? [*Pulls a newspaper from his coat pocket*]
MIELKE [*Serving* FUTTERKNECHT *coffee*]: I can only tell you what I've already said. I was in the kitchen, with Reinhold.
FUTTERKNECHT: The coffee's good. Still in her room, I guess?
MIELKE: Reinhold?
FUTTERKNECHT: The foreign lady.
MIELKE: Is it her who called you?
FUTTERKNECHT: That's right.
MIELKE: The things those muckrakers splash all over their paper. It's wrong from top to bottom.
FUTTERKNECHT: Well, my dear Frau Mielke, let's not waste our time. Won't you be so kind and tell the foreign lady? Please.
MIELKE: I'll kick her out of here. The whore!

2

THE STRANGER *comes down the stairs*

FUTTERKNECHT: That's her?

[*Exit* MIELKE]

[*Enter* THE STRANGER]

FUTTERKNECHT [*Gets up quickly, adjusting his tie*]: Good morning.
THE STRANGER: Good morning. Was it you I was talking to on the phone?
FUTTERKNECHT: Yes. Dr. Gustav Futterknecht.
THE STRANGER: Shall we sit down?
FUTTERKNECHT: Please.

[*They sit down*]

THE STRANGER: You're a lawyer?
FUTTERKNECHT: Lawyer and notary public.
THE STRANGER: I'd just like to know to what extent you're familiar with the local situation.
FUTTERKNECHT: I'm a Bebran. From the day I learned to read.
THE STRANGER: From the day you learned to read. Bebran. In this awful Bebra! In this utterly disgusting hick town. I'd like to file a complaint against a person everyone around here seems to call Lutter. For sexual assault, that is. Furthermore I'd like to file a complaint against the owner of the hotel for making a false statement and for conspiracy to obstruct justice. I want to file complaints against the Maul brothers and said Lutter for committing manslaughter. I won't leave this town until charges have been pressed against all of these persons.
FUTTERKNECHT: Whoa! Whoa! That doesn't sound very good. Not at all. Wait a minute. I'm just counting. Complaint against Lutter. Number one. Number two: Frau Mielke. For conspiracy to obstruct justice. The Maul brothers for manslaughter. Makes four. Four complaints. My dear madame. That's a big chunk you'd like to bite off.
THE STRANGER: Would two thousand marks be enough to cover your expenses for the time being?
FUTTERKNECHT: I'm fully convinced, of course, that you're in command of the necessary funds. Nonetheless, I have to point out right away that such

an accumulation of complaints would, shall we say, rather weaken your position in court than strengthen it. Even from a purely tactical position, five complaints is ill advised. I'd drop Mielke. Go for Lutter and the Mauls. Then I'll be glad to take the case. Believe me. We have to plant the germ that will divide them and set them against each other. Otherwise, they'll stonewall. And you won't achieve anything.

THE STRANGER: Have you any idea what happened here last night? After the Pole passed away.

FUTTERKNECHT: Excuse me. Would you mind a straightforward question?

THE STRANGER: Of course.

FUTTERKNECHT: What brought you here? Of all places?

THE STRANGER: Beg your pardon? [*Very agitated*] But that's preposterous!

FUTTERKNECHT: There are certain rumors circulating.

THE STRANGER: What rumors?

FUTTERKNECHT: About the reason for your visit to our town.

THE STRANGER: What kind of rumors? I don't know of any rumors! It was snowing . . .

FUTTERKNECHT: Of course, of course. Sure. The snow. But as an unattached lady—don't get me wrong, please—that's attracting attention.

THE STRANGER: Does it?

FUTTERKNECHT: Don't make this more difficult than necessary.

THE STRANGER: Why should I be supposed to offer any explanations, why me, of all people . . .

FUTTERKNECHT: You don't want to tell me. I understand. I just hope we won't have the same difficulties with other items. Otherwise, we won't have a fighting chance against the Mauls.

THE STRANGER: That's what I'd like to see, that they get off scot free. [*Enter* LUTTER *and* GERO] Right here, in front of my very eyes, a man has been killed! Only because he's a foreigner. And in my room I've been sexually molested in a most revolting manner.

3

LUTTER *sits down at the bar in a provocative manner.* GERO *crouches at his feet.*

LUTTER: Frau Mielke! A pilsner!

THE STRANGER: Tell him he should put the dog on the leash. Tell him that!

LUTTER [*Calls again*]: Frau Mielke! I can see you! There you are, hiding behind the door, listening!

FUTTERKNECHT: Herr Goedeke!

LUTTER: "Herr Goedeke? Herr Goedeke! Futterknecht wants to talk to you." [*Turns around to* FUTTERKNECHT] I'm sorry. Herr Goedeke isn't in.

FUTTERKNECHT: Lutter! Please, take your dog outside!

LUTTER: But he doesn't harm anyone. [GERO *gets up*]

FUTTERKNECHT: Please. [GERO *barks*]

4

MIELKE *steps behind the bar*

LUTTER [*Laughs*]: A pilsner! Did you hear me? [*Bends down to* GERO] Search! [GERO *sniffs around the lobby*]

FUTTERKNECHT: Herr Goedeke!

LUTTER [*To* THE STRANGER]: If you're going to tell that kind of shit once again, you snake!—like, I had done things to you—I'll skin your hide. Understood? Herr Futterknecht. I paid her the proper rate. She's advertising for johns. Frau Mielke here knows. And the Mauls know it. Mielke. You tell 'em!

MIELKE: Yes. She's advertising. I've read the ad myself.

FUTTERKNECHT: Where?

MIELKE: Herr Maul showed it to me. And all that sexy lingerie of hers! I've seen that also, with my own two eyes.

THE STRANGER: This is hysterical! This is absolutely hysterical! [*Has a fit of hysterical laughter*]

MIELKE: I can go and bring the suitcase with her hooker's underwear down, if you like.

LUTTER: I'll take care of that.

THE STRANGER: No, you won't! You can't allow this!

FUTTERKNECHT: But you're responsible for these rumors, aren't you! I asked why you had come here.

THE STRANGER: Because the train got stuck in the snow.

[LUTTER *and* MIELKE *burst into laughter*]

LUTTER: I'll get the suitcase.

FUTTERKNECHT: You say one thing. He's saying something else. Who am I supposed to believe?

THE STRANGER [*To* LUTTER]: You're not going to do that.

LUTTER: All by myself I'm going upstairs. And then I'll put every single piece on the table, right in front of the lawyer. [*Picks up the key*] Gero. [GERO *runs to* LUTTER]

THE STRANGER: Why don't you do anything against this . . . brute.

LUTTER: Gero. [*Exits with* GERO]

MIELKE: Nothing but trouble! She's turning my hotel into a brothel!

5

Enter the MAUL BROTHERS

CHRISTIAN: Good afternoon!

ULRICH: Good afternoon! Thanks for calling, Jutta!

CHRISTIAN: Exactly what we've been thinking. Right, Mousey? Exactly what we've been thinking.

ULRICH [*Pulls a newspaper from his coat pocket. Reads aloud.*]: "Quite different is the view a foreign visitor takes of the tragic accident. According to her, the Maul brothers couldn't move their car from its space because the Polish vehicle was blocking it. As the eyewitness, who is staying at the Reichsapfel Hotel, reports, the M. brothers, together with a certain Lutter, beat up the Pole in such a brutal manner . . ." And so forth! And so forth!

CHRISTIAN: Is that your doing? [*Grabs* THE STRANGER *roughly by the nape*] She won't pin manslaughter on us! Not someone like her!

ULRICH: Frau Mielke!

THE STRANGER: Take your dirty paws off me!

ULRICH: Quiet! We didn't beat up any Pole.

CHRISTIAN: Quiet, you hooker! [*Stuffs the newspaper into* THE STRANGER'*s mouth*] Eat that! Eat that crap! [THE STRANGER *is choking on the paper*]

ULRICH: Quiet! Frau Mielke, why don't you tell us. Or else Herr Futterknecht will get a completely false impression about us.

FUTTERKNECHT: Leave the woman alone! I beg you!

MIELKE: The Maul brothers were eating their Advent dinner. Goose. Like every year. Until Lutter came in. Because of the dogs.

ULRICH: Because the animals were snowed in!

MIELKE: But that's what I'm saying, Herr Maul! And as the gentlemen were getting ready to leave, there is this crash out there. We run outside and saw the gentleman from Poland had driven his car into the lamppost. His head's down on the steering wheel.

ULRICH: Slippery as it was! And hadn't buckled up.

MIELKE: We moved the gentleman from the car. He had already passed out. And then we put him on the chair, there. The blood is still . . . And I called Dr. Sausen . . .

CHRISTIAN: But she says the gentleman died here! In the hospital, that's where he died! This morning at 5:24 A.M. As the death certificate says. Died of heart failure at 5:24 A.M.!

ULRICH: There! And she claims we committed manslaughter!

CHRISTIAN: Herr Futterknecht. We all tried whatever we could do for the gentleman. It's really galling if you later read stuff like that in the paper about yourself. The way we're made to look now! [*Plucks the shreds of paper from* THE STRANGER*'s mouth*] I apologize! But that really was out of order. First of all, you were in your room when we heard the crash outside. Frau Mielke can corroborate that.

FRAU MIELKE: She was in her room.

FUTTERKNECHT: Excuse me, Herr Maul. But I didn't know anything about that.

6

LUTTER *returns with the suitcase*

LUTTER: Here. Let's have a look! [*Opens the suitcase. Pulls items of lingerie out and throws them all over the lobby.*] Black panties. White lace panties. Oh. And what do we have here! [*Pulls a thousand-mark banknote from between the lingerie*] That's what I paid her with last night, Herr Futterknecht! And Herr Maul certainly can confirm that, 'cause he lent me this banknote. [*To* THE STRANGER] No, don't get upset. I won't keep it. It was earned the old-fashioned way. And I'll work it off in due time with Herr Maul. Right, Herr Maul?

CHRISTIAN: I'm sure of it, Lutter.

[*A sudden silence.* CHRISTIAN *nods.* ULRICH *nods.* MIELKE *is stubbornly polishing one spot on the bar.*]

ULRICH: I think this is appalling, quite appalling, Herr Futterknecht, that one is forced to defend oneself in this way. Good afternoon.

FUTTERKNECHT [*Turns to* THE STRANGER]: There is one thing I have to tell you quite clearly: the business with the suitcase was in bad taste. On the one hand. No, Herr Maul. It's my turn now. On the other hand, we have here four statements against yours. I mean concerning the events of last night.

ULRICH: And the time of death!

FUTTERKNECHT: You're silent?

ULRICH: Speak up!

FUTTERKNECHT: I see! You prefer to say nothing! Paragraph 153 and Paragraph 164 of the Criminal Code. Deliberate false accusation. That's German law, Madame. Are you aware of this?

CHRISTIAN: Let her grit her teeth and scram! Come on, Mousey! We prefer to be with our own kind! Lutter. Let her pack her lingerie. And then you take her to the station.

FUTTERKNECHT: Herr Maul. Please. Yes. I'm terribly sorry. But with the best intentions, I couldn't have guessed this. Is the paper going to print a retraction?

ULRICH: That's already been written.

FUTTERKNECHT: We should put our heads together whether we should introduce a charge of false statement, after all . . .

[*Exit* BROTHERS *and* FUTTERKNECHT]

LUTTER [*Looks steadily at* THE STRANGER]: Come, Gero. [GERO *runs to him*] We'll be waiting outside. [*Exits with* GERO]

7

MIELKE [*Steps from behind the bar and begins, in a surly and aggressive manner, putting the lingerie into the suitcase*]: Pigs, the whole lot of 'em! You can't trust anyone. It's disgusting! Get richer and richer, that's all they want! [*Pushes the suitcase in front of* THE STRANGER's *feet. Closes the suitcase.*] Why did you want to file a complaint against me? You wanted to file a complaint against me! The Maul brothers are untouchable in Bebra, for anyone! For anyone! I've got my hotel, don't I? [*Lifts the suitcase and holds it out to* THE STRANGER] Here! Where are you going? I can check the schedule. Woman! You want me to hold your suitcase like this forever? I don't want your money. [*Puts the suitcase down*] All right, then! If you've got no feelings! [*Runs behind the bar. Rummages for matches. Comes back with them. Walks up to a table. Lights a match and holds it to the tablecloth until it catches fire.*] Now I'm setting the hotel on fire! Now I don't care shit anymore! [*Tablecloth is burning.* MIELKE *is terrified and comes to her senses again.*] Oh God! [*Tries to extinguish the flames with her bare hands. Burns herself, screams. Runs back behind the bar and gets water.*] If you won't say one

155

single word! [*Brings the water to the burning table and extinguishes the fire*] You're really a wicked devil! [*Screams*] Get going now! What do you want here? [*Calls*] Lutter!

[LUTTER *appears in the doorway*]

LUTTER: Yes?
MIELKE: Yes. Take her . . .
LUTTER: Yes.
MIELKE: Yes. Take her away.
LUTTER: To the Federal Railways. [*Laughs*] I'll take her.

[*Exit* LUTTER *and* THE STRANGER]

MIELKE [*Calls to the kitchen in the back*]: Reinhold! She's left the suitcase behind. [*Silence*] With all the underwear. Yes. [*Silence*] She'll be back. Yes.

[*Blackout*]

Act IV

Copenhagen. A room with a view of the sea. A big window. On the walls, paintings by Beckmann and Oelze. No furniture, except for some chairs. From the adjoining rooms a band can be heard playing Jewish wedding tunes.

1

THE STRANGER *in a bright white wedding dress.* LEON *enters.*

LEON: You're here, Margrit? They're dancing, they're enjoying themselves. The beautiful bride shouldn't be missing. Shorty is very amusing. Don't you want to dance? Shorty is terribly envious of me. Because of you. What are you reading?
THE STRANGER: I found it with the wedding mail.
LEON: Mail from Germany. Oh, my God. [*Reads cursorily*] Did you take a look at the sunset? The light is indescribable.
THE STRANGER: No.
LEON: No? You know what's been the funniest of all? Shorty's beginning to get on my nerves with his philosophers. "You've got the most beautiful bride," says he. "You little baby face always were the one who got the

most beautiful women. But this one is so beautiful that I'll probably have to snatch her away from you." I laugh. In reply he's quoting Kierkegaard: "Once reason alone has been baptized, all human passions are mere heathen." And those human passions are supposed to be his own, of course. Which he intends to aim at you now.

THE STRANGER: What do you think?

LEON: Skimpy. [*Hands the paper back to* THE STRANGER] There isn't much to be done with this information. Two hundred dollars down the drain. And that's enough of that. Let's go and dance. Of all people, it is my brother Shorty who's quoting Kierkegaard. You know what kind of money bought him this mansion?

THE STRANGER: Don't be cross at me.

LEON: Cobalt futures. Let's go to the drawing room. You've got to get this out of your mind. I understand why it isn't easy for you. So what. I'm too much of a realist. Even the greatest lawyer won't get anywhere in that German cesspool.

THE STRANGER: You think I should simply forget it now?

LEON: Yes, that's what I think. For your sake. For my sake. For our happiness.

THE STRANGER: Oh no!

LEON: What? You'd like to turn our wedding day into an endless quarrel?

THE STRANGER: Don't talk to me like that.

LEON: Sorry! Please, don't get that fanatical stare of yours. You know how much it scares me. Not today.

THE STRANGER: I'm going to get them! All three of them! There's got to be a way. So, we'll just postpone our trip to Mexico. I wouldn't enjoy it anyway. First, I have to get this out of my system.

LEON: But how? That's sheer madness.

THE STRANGER: What is madness?

LEON: Picking a fight with filthy bigots like that. In that horror country. It makes me puke! You know what I think of it? It's a stinking gutter. That's what the country's like.

THE STRANGER: It's like a festering boil inside me.

LEON: Now you listen, my beautiful passionate wife. Even if, as you said, you're going to "get them," it won't bring the Pole back to life. You see that, don't you?

THE STRANGER: I want to see them pay for it.

LEON: You aren't going to help anyone, love. If you take the train back there . . . [*Takes* THE STRANGER *into his arms*] You'll only be sullying yourself.

THE STRANGER: That's what I am since that night.

LEON: This absolutely unnecessary and senseless trip you made by train.

THE STRANGER: I wanted to see Germany. For once. My mother was born there. [*Pause*]

LEON [*Impatiently*]: Yes.

THE STRANGER: It was terrific. The train was totally empty. I was sitting in my compartment and I looked and looked. The white woods . . . as if half the world were but one snowed-in German forest. . . . I was thinking of so many things . . . all the stories of Germany my mother used to tell me . . . about the Spider Man who was sitting at the open window for days on end, looking at his bare chest in a mirror so he could count the spiders on it. Because he believed the hairs were spiders. Or the story of the witch who crippled the German Emperor's left arm when his mother was in childbed with him. And the other story! Of the dead girl in Lake Mauer. Until the train got stuck in the snow . . . Everyone had to get out. They took us into town by bus. They had laid out mattresses in a gym. When I saw the mattresses in that huge space with its high ceiling and the neon lights and the smell. It all looked like in those pictures Papa used to show us. When he'd come to Germany during the war. I thought I had ended up in one of those camps. And then I rushed into the street with my suitcase. I only thought: "I've got to get away! Away! Or else they'll lock me in." I ran through the snowy streets . . . I could see lights in the windows. They were candles. Everywhere, they had lit candles. It was like being among hundreds of old toys. Until I met the Pole. Without him I'd never have found the hotel. And now he's dead.

LEON [*Helpless*]: Yes. [*Pause. Dance music.*] Germany. An empty skull on top of a full stomach. Let's dance.

THE STRANGER: You're making your money there.

LEON: There and in the States and in France. And I've got a beautiful wife.

THE STRANGER: Stop trying to be clever. Leon! We've got to do something. We cannot dance and do nothing at all.

LEON: And what shall we do? If you please?!

THE STRANGER: I don't want to be your wife otherwise.

LEON: You're crazy. "Don't want to be your wife!" Does this mean more to you than I do? Cutting the rotten spots out of three German potatoes? I don't believe this.

THE STRANGER: Because you don't know everything yet.

LEON: Teaching culture to German beer guzzlers. You know, I'd have a better chance of winning the New York marathon. And what is it that I don't know yet? [*The music is getting ever more joyous*]

THE STRANGER [*Simultaneously with* LEON]: I've been raped.

LEON: You've been raped. Five times you've told me the story! Every time differently, and every time something new is added . . . What? What was that? You've been what? What did you just say? You've been ra . . . you've been ra . . . No. No, that's not true? [*Pause*] I've misunderstood what you said.

THE STRANGER: No. You didn't misunderstand. [*Pause*] He raped me. He stuck money to my forehead with his spit . . .

LEON [*Softly*]: Stop it.

THE STRANGER: And said . . .

LEON [*Screams*]: Who?

THE STRANGER: And said I had done it with him for that. I am a hooker.

LEON: Who stuck money to your forehead? With his spit? Fuck it! Who? [*Pause*] Come here, Margrit.

THE STRANGER: The one I've told you about. The one with the dog.

LEON: The one with the dog.

THE STRANGER: Him.

LEON: He has . . .

THE STRANGER: Yes.

LEON: He stuck the money to your forehead and has . . .

THE STRANGER: Yes.

LEON: When?

THE STRANGER: What?

LEON: When? When did that happen?

THE STRANGER [*Confused by his question*]: After the Pole had died. A bit later. Some time later. I didn't look at my watch, of course.

LEON: Of course not! [*Pause*] Outside? [*Pause*] Outside?!

THE STRANGER: In my room.

LEON: Couldn't you lock it?

THE STRANGER: He brought the dog along!

LEON [*Shouts*]: I've asked you if you couldn't lock the door! If you couldn't have locked yourself in this goddamned room! Excuse me.

THE STRANGER: No.

LEON: I'm sorry.

THE STRANGER: It's OK.

LEON: It's not OK.

THE STRANGER: Do you understand me now? Do you understand that I simply can't forget it and fly away to Mexico? Leon. You do understand that, don't you?

LEON: I don't understand anything. Not one single thing. I'm going to kill him. Do we have any whisky here? These German monsters. A stinking gutter. This is horrible. Horrible! This music is getting on my nerves. Make that music stop! You know something? I'm a coward. I'm a miserable coward. Can't they stop playing these happy tunes? They make me cry! [*Finds some whisky. Pours himself a shot.*] I'm going to kill them. I'm going to kill all of them. *Raped.* By a German dog trainer. [*Drinks*] By some stinking German dog trainer. [*Drinks*] The idea's simply killing me. [*Drinks*] My name is Leon Rauch. Leon Rauch. They've taken your wife . . . in Germany . . . where you're making your money . . .

THE STRANGER: Leon. [*Pause*] Would you pour me a drink too?

LEON [*Doesn't respond, stares*]: If this really happened the way you've said . . . if it happened that way.—No! Damn it! No! [*Stares at her, speaks softly*] I don't believe you. I don't believe you. What do you want? Tell me. What's behind all of this? [*Pause*] Do you want me to go to that place of horror? Because you've set your mind on it? So I make these monsters pay for it? No.

THE STRANGER: No?

LEON: No. [*Suddenly changes. Cold. Trying to compose himself, to regain normality.*] I can't cancel Mexico.

THE STRANGER: Was this supposed to be a honeymoon or a business trip, Darling?

LEON: Don't ask me such a stupid question. What's the difference? I'm going to meet—we're going to meet Gregory in Mexico. Gregory is immensely important for my research project. We can't cancel Gregory! And then I have to give a lecture in Boston, a trivial lecture—I know what you're thinking, a trivial lecture on the coiling of nucleic acids. But to me, Gregory and this trivial lecture aren't quite the useless projects they are to you, maybe. Even—excuse me—even compared to the monstrosity that happened.

THE STRANGER: It's simply cruel, what you're saying. It's cruel, and it hurts me. Yes, Leon, that's what it is. You refuse to believe me. Let me finish. You don't believe me. Because it's much more convenient.

LEON: Beg your pardon! Five days go by and I'm told nothing. Here. Today. That's when the wrapping is taken off my wedding present. With the proviso that I cancel Gregory, cancel Boston, and wade into the German morass instead. No. Definitely not. Do you understand that I don't understand all this? How could it have gone as far as that? That's what I'm asking you. How could you let creatures like that get close to you? I know you. I know how you often provoke such things. The thought of it is driving me mad. When I look at you and imagine some Kraut is fingering your body, touching you . . .

THE STRANGER: And is doing it to me!

LEON: No, please don't ever again! Don't let me ever again hear that from you.

THE STRANGER: What a coward you are.

LEON: I am a coward. And I've always been very successful. Being a coward. [*Pause*] Get out of this dress. He came to your room. And then? He must have said something, after all. And you. Couldn't you scream? I don't get it! Why hadn't you locked yourself in?

THE STRANGER: I wanted to get something to drink.

LEON: That's absurd! Just like that train trip! Absurd!

THE STRANGER: Yes.

LEON: Why are *you* saying yes? When *you* hadn't locked the door! Our flight to Mexico City is leaving tomorrow morning. Don't you understand that there is nothing we can do about it now? Who are your witnesses anyway? And at which court?

THE STRANGER: There are other ways.

LEON: What ways? [*Pause*] What other ways, if you please. Enlighten me, will you! Am I to hire two hit men? Ridiculous! Childish! Moronic! I'm not going to chase after my rage all the way to Bebra! Because you have fun running around half naked in your spiffy dresses, teasing the world with your skin!

THE STRANGER [*Slaps his face*]: You're talking the way they do. Just like them. [*Pause*] I'm sorry. No, I'm not sorry. I love you and I don't love you, right now.

LEON: No. You're in love with God knows what.—With your hatred . . .

THE STRANGER: And so what? I'm like dead since that happened. I wanted to put it away, I wanted to wipe it off, I wanted to forget it and, if the memories were crowding in on me, think of it as of a bad dream. When you were there waiting for me at the station, I felt fine, I thought, "it's gone now." But during the night I prayed, I begged God to erase the spot in my memory, and God showed his face to me and it was a stone. Let me go. I've got to wash myself.

LEON: You beautiful woman. What shall I say? I have to say something now. Where you are. Give me one day's time.

THE STRANGER: No.

LEON: It was always the same. Every day. In New York. Frankfurt on the Hudson. In Washington Heights. Long after they were gone. Homesick. A perpetual shadow. It's like that with your mother. It was like that with my father. Beautiful Germany. It's like that with you. What an unexplainable, sick kind of love.

THE STRANGER: What are you talking about?

LEON: About beautiful Germany! [*In a singsong*]

> There were three gypsies I once saw
> They were resting in the heather
> When a wagon came oh so slowly drawn
> By a weary nag through the heather

It's by Lenau. My father used to sing it . . . when he was hiking with us . . . I never understood this love . . . it seemed like an addiction to me . . . after all that had happened . . . this love for that horror land. [THE STRANGER *tenderly strokes his head*] Don't go.

THE STRANGER: Not because I'm so much in love with Germany. No.

LEON [*Pushes her hand away*]: But you are! You are in love with that sinister Germany! You were always talking about it in a strange way. It never would have happened! You were provoking it. Yes! You felt the shadow. This addictive love. Why don't you go to him who screwed you. A goy with a dog. Go and crawl under his jackboot heel! Like so many of our people . . .

[*Suddenly* LEON *and* THE STRANGER *are surrounded by dancing couples. The music is merry and joyful. Then blackness.*]

Act V

The lobby of the Reichsapfel Hotel. One week later. Evening.

1

ULRICH *and* CHRISTIAN, FUTTERKNECHT, LUTTER. *They are eating and drinking.*

ULRICH: I couldn't care less!

CHRISTIAN: No way!

ULRICH: We don't give a shit, no way!

CHRISTIAN: We had no need for love!

ULRICH: I hate the mere word already!

CHRISTIAN: I hate God and his love! And why? Because God never had any love for us!

ULRICH: Squeeze 'em hard! We've shut up the foreign slut's big mouth and took care of the Polack, too. Cheers!

CHRISTIAN: Cheers, Mousey!

ULRICH: And now we'll drink to that. Cheers! There ain't no justice. Right?

CHRISTIAN: No! One time we were in need of him. But he didn't show up. God, with his famous love!

ULRICH: That's a bitter lesson we had to learn!

CHRISTIAN: And he was—well, where the fuck was he? Well, Mousey?

ULRICH: Gone for a piss! God and his love were gone for a piss. Just when we were in need of God's love.

CHRISTIAN: They're telling all kind of shit about us. We're human beings too, aren't we!

2

Enter THE STRANGER. *She walks up to the bar, where she waits for Mielke. The men do not notice.*

ULRICH: The other guys aren't sleeping! Better bite. Or else you get bitten!

CHRISTIAN: It's a shame! It's a crying shame our mother couldn't see this! The way we've been biting back. Right, Mousey!

ULRICH: I'd like to holler it right into the women's grave! Mother! We've paid them back, those fucks!

CHRISTIAN: Them.

ULRICH: Yes. [*Pause*]

CHRISTIAN: We're nursing that hate in our gut. [*Drinks*] Our beautiful Hesse! At home I sometimes feel plain homesick for my Hesse! That's because it's become so foreign to me. Mousey! I cross the street and feel homesick!

ULRICH [*Shouts*]: Mielke! You're so quiet, Lutter. Don't you like the goose? Mielke!

LUTTER [*Darkly*]: Better to burn down the house than leave it to the rats.

FUTTERKNECHT: No use in going to extremes. In any direction.

LUTTER: Who's going to extremes? Stalin? Hitler? Who!! "We must get used to the fact that there will also be black Germans."

FUTTERKNECHT: But that hasn't been stated by anyone in public! Not in this way!

LUTTER: No one's going to get me used to that! [*Pause*] Black skin. We Germans! [*Pause*] We're the most unfortunate among the nations! I hate the Jews! I hate them! And I won't hide it! What am I living in a democracy for! I want my share of it, too. The Jews aren't any better than us Germans are!

ULRICH: You! Always carrying on about your Jews! The gypsies! The niggers! It's them! They're bringing the plague to the country!

MIELKE [*Comes with a wine bottle from the back*]: And is it all right? The goose? [*Opens the bottle*]

ULRICH: As right as Futterknecht's law is right!

FUTTERKNECHT: Well, Herr Maul. The law! The law has a backbone. And you've got a backbone!

CHRISTIAN: The truth is always in the middle.

ULRICH: And that's where it's getting screwed! Right in the middle!

FUTTERKNECHT: Well now, Herr Maul! Even though I'm eating your Christmas goose here, I wouldn't like to hear that word again as long as I'm present.

CHRISTIAN: I don't get it. Do you get it, Mousey?

ULRICH: Homesick! In my own hometown! That's what it has come to!

MIELKE [*Comes to the bar. Sees* THE STRANGER.]: You! Yes! Just a minute! [*Exits behind the bar*]

ULRICH: Sometimes I'm thinking all kinds of things. And I think, "Ulrich! The whole world is raging right in your own breast!" You know that?

CHRISTIAN: You aren't feeling well? [*Drinks*]

ULRICH: Black Germans.

MIELKE [*Comes back with the suitcase and places it in front of* THE STRANGER. *Speaks to* THE MEN.]: Like that Neboah. Or whatever they call him. That soccer player! Black! German! Right away they've made him a citizen! That Bimbo!

FUTTERKNECHT: But my dear Frau Mielke! This negro is playing a fantastic game.

MIELKE: So what? Aren't there any German players left? No honest German soccer players?

THE STRANGER: Would it be possible to get a room for one night?

MIELKE [*Very loud, aimed at the men's table, as if she's asking for permission*]: Here?

LUTTER: All kind of strings are being pulled, underground.

FUTTERKNECHT: In politics you get paid for your stupidity!

MIELKE [*Takes a key from the board and slams it down on the bar*]: The train's gotten stuck again?

ULRICH: Right. Lutter. Shut up! Why? 'Cause of it!

THE STRANGER: May I have a cup of tea?

MIELKE: Tea! [*Surly. Exits to the back.* THE STRANGER *sits down at a table close to the bar.*]

LUTTER: Deep down in our German soil! The way everything's being undermined! Back in the fifties. Who cares! Could be it's all for the sake of money: I love my German fatherland!

ULRICH: He's right, our Lutter! [*Raises his glass*] I'll drink to our country! And Dr. Futterknecht is right. Why? What's that? [*Pause*] I'd like to meet the good Lord . . . if he's loving or whatever the devil says . . . once I'd like to meet God. I'd tell him a thing or two. What's this with the love you're preaching? What's this with the Golden Calf? What about your German fatherland? Who invented all that stuff? Oh Lord, you? Herr Hitler? Herr . . . whatever all those kaisers were called? Well now, Herr God! Who's invented this German thing? [*Pause*] Not a sound! Just hate! Hate! Silence speaks a clear and loud language! Hate! [*Pause*] I'm saying one more thing. And if you all kill me for it! This God! [*Pause*] Whose love is for sale! [*Pause*] I don't give a shit about the Jews. The niggers. The Chinese. [*Pause*] I feel different. I talk different. And that is what I'd like to . . . for my dead mother and my three and a half bits of feeling . . . I'd like to . . . preserve that for me. My mother! Our mother, Christian . . . the super and the good Lord. [*Pause*] Everyone's laughing. The super at our school, Christian. With his black headband. "Wipe your feet." He was the good Lord! That's what he was called at least. [*Pause*]

CHRISTIAN: Lost wars!

ULRICH: Me too. [*Sneezes several times*]

CHRISTIAN: Gesundheit. Gesundheit! [*Pause*]

ULRICH [*Notices* THE STRANGER]: Gooood eeevening! [*Raises his glass to* THE STRANGER]

CHRISTIAN: Mousey!

ULRICH [*To* THE STRANGER]: God bless you!

CHRISTIAN: Don't start a conversation!

ULRICH: Back in town? [*Pause*] Back in town?

THE STRANGER: Just passing through, as it were!

FUTTERKNECHT: Good evening!

ULRICH: Lutter! She's forgotten the lingerie! She's come for her lingerie!

[MIELKE *comes back with the tea and serves it to* THE STRANGER]

CHRISTIAN: Mousey! Sin. [*All* FOUR MEN, *each in his own manner, stare in the direction of* THE STRANGER, *as if she were an apparition. The Stranger slips out of her coat.*]

FUTTERKNECHT: Please keep your voices down a bit.

CHRISTIAN: Mousey! I want to jump into the sauna now!

ULRICH: I hear you!

CHRISTIAN: That chassis! Mousey! I'd like to see that sweating for once. Right in its skin.

FUTTERKNECHT: Please. We won't behave like little rascals now, will we!

ULRICH: Lutter! What are you making eyes at?

LUTTER: The great beyond.

FUTTERKNECHT: So. Yes. So you've made it back to us once more. To our beautiful Bebra. The health spa.

THE STRANGER [*Sighs*]: Yes.

CHRISTIAN: Cold. Isn't it.

THE STRANGER [*With a girlish allure*]: Pooh.

CHRISTIAN: Winter.

FUTTERKNECHT: Harsh winters. Sweltering summers! Fortunately, we aren't responsible for the weather. Ha, people would start to kill each other.

THE STRANGER: I'm sure.

CHRISTIAN: There's a sauna in the building! If you're feeling as cold as that.

[*Silence*]

FUTTERKNECHT: During the day, it's wonderful. The clear frosty weather and the white roofs glittering under a steel-blue sky. Wonderful. Life! And you really ought to read our Goethe. The mischievous fun he thought up in his *Faust*. For the witches' sabbath during Walpurgis night. It's just a thought. Since we're so close to Brocken Mountain here.

CHRISTIAN: You must be frozen stiff, aren't you?

THE STRANGER: Beg your pardon?

CHRISTIAN: You must be really frozen stiff.

THE STRANGER: Oh yes! I sure am!

CHRISTIAN: There's a sauna in the building! As I've said! Wouldn't you like to come and sit at our table?

THE STRANGER: Don't trouble yourself. I'm just going to finish my tea.

FUTTERKNECHT: Tea isn't a healthy beverage if taken after 9 P.M.!

CHRISTIAN: Positively unhealthy! Wine is healthy! Mousey!

ULRICH: As long as she isn't cross with us, like she was the other week! Let her join us!

CHRISTIAN: Mousey! We want to forget that. Don't we? Beautiful lady. We won't think of it anymore tonight.

FUTTERKNECHT: Life! Sometimes it's really playing . . . it's odd. We're having today . . . we've come together here tonight because a German shepherd from the Maul Brothers Kennel has won the gold medal at the

Osnabrück dog show. And there'll be a winter night drill of the dogs later on.

THE STRANGER: At Osnabrück!

FUTTERKNECHT: Gold in Osnabrück!

CHRISTIAN: Well, why don't you come over and join us. We won't bite. Right, Lutter? Cheers! Mousey! Cheers! To our fatherland! [*Raises his glass.* THE OTHER MEN *follow suit. They clink glasses and drink.*] You too. It's cozy here. A glass, Frau Mielke. [THE STRANGER *sits down at the men's table*] Last Sunday before Christmas!

FUTTERKNECHT: You see. Once the misunderstandings have been dispelled. As I'd like to put it. Well, yes. There shall be fun. Ought to be.

CHRISTIAN: Two more weeks and Santa Claus is coming to visit. Frau Mielke! We need another glass here! Why is it that Santa Claus has those big nuts?

THE STRANGER: Beg your pardon?

CHRISTIAN: Why is it that Santa Claus has those big nuts?

FUTTERKNECHT: I beg you! Herr Maul!

ULRICH: Quiet, Futterknecht! Precisely! That's what we'd like to know. [*Drinks*] Why!

[*Silence*]

LUTTER: Why what?

[*Silence.* MIELKE *brings a wine glass.*]

CHRISTIAN: Why Santa Claus's nuts are as big as they are. You dumbbell! Because he comes only once a year! Because he comes only once a year! [*Expectant silence*]

ULRICH: Let it be! Let's try the goose! Frau Mielke! One more plate. What? You won't even try it?

THE STRANGER: Sure. I'd like that.

ULRICH: No?

THE STRANGER: I'd like that.

ULRICH: Mielke! She should try it too! A taste of what your Reinhold is cooking up in his kitchen!

MIELKE: Certainly. [*Exits behind the bar*]

FUTTERKNECHT: Oli-ola! A great goose! A tasty goose!

CHRISTIAN: First eat the goose. And then into the sauna to sweat that goose all out again! That's cool!

FUTTERKNECHT: Up-to-date. Makes your body fit!

THE STRANGER: Yes? [*Pause*] Is that what makes you fit?

FUTTERKNECHT: We're not like that.

THE STRANGER: Like what? [*Pause*] You aren't like what?

FUTTERKNECHT: Well, like . . . that we're . . . in that respect . . . No!

CHRISTIAN: To fuck! [*Laughs*] Hessians won't fuck anyone. Unless they've caught her alive!

FUTTERKNECHT: I must say, Herr Maul. Where are we here? That's a very uncouth expression. We don't like to hear it here ever again! [*To* THE STRANGER] I apologize.

[MIELKE *arrives with a plate*]

ULRICH: Frau Mielke. What's the problem?

MIELKE: That's what I'm asking you.

ULRICH: Me? No one's going to ask me anything tonight. Now we'll have the goose! [*Puts a helping on* THE STRANGER's *plate*]

CHRISTIAN: Well!

THE STRANGER [*Puts the first bite into her mouth*]: Tell me. There's really a sauna in the building?

CHRISTIAN: And a great one too. Frau Mielke!

MIELKE: No. At this hour I won't put the sauna on!

CHRISTIAN: But our foreign visitor is frozen stiff . . . Hooh!

MIELKE: Hooh! Yeah. Hooh-hooh! Nixi-pixy. No sauna!

CHRISTIAN: Mousey! Sauna! What do you say!

ULRICH: Naked in the sauna! Frau Mielke! Close the restaurant and heat up the sauna. As young and as—[*A gesture*] Hmm . . . in this life we'll never get that again. Cheers. [*Clinks his glass against that of* THE STRANGER] You like the goose? Do you like our goose?

CHRISTIAN: You dirty dog!

FUTTERKNECHT: Well, a little turn in the steam bath, Frau Mielke, I wouldn't mind it at all. It's healthy for sure.

MIELKE: It's late.

FUTTERKNECHT: Not at all. We're all in such a great mood. No?

ULRICH: You really look frozen stiff! Sa-hara! I won't even talk about us!

CHRISTIAN: Give us a kiss, Mousey!

ULRICH: Bravo. Brother mine. You know something? First I'll kiss you. Then I'll kiss her. Great. What now, Frau Mielke?

MIELKE: I'm on my way. [*Exits behind the bar*]

FUTTERKNECHT [*After a pause*]: Splendid. It's quite a splendid evening, I think. Exciting. Caribbean. Oh well. Salut! [*Drinks*] What game shall we play? Strip poker? Oh, nonsense! Sometimes you've got this itch to jump right out of . . . oh, well.

THE STRANGER: We'd need some music. Don't you think? Don't you think?

ULRICH [*After a pause, loudly*]: What?

CHRISTIAN: Before getting into the sauna!

FUTTERKNECHT: Absolutely!

THE STRANGER: Don't they have any music here?

FUTTERKNECHT: Absolutely! Into the sauna!

THE STRANGER: Lutter. What's the matter? What are you afraid of?

LUTTER: Afraid?

THE STRANGER: How's your dog doing? [*Pause*] Where is your dog?

LUTTER: What do you want? [*Pause*] What are you doing here?

ULRICH: Soliciting! You dumbbell! Soli-cit-ing!!!!!

THE STRANGER: I've come to get my luggage. I'll take the first train in the morning. Any kind of music.

CHRISTIAN: Precisely! [*Drinks. Slaps his hand on the table.*] That's it precisely! [*Silence. Again slaps his hand on the table, with a very loud slam.*] Precisely!

FUTTERKNECHT: Would you please stop it, Herr Maul! Please.

THE STRANGER: Isn't there any more dancing here? In the ballroom? [*Pause*] Isn't there any more dancing at all in the ballroom? Like there used to be?

ULRICH [*Gets up and raises his glass*]: I love hookers! [*Pause*] I just love and adore whores. Well?

FUTTERKNECHT: That's going too far, Herr Maul. Even with Goethe in our pocket, we shouldn't lose all control.

THE STRANGER: I've had enough to eat. Sorry.

ULRICH: *I love hookers!!* Without 'em I wouldn't have learned what love is.

CHRISTIAN: All right, Mousey!

ULRICH [*With an unexpectedly graceful gesture he takes* THE STRANGER's *hand, brings it to his lips, and kisses it*]: I only love . . . I only love what can be bought . . . that's what I learned from our mother. Right, Christian?

CHRISTIAN: Leave Mother out of this!

ULRICH [*Sings rather stupidly*]: Leave Mother out of this . . . tem . . . tem. We don't have that many of them! Frau Mielke! Wine! We're going to guzzle it till blood's spilling from our ears! When will the sauna be hot? I'm already hot as hell!

THE STRANGER: Do they really have no music here? German music!

LUTTER: What? [*Pause. Leans close to* THE STRANGER's *face.*] In the attic, I know, there's a box with old records. All of 'em broken.

169

FUTTERKNECHT: Straight away, into the sauna! That's what my metabolism needs.

THE STRANGER: I would have loved to dance. Are all of them actually broken? All those records? Prince Lutter.

LUTTER: Don't call me that. Stop it!

THE STRANGER: German music. That sad German music.

ULRICH: You shouldn't stop eating!

CHRISTIAN: Bravo! Whoever works as hard as we do is entitled to go ape once in a while.

FUTTERKNECHT: I really must beg your pardon. No one here wants to go ape. [*Pause*] Those floppy little rubbers! [*Pause*] I can't get all those floppy little rubbers out of my mind. Sorry. I'm really very sorry. [*Pause. He drinks.*] Let's just rip off all our clothes!

LUTTER [*Again leans toward* THE STRANGER]: If you care for my advice: Beat it!

ULRICH: Shut your trap, Lutter! Are you queer, or something? Maybe Lutter's queer! [*Laughs*]

CHRISTIAN: Goering was queer too! [*Laughs*] Cheers, Mousey!

FUTTERKNECHT: Frau Mielke! You really must tell us . . . [*Hiccups*] te-he-hell . . . if we're getting out of bounds . . . like pigs!

LUTTER [*Close to* THE STRANGER, *unpredictable*]: Hush—hush. Ff-Ff. You shall get your music. [*Goes to the bandstand. Sits down behind the old percussion set. Begins to play the drums slowly.*]

THE STRANGER: Truly.

CHRISTIAN: That whole shitty Catholic Church is queer!

ULRICH: And probably that naked joker with his crown of thorns was queer too!

FUTTERKNECHT: Beautiful! Beautiful that you think this is fun. Really beautiful!

THE STRANGER: Did I say that?

ULRICH: I love you. *I love hookers!* Once and for all. Christian! What I'm saying now I also say to honor our mother! They wiped her out in this miserable town, put her down, despised her, humiliated, and insulted her. They made our mother a hooker. There was no end to what our mother suffered from these squares. Because she was proud of what she was doing. Until she couldn't suffer it any longer. Until she had to leave and put her boys into a home. Her boys! Whom she loved so much.

FUTTERKNECHT: You must tell us if we're going too far. Won't you?

ULRICH: And now everyone's going to have fun on the bandstand! Wine! And music! Or else I'm going to buy this whole fucking Reichsapfel

Hotel, and three days from now there'll be a fucking building site here where I'll plunk down a fucking warehouse for my fucking paints! And our fucking shyster here can prepare the papers, and then he'll get his fucking money he's been dying for. Satisfied? Satisfied with my fucking address?

CHRISTIAN: Great, Mousey. That's the way! Let me give you a kiss for that!!! [*Kisses* ULRICH]

THE STRANGER: And? What about me?

ULRICH: What? Christian. What's that she said? [*Pause*]

FUTTERKNECHT [*Reciting the words*]: "Close your eyes!" I closed mine long ago! [*With closed eyes and arms stretched out, he is groping for* THE STRANGER] I don't know! I don't know! Them there hills are looking for me!

LUTTER: No.

[*Pause.* FUTTERKNECHT *touches* THE STRANGER. ULRICH *and* CHRISTIAN *try to kiss her. She puts bits of potato into their mouths.*]

FUTTERKNECHT: Oh! May I please be first in line! What really turns me on like crazy: give me an order. Anything! Give me, for instance, an order to climb the bandstand and strip for the sauna, and then make me sweat as your sh-shlave, and then let me, let's say, scrub the floor, the ground beneath your feet. Or, even better! Give me one of your many little rubbers!

THE STRANGER: Why?

FUTTERKNECHT: No! Holy shit! Aren't you afraid?

CHRISTIAN: That's class!

FUTTERKNECHT: Just say it! [*Pause*] Give me the order! [*Pause*] "Go up and strip and scrub!" [*Pause*]

THE STRANGER: What should I do?

FUTTERKNECHT: Go on! Say it! Say it!

[CHRISTIAN *is kneeling before* THE STRANGER]

FUTTERKNECHT: We're waiting for your orders! "Strip! Scrub! Submission!"

CHRISTIAN: Enema! [*Howls like a dog*]

ULRICH: Why don't we hear one single word? Is there someone here who refuses to kneel before our Queen Sahara! That swine should speak up! Mine's touching my belly button!

CHRISTIAN: Mine's touching my chin! Mousey!

LUTTER [*To* THE STRANGER]: Well? What's on your mind? With all that hate in your heart?

FUTTERKNECHT: To the sauna! "Sweat! Scrub!" [*Starts taking off his clothes*]

THE STRANGER [*Coldly*]: You swine.

ULRICH: Yes! That's the right lingo! "Kneel down, you swine!" [*Shouts*] Say it! Say it! Come on!

THE STRANGER: Kneel . . . kneel down, you German swine.

ULRICH: Yes, that's me! [*Embraces* THE STRANGER's *legs*]

FUTTERKNECHT: To the steam bath! To the steam bath! [*Takes off all his clothes*]

THE STRANGER: My German swine! Now trot around in a circle. And grunt and lick the floor. That's what I want to see. [BROTHERS *and* FUTTERKNECHT *crawl on all fours in a small circle and grunt a little*] Louder! Much louder! It's truly disgusting.

[MIELKE *comes behind the bar and watches the strange spectacle with a dim and angry eye*]

THE STRANGER [*As she pours wine on the floor*]: Lick it up. [*The* THREE MEN *lick the puddles of wine from the floor*] Let's have a look at you! Let me have a look at your swine snouts!

BROTHERS [*Holding their wine-slobbered faces up to* THE STRANGER *breaking into song*]: And where has gone my dick to hunt, my dick to hunt, my dick to hunt? You've got it right inside your cunt, inside your cunt, inside your cunt. [*As* FUTTERKNECHT *opens the tablecloth he has wrapped himself in*] Oh, look at him. The doctor. How white he is!

MIELKE: Very funny, Herr Doctor. Very funny!

FUTTERKNECHT: Are we a tad too naughty, Frau Mielke?

THE STRANGER: The white German animal! Hasn't any pants to wear! [*Claps her hands*] Come on, you swine. One of you shall have me tonight! [*Claps her hands*]

[FUTTERKNECHT *has wrapped himself in his tablecloth again.* THE MEN *crawl, singing, toward the bandstand.*]

BROTHERS: Take off your shift, Frau Nightingale! We'll screw you silly without fail. Olé! Olé! Olé! We're the greatest. Germany! Germany! Victory! Victory!

[THE MEN *are on the bandstand.* THE STRANGER *has closed the curtain. Silence.*]

THE STRANGER: When I clap my hands, send the first one out. He who pays the fairest price shall do it to me tonight. Well? Are you ready? [*Sits on a chair and begins to open her dress. Suddenly, she is shivering. She notices that* MIELKE *is watching her with a dark, brooding look. She wants to say something, but doesn't—and lightly claps her hands at last. Pushing and shoving behind the bandstand curtain.*] Well?

ULRICH [*Offstage*]: Let our dumbbell go first. [LUTTER *is pushed forward.* BROTHERS *stand in the opening of the curtain and watch as Lutter walks up to* THE STRANGER.]

THE STRANGER: Well?

LUTTER: Well? [*Grins*]

THE STRANGER: Here. I'm still smelling of you.

LUTTER: Don't you know your way back?

THE STRANGER [*Pause*]: You want to, don't you? Sniff. Come on. You can still smell your stink on my skin. You dirty swine! [*Bends her head to one side*] Afraid? Where's your dog? Where's your four-legged courage. You want me?

LUTTER: Yes.

THE STRANGER: Can you smell yourself?

LUTTER: I smell you.

THE STRANGER: How are you going to pay me?

LUTTER: Tell me.

THE STRANGER: I want you.

LUTTER: Me?

THE STRANGER: Your dog.

LUTTER: It's him you want?

THE STRANGER [*Takes one of* LUTTER*'s hands and brings it to her throat*]: No?

LUTTER: You witch! [*Softly whistles between his teeth.* GERO *comes from the other room and runs to Lutter.*] Sit, Gero. Good boy.

THE STRANGER: What a beautiful animal! There's my suitcase with the lingerie. Take it up to my room. You like seeing me in my undies, don't you? [*Claps her hands*] Go to it. When you're ready, come and get me.

LUTTER: You bet. You bet I'll come and get you. [*Grins broadly, showing his rotten teeth*]

THE STRANGER [*To* MIELKE]: Bring us some wine. Isn't the sauna heated yet? I'm really cold!

LUTTER [*To* GERO]: Sit! [*Picks up the suitcase and exits upstairs.* CHRISTIAN *and* ULRICH *step out from behind the curtain.*]

THE STRANGER: Yes, my swine. Come here to me, both of you. [*Very softly*] Or . . . aren't you my German swine anymore?

CHRISTIAN: Oh yes! Your swine! We're your German swine!

THE STRANGER: There are others, after all!

ULRICH [*Shouts*]: But they aren't here! But they aren't here! They're busy being respectable!

CHRISTIAN: Nature's own champagne! We like it the Greek way! Real swinish!

THE STRANGER: No. I don't want it with you!

ULRICH: Why not?

CHRISTIAN: Why not with us?

ULRICH: Now I'm getting riled! You slut!

THE STRANGER: You're not playing the game!

ULRICH: Not playing? [*Burps*]

CHRISTIAN: Your price! You dirty slut! Tell us what you're asking. Go on!

THE STRANGER: You should . . . this dog, the dog . . .

CHRISTIAN: What?

THE STRANGER: You should kill him! Off him. Any way you'd like. Then you shall have me. [*Pause*] Oh no! What am I saying! What is it I want! Not killing the dog. Don't. I'm crazy. It . . . it just turned me on really hot . . .

ULRICH: That's the way you shall stay! Hot as hell! That's the way we want you, slut! If that's what turns you on—come on, Christian. I'll pay that price for a real dirty game.

CHRISTIAN: Come here, doggy. We'll put you into the gas oven! Won't hurt you much!

ULRICH: Won't have to wipe off the blood.

CHRISTIAN: Come, doggy. Good boy! Into the gas oven with your little head.

ULRICH: Sodom and Gomorrah! You're Sodom and I'm Gomorrah. Come, Gero.

[BROTHERS *exit with* GERO *behind the bar.* FUTTERKNECHT, *now fully dressed, slips through the curtain and steps down from the bandstand.*]

FUTTERKNECHT: That's the carnal instinct for you. Good God. I've gone too far. But . . . but . . . a crazy night. You're so . . . you're stimulating quite beastly urges in me. Believe me. Just a moment ago I swore to myself: "Gustav! You'll leave now!" You've got a peculiar attraction. Tell me, please: How much. I've got to be your slave once without any clothes at all. Be your abject creature . . . God, you're driving me mad! A hundred and fifty marks? Two hundred? Two hundred marks! [*Gulps*]

THE STRANGER: No.

FUTTERKNECHT: Four hundred! For God's sake! A travelers check!

THE STRANGER: Too much! Too much, my dear. Nothing at all.

FUTTERKNECHT: For free. [*Gulps*] Ah! Aha!! No! If you assume I would reopen the case for you—no! The Pole has long gone to his Maker. Dead and forgotten!

THE STRANGER [*Pause. Then softly and intensely.*]: The brothers are killing the dog. [*Pause*]

MIELKE [*Standing half hidden behind the bar, trying to stay out of this as much as possible*]: In your place I'd get out of here.

THE STRANGER: A human being was killed here!

MIELKE [*With a grandiose simplicity*]: Because this is our Germany! And because he parked in the wrong spot! But why am I wasting my words! Beat it! You've got what you wanted! Just wait until Lutter knows!

THE STRANGER [*Coldly*]: That mangy dog!

[BROTHERS *return each with a bleeding dog's ear, Ulrich swinging the bloody dog tail triumphantly, like a lasso*]

ULRICH: Here, slut.

CHRISTIAN: Here, Nightingale. Dead as a doornail! [*Hands* THE STRANGER *an ear*]

ULRICH: The Mauls always pay promptly. [*Hands* THE STRANGER *an ear*]

CHRISTIAN: The Mauls have always paid promptly!

ULRICH: Promptly and on time!

CHRISTIAN: As it should be!

[*During the last exchange,* LUTTER *has returned. He looks at the two ears in* THE STRANGER'*s hands.*]

LUTTER: What is this?

[CHRISTIAN *and* ULRICH *explode with howling laughter*]

ULRICH: Is?! Was! Was!! You dumbbell!!!

CHRISTIAN: Quiet, Lutter! We had to send your Gero into the gas! The wages of sin! [*Laughs*] It wasn't a happy parting. [*Pause*]

ULRICH: That with the dog . . . that was a mistake . . . we shouldn't have
   done it . . . we won't do anything like that again. A pilsner.
CHRISTIAN: Two pilsners. [*Pause.* MIELKE *goes behind the bar and draws the
   beers.*]
FUTTERKNECHT: She turns men into swine, that one.
ULRICH: Pick yourself another one tomorrow! Osnabrück! Gold medal!
LUTTER [*Pulls a knife, stabs* CHRISTIAN. *Christian falls into* ULRICH's *arms.*
   LUTTER *turns to* THE STRANGER *and holds the knife to her throat.*]: The
   way I feel you burning on my skin . . . I've got to wash you off my
   skin . . .
ULRICH [*Lets go of* CHRISTIAN *and jumps at* LUTTER, *tearing him away from*
   THE STRANGER]: What? What have you done now?

3

Enter LEON. *He takes* THE STRANGER *into his arms.*

LEON: Come. Margrit! [*Screams*] Margrit!!

[LEON *quickly leaves with* THE STRANGER]

ULRICH [*Hitting* LUTTER *in the face*]: What have you done!!
MIELKE: Those foreigners. All the trouble's caused by those foreigners!

[*Silence. Blackout. Curtain.*]

THE END

Fernando Krapp Wrote Me This Letter

An Assaying of the Truth

TANKRED DORST
in collaboration with Ursula Ehler

•

Translated by Michael Roloff

Editor's Note

•

The Akademie Theater, Vienna Burg Theater's smaller house, was the site of the premiere of *Fernando Krapp Wrote Me This Letter* on May 15, 1992.

Tankred Dorst once remarked that he always was intrigued by "the overwhelming power of the imagination, of fears and also of utopian dreams, and its conquest of reality . . . the discrepancy between utopia and reality, between the person you would like to be and the one you are." This "power of the imagination" has become a theme of many of his texts. *Fernando Krapp Wrote Me This Letter* presents a protagonist who decides to shape himself, the world, and the people who surround him according to a dream he desires to live. But he destroys the object of his desire as well as himself in the pursuit of this impossible project.

The play's narrative is derived from a novella by the Spanish Basque writer and philosopher Miguel de Unamuno (1864–1936) entitled *Nada menos que todo un hombre* (Nothing Less Than a Man). Michael Roloff, the translator, comments on the connection:

> Reencountering, in Tankred Dorst's adaptation, one of my favorite stark works, Unamuno's novella *Nothing Less Than a Man,* came as a pleasurable surprise. Meanwhile, subsequent to doing the translation, in Mexico, I took a fresh look at the novella itself. This, then, proved to me that my idea that it lacked a single adjective must have been a notion fed by an ascetically sublimating, idealizing strain of mine; the work, unread for thirty years, had taken on a life of its own. Yet my memory was not far off the mark. *Nothing Less Than a Man* does contain a handful of dramatic adjectives, but these are sloughed off on the way to an even greater minimalization at the hands of Tankred Dorst.
>
> However, time had not distorted the "fable" in my mind; it is intact, in boiled-down fashion, in Dorst's dramatization; unless you consider arguable some of Dorst and his collaborator's emphases and deemphases and matters retained verbatim from the original. Some of these matters make utterly good sense, especially dramatically—to enumerate and speculate is fascinating but is not my task; the change in title itself points to the

currents of time in this dramatization. Who is whose victim, and of what, in this Liebestod? So I suggest to the readers, actors, and directors of the play to make their own fruitful comparison with the original or with Angel Flores's Grove Press (1956) translation. Unamuno's highly stylized Spanish, fidelity to whose syntax has some odd consequences for Flores's work, also exerts itself there, as the stylization does in the German play, and I hope in this translation.

Tankred Dorst was born in 1925, in a small town in Thuringia, the son of an engineer and factory owner; his father died when the boy was five. In 1943 while still in high school, Dorst was drafted into the Labor Service and then into the army at the Western Front, where he became a prisoner of war in 1944. After three years in prison camps, briefly in England but mainly the United States, he returned to West Germany, where he finished high school. He studied art history, literature, and theater at Bamberg and Munich universities during the early fifties. In Munich, he was a member of a student marionette theater group, for which he wrote a number of plays. In 1960, the first three of his theater texts received their premieres at city theaters in Lübeck, Mannheim, and Bielefeld.

Dorst has become one of the most prolific and widely performed playwrights in the language. His work encompasses a variety of genres: absurdist comedies, like *The Curve* (1960); realistic family plays, such as *On Chimborazo Mountain* (1975); epic pieces on political themes, such as *Toller* (1968), *Little Man—What Now?* (1972), and *Ice Age* (1973); large-scale works based on myth and fairy tale, like *Merlin: or the Waste Land* (1981) and *Parzival on the Other Side of the Lake* (1987), the latter with Robert Wilson; and plays of pure fantasy, such as *Korbes* (1988) and the present play. Dorst also has written several opera libretti, prose works, and films; some of the latter he also directed. During 1970, Dorst was a writer in residence at Oberlin College. The same year, he began his collaboration with Ursula Ehler, who was to become his wife.

Much of Dorst's writing focuses on the confrontation of the personal with general history, the ways societal forces intrude upon the private realm. His own biography has clearly left its mark on many of his plays: the experiences of his youth in Nazi Germany, the war, and the events that shaped his country's history during the forty years of the two German states. When he was invited to join the (West) German Academy of Sciences and Letters in 1983, he ended his acceptance speech with the words: "How can we live? is what all of my theater pieces ask: What power is driving us into our deeds and our crimes, into our madness? What dark move of our imagination will drive us eventually into war and the end of it all? Nothing is certain, and the truth that we are striving for in our lives and our writings is not to be found."

Carl Weber

Fernando Krapp Wrote Me This Letter

CHARACTERS

The Father
Julia
Fernando Krapp
The Count
Two Psychiatrists

●

1

JULIA. THE FATHER.

JULIA: Fernando Krapp wrote me this letter. [*She offers the letter to her* FATHER]

THE FATHER [*Pretending to be astonished*]: Really?

JULIA: Read it!

THE FATHER: So, what did you reply?

JULIA [*Impatiently*]: Read it.

THE FATHER: He is much sought after. Everyone is talking about him since he returned a millionaire from America. Quite a few damsels would be more than glad to get a letter from him—all of them would.

JULIA: Read!

THE FATHER: No. The letter is addressed to you, you only need to tell me what it says. I know that you have read it.

JULIA: It's not long.

THE FATHER: The man doesn't beat around the bush, he is a very energetic person. I can tell as much from the handwriting.

JULIA [*Reading it to him*]: "Dear Miss . . . "

THE FATHER: Is that how he addresses you? "Dear Miss," that informally?

JULIA [*Reading out loud*]: "I have been told that you are the most beautiful girl in the city where I settled a short while back. I took a look at you when you went walking with your father in the park."

THE FATHER: Really? He saw us there?

JULIA [*Reading out loud*]: "It is true. You are the most beautiful of them all. I will marry you. Fernando Krapp."

THE FATHER: He has a firm grasp of his objective. The sign of a strong character.

JULIA: How long were we at the park on Saturday?

THE FATHER: Oh, I don't know any more.

JULIA: I wanted to go home, but I had to walk the length of the alley—two more times; you insisted.

THE FATHER: Fresh air is healthy. You're sitting too much at home, reading, spinning your dreams.

JULIA: You arranged everything with him! [*She throws the letter in* THE FATHER's *face*]

THE FATHER: Julia, darling! Tell me, what did you answer him.

JULIA: Ha!

THE FATHER: I don't believe that you replied a mere "Ha!" I know you to be a very adroit, imaginative letter writer.

JULIA: I will tell you what I wrote Fernando Krapp: "Dear Sir, I infer from your letter that you have bought me from my father. What was the asking price for each pound of my flesh? What was the price per kilo of living flesh? And did you immediately agree to the asked-for price? Or did you try to bargain him down? I can imagine my father's face pinching anxiously, the trembling of his lips, and isn't that a tear running down his blue-veined cheek? And all because you hesitate to pay the asking price! But you know that the poor man is like putty in your hands, his debts are sky high, he has to sell the goods at any price."

THE FATHER [*Moaning*]: You are joking, you must be joking, Julia!

JULIA: "Or did you happen to catch me smile while you were watching, and that was worth a few extra thousand, which you threw in of your own accord? I can assure you, dear Sir, I have normal teeth and pretty earlobes, not to mention other features, which good taste prohibits from revealing unadornedly. But if you come to my father's, the salesman's, house, you may inspect the goods before fixing the exact amount to be entered in the contract."

THE FATHER [*Horrified*]: Julia!

JULIA: Don't tell me that I did not write the letter in your spirit, father? *I* thought so.

THE FATHER: You are cruel, are making fun of my blue-veined cheeks . . . I am so close to death, yes, to death, from worrying about you.

JULIA: Don't complain! Otherwise I will get a headache! And black rings under my eyes—that might diminish the asking price.

THE FATHER: You poor child. Can't you see what danger you are in if I don't assure your future! You are as beautiful as one of God's thoughts; but as beautiful as you are, the thoughts inside your head are so odd they make me anxious for you. You offend people with your bizarre ideas.

JULIA: Ideas?

THE FATHER: What kind of woman will reply to a rich and respected man's marriage proposal with such insults. What a job it will be to straighten it all out again.

JULIA: No need to.

THE FATHER: What bizarre ideas you have! There you go asking a poor student, who has nothing and isn't anyone, and whom you scarcely know: "abduct me!" That is what I call bizarre. And he says, says so in his fright: "All right, I'll do it. But what are we going to live on?" And you, what do you reply?

JULIA: Well, what?

THE FATHER: "We'll commit suicide together," is what you said.

JULIA: There's no way you could know this.

THE FATHER: I know it. Everyone knows it. He told everyone, the poor confused boy. The whole town knows it. And he didn't come back here, did he? He thought to himself: "I don't want to die."

JULIA: A blabbermouth!

THE FATHER: Listen: who wants to die, darling? No one wants to die; me neither. You want to make your fortune, hope for a little bit of something. Take a look at your old father! He can still laugh, hasn't given up all hope; although, to put it mildly, he is short of liquid capital, at the moment. [*Snaps his fingers, grins*]

JULIA: Stop snapping your fingers like that.

THE FATHER: Indeed, I am snapping! A stupid habit of mine.—If Fernando Krapp bails out, as he just might because you wrote him this letter, I will hang myself! [*Walks off*]

2

JULIA. FERNANDO KRAPP.

FERNANDO KRAPP [*Entering*]: You wrote me a letter, I really liked it.

JULIA: You were not supposed to.

FERNANDO KRAPP: I can see from this letter that we will get along very well.

JULIA: But I didn't like *your* letter!

FERNANDO KRAPP: Most everybody knows that Fernando Krapp achieves everything he sets out to do. You are the most beautiful woman in town and probably in the whole country. I want to marry you. Here I am.

[JULIA *sits for a long time without moving or saying anything*]

FERNANDO KRAPP [*Made uneasy by her silence. After awhile he walks up to her and looks at her. Matter-of-factly.*]: Are you all right?

JULIA: Sure . . . I'm fine.

FERNANDO KRAPP: But you are trembling, I can tell.

JULIA: It's cold . . . it is quite cold.

FERNANDO KRAPP: You are mistaken, it is warm.

JULIA: Really?

FERNANDO KRAPP: You are trembling because you are afraid?

JULIA: Afraid of what?

FERNANDO KRAPP: Of me.

JULIA: Why should I be afraid of you? No, certainly not.

FERNANDO KRAPP: Sure. You are afraid of me.

[JULIA *starts to cry*]

FERNANDO KRAPP [*Watches* JULIA *quietly; after a while*]: Am I a monster? Take your hands away from your face! Look at me!—Only my enemies fear me.

JULIA: I am being sold.

FERNANDO KRAPP: Really? Who says so?

JULIA: I say so.—What choice does my poor father have?—He is bankrupt and has to go to prison. But before the police fetch him, before he will let himself be dragged shackled through the wild-eyed inquisitive crowd, before that happens to him, he will hang himself. I know it.

FERNANDO KRAPP: None of that need be.

JULIA: You with all your money, showing it off everywhere. Your money. You open your billfold, waving banknotes around, tossing them from the balcony down to the people so that they grovel for them, scrape the last banknote out of the mud!

FERNANDO KRAPP: Your father was in a fine fettle. I took care of everything, paid everything.

JULIA: Paid everything?

FERNANDO KRAPP: Yes. How much was it? I've actually forgotten the sum, meanwhile.

JULIA: Really. So you've already acquired us, we are already living off your money? [*Tears off her scarf*] This scarf that my father brought home for me yesterday, it was paid for with your money?—And the shoes?—The shoes too. [*She takes off the shoes and flings them at* FERNANDO KRAPP's *head*]

FERNANDO KRAPP: I can see, Julia, what pretty feet you have.

JULIA: You'll never have me! Never, never! Only when I am dead.

FERNANDO KRAPP: But you love me, Julia. You love me even now! That is why you will marry me.

JULIA: Bought! Like a pig in a poke!

FERNANDO KRAPP: You seem to think you are the merchandise and that I have the money.

JULIA [*Screaming*]: Yes! Yes!

FERNANDO KRAPP: I stipulated no conditions when I gave your father the money. Made no demands.—You do not want to love me? But that is impossible! Not to love me, that is impossible!

[*A long silence.* JULIA *is crying. Silence.*]

JULIA [*Softly*]: Do with me as you like.
FERNANDO KRAPP: What do you mean by that? What are you saying?
JULIA: I don't know . . . I don't know what I am saying.
FERNANDO KRAPP: What does that mean, I should do with you as I like?
JULIA: It means . . . I don't know . . .
FERNANDO KRAPP: I don't want to buy a whore—"bought"—Nonsense!—
It is a marriage of love. You love me, that is why you are crying! You are
beginning to understand it.

JULIA: She marries him.

3

JULIA. FERNANDO KRAPP.

JULIA: What kind of man are you?
FERNANDO KRAPP: What should I be like? I am I, *Fernando Krapp*.
JULIA: You keep saying that. You never talk about your past. I don't know
anything about your parents.
FERNANDO KRAPP: I have no parents. My family begins with me. I am the
beginning of my family. I made myself.
JULIA: Take a look at my hands.
FERNANDO KRAPP: Slim, elegant fingers.
JULIA: They are my mother's.
FERNANDO KRAPP: Inadvertently, they become small hard, furious fists. That
amuses me.
JULIA: Yes, it's true; when I think about something I make a fist.
FERNANDO KRAPP: And you don't knock before you step into my room, the
way others do, with the knuckles, but your fingernails tickle the wood.
JULIA: Like my grandmother! She did it like that. But the beautiful nose is
my father's.
FERNANDO KRAPP: I am not interested in that. It is beautiful, it is unique.
JULIA: My imagination is my mother's, too. The pleasure in fantasy runs in the
family. There's a story about an aunt who never crossed the threshold to go
outside her house, saying: "Why should I go bother going out: I can imagine
everything, that is far more interesting."—And from whom did you get
your nose, Fernando, and that chin with that notch that I like so much?

FERNANDO KRAPP: So you like that!

JULIA: Don't you remember anything about your childhood?

FERNANDO KRAPP: I am not interested in childhood. I am who I want to be.

[*Silence*]

JULIA [*Carefully*]: There was something else I wanted to ask you, Fernando. But I lack the courage to do so.

FERNANDO KRAPP: Why not? I'm not going to eat you. So far, you've not insulted me, no matter what you've said. You know that!

JULIA: I am not complaining.

FERNANDO KRAPP: That would be something, you starting to complain.

JULIA: No, of course I'm not complaining, but . . .

FERNANDO KRAPP: Come, ask your question, be done with it!

JULIA: I think I better not . . .

FERNANDO KRAPP: Ask, dammit! I want you to ask the question.

JULIA: All right; I'll ask it: Is it true that you've been married once before?

FERNANDO KRAPP [*Wrinkling his brow*]: Yes.

JULIA: And your first wife?

FERNANDO KRAPP: She has been dead for years. I was a widower when I married you. [*Suspiciously*] People probably have told you stories?

JULIA: No, but . . . oh, forget it.

FERNANDO KRAPP: People told you stories—out with it!

JULIA: Well yes—there was something that I heard.

FERNANDO KRAPP: And you believed it?

JULIA: No. Believe it? No, not exactly.

FERNANDO KRAPP: Of course not! You couldn't allow yourself to. That you couldn't do!

JULIA: No, of course not, I didn't believe it.

FERNANDO KRAPP: That is completely natural! Anyone who loves me the way you do and who is so completely mine can't believe a fat lie like that.

JULIA: Yes, I do love you.—There's just one thing I wish.

FERNANDO KRAPP: Wish for anything!

JULIA: Oh—If just once you would say so to me.

FERNANDO KRAPP: "Sweetheart, my darling, my little salad leaf." That is what you want me to say? Useless, silly words. You find them in novels. I know, you like to read books.

JULIA: And I still like reading them.

FERNANDO KRAPP: Read, read on! As much as you like! I'll have them build a pavilion, in the back of the garden near the rose hedges. I'll bring you your books there, every book that's been written since Adam and Eve.

JULIA: How lovely!

FERNANDO KRAPP: The less people tell each other how much they love each other, the better.

JULIA: Oh, Fernando!

FERNANDO KRAPP: What did people tell you? That I was married in Mexico, in my youth?

JULIA: What did she look like?

FERNANDO KRAPP: To a very wealthy woman, who was older than I, to an aging millionairess? Yes?

JULIA: Yes.

FERNANDO KRAPP: And people told you that I forced her to make me her sole heir, and that then I murdered her? Is that the sort of thing people told you?

JULIA: That you choked her to death in her bed. And even that you did it with your hat.

FERNANDO KRAPP: And you believed that?

JULIA: No, of course not.

FERNANDO KRAPP: With my hat! With my hat! [*He waves his hat around*]

JULIA: I can't even imagine you ever killing your wife.

FERNANDO KRAPP: I can see that you have a better mind than I gave you credit for. Why should I have killed my wife, something that is mine?

JULIA [*Imitating him with an emotionless voice*]: "Why should I have killed my wife, something that is mine?"

FERNANDO KRAPP: Are you a parrot? Why do you repeat what I say to you?

JULIA: I don't know.

FERNANDO KRAPP: What reason did I have for doing so? I already had her money, and her copper mines I had too. So why kill your own wife? That would have been completely unnecessary.

JULIA: Still, some husbands kill their women.

FERNANDO KRAPP: May be, may be. That's of no concern to me.

JULIA: Out of jealousy for example. Or out of revenge, because the woman has a lover.

FERNANDO KRAPP: Only morons are jealous. Impotent excitable fools. And they have reason to be! But I . . . I don't know what that is: jealousy. A feeling . . . it must be a strange feeling . . . I don't know what you feel, feeling that. My woman won't cheat on me. My first wife was never able to, nor will you, no one will!

JULIA: Don't talk like that, let us talk about something else . . .

FERNANDO KRAPP: But why?

JULIA: It hurts me when you talk to me like that. It seems as though you might suspect me. And that makes me unhappy.

FERNANDO KRAPP: Actually, the subject halfway amuses me.

JULIA: Not in a dream would I think of cheating on you!

FERNANDO KRAPP: But I know that, that's what I am saying.

JULIA: Never!

FERNANDO KRAPP: It isn't even possible, I know that. You can't cheat on me.—The first wife died a natural death. I didn't need to kill her. Now you know everything, Julia.

JULIA: Yes.

[*Silence*]

FERNANDO KRAPP: You can be moody.

JULIA: I am all right.

FERNANDO KRAPP: Your eyelids are swollen. Let me see!

JULIA: Fernando . . .

FERNANDO KRAPP: Now that I look at you, your eyes are closed. Are you still thinking about that stupid story? I explained everything, and you understood everything.

JULIA: I am pregnant.

FERNANDO KRAPP: Yes—I expected that. Now I have my heir, I will make my son into a man like myself.

JULIA: We don't know whether it is a son or a daughter.

FERNANDO KRAPP: It will be a son, I know it.

JULIA: But what if it is a girl?

FERNANDO KRAPP: No, it is a son!

JULIA: They had a child, and it was a son.

FERNANDO KRAPP: What a marvelous child you gave me!

JULIA: Why don't you kiss your child? You made him such marvelous presents when he was born, and lavished money on the people, and showered me with presents so that I thought that you are truly happy about your child, and now you never take him into your arms or kiss him.

FERNANDO KRAPP: All that kissing and stuff is nothing but a bother for children. I will wait until he understands me. There is much I will have to say to him then.

JULIA: I talk to him all the time, with my hands and kisses.

4

JULIA. FERNANDO KRAPP.

FERNANDO KRAPP: Did this Count come by again?

JULIA: "This Count"? What Count are you talking about?

FERNANDO KRAPP: Well, that one, who's been coming recently. One of those useless busybodies. Does nothing but talk but doesn't have it in him to repair the family palace. The roof is caving in, the window shutters are falling off their hinges, the pompous gate is blocked with barbed wire, he has to enter and leave through the back door. I took a look at it; it was offered to me too, to tear it down.

JULIA: Yes "that one" came by.

FERNANDO KRAPP: If it amuses you, go ahead. In that case, the fellow is not completely useless, that jerk.

JULIA [*Offended*]: At least he is very polite and considerate.

FERNANDO KRAPP: Polite, but a jerk.

JULIA: And he is very well educated. He even writes.

FERNANDO KRAPP: Cultured, still a jerk.

JULIA: He has even written poems.

FERNANDO KRAPP: Poems.—Just like him!

JULIA: And he's such a good conversationalist. He really knows his literature. Other things too.

FERNANDO KRAPP: So much the better that he amuses you . . .

JULIA: "Amuse" isn't the right word. He is very unhappy.

FERNANDO KRAPP: Ah, so he makes himself out to be a bit interesting—he suffers! I bet he's composed a poem about his suffering and slipped it to you for you to find. Say, under the saucer of the teacup? So few people understand his pain, he has to be consoled, people must have understanding.

JULIA: He is very sensitive.

FERNANDO KRAPP: Very! Console him, talk to him about his interesting psychological problems.

JULIA: You misunderstand him. He really is a special person. And his secret wound is that his wife cheats on him.

FERNANDO KRAPP: Well, "secret"! Everybody knows about that. He tells that story to everybody because he hopes to make a pitiable impression on the ladies.

JULIA: I can't imagine a woman doing something like that to her husband, embarrassing her husband like that in public.

FERNANDO KRAPP: I understand that only too well. Because he's a jerk. Probably she only married him for his title and now is bored to death. A woman wouldn't get away with that with me.

JULIA [*After hesitating momentarily*]: And if she did? How would things go on then?

FERNANDO KRAPP: Nonsense. I am not a serial novel! Our life isn't something we make up out of whole cloth! About which you can have interesting conversations with this Count! Life is normal. And if you think that you are making me jealous, you are mistaken! To start playing games like that! With me! Amuse yourself all you like with this jerk. It means nothing to me.

JULIA [*As an aside*]: Really, doesn't he give a moment's thought to the Count visiting me so frequently? That we sit talking in the pavilion afternoons at a time? Is he that blasé? Does he love me? Doesn't he love me? The question tortures me. [*To* FERNANDO KRAPP] We have an invitation to visit his palace tomorrow.

FERNANDO KRAPP: What should I do there?

JULIA: For tea.—Don't you want to come?

FERNANDO KRAPP: Teatime! No. I only drink tea when I have a stomachache. Go by yourself, console the Count. The Countess probably will be there too, and with her guy, whosoever's turn it is now. A modern marriage! Interesting! Go ahead.

5

JULIA. THE COUNT.

THE COUNT [*Worriedly*]: It is just like the most banal of farces. Milady is wearing a little shirt, nothing but a little shirt, and walks back and forth between the bedroom and the salon, is literally hopping back and forth. And goes "la-la-la-la." "So why are you trilling like that all the time?" "I go la-la-la-la because I am so alone and the sun is shining through the window." "Two dishes, two glasses. For whom?" "For you!" "A fresh melon. But someone has already taken a bite." "Of course! How funny!" Then I hear half-suppressed sneezing. Did that really come from the closet? I open the closet as though I want to change my necktie. There's no one there. Should I look under the bed? Should I lower myself that far and participate in this farce? Draw back the curtain with one fell swoop, so as to look into the stupidly grinning face of some man, whom I don't know, or who is my best friend, or is the postman or the tennis coach. I could toss the lover out the window, drive her out onto the street. That is what she wants, she loves scandal, the excitement, the screaming. But I don't say anything, I flee. I'm unfit for such an ordinary farce.

JULIA: How did this misfortune befall you?

THE COUNT: Why I married this woman, is what you are asking?

JULIA: Yes, why?

THE COUNT: Don't condemn me!

JULIA: She must have been very attractive?

THE COUNT: Yes, and she still is. But that wasn't what mattered. She was completely uncultured, I liked that. A creature of nature! She didn't know anything, and I thought I would be able to teach her everything, from the ground up as it were. I thought I could wake her up, form her intellect, make her soul sensitive. I imagined that I could, so to speak, breathe life into her. Awaken interests in her of which, previously, she had no idea, warm her heart to the wonders of music, the beauty of language, perhaps even to philosophy. Really, that's what I thought.

JULIA: Pygmalion!

THE COUNT: Until I found out that her beautiful naïveté was that of a moron, her lightheartedness that of a soubrette.

JULIA: I feel sorry for you, dear Count.

THE COUNT: I, who so suffer under banalities!

JULIA: What a terrible deception.

THE COUNT: My soul is mortally exhausted, but I am not complaining. I have no right to. I should have known that there are people who, themselves callous, may perceive this lack of the capacity to feel as a grievous absence and therefore have the need, perhaps even take pleasure, in torturing others, so as to warm their cold hearts in the other's pain.

JULIA: But dear Count, how cleverly you look through everything!

THE COUNT: A life full of pain affords insights and knowledge from which the happier and more self-satisfied are excluded. Read Leopardi, read the poets who are our contemporaries—all great poetry draws on a painful feeling for life, on melancholy.

JULIA [*Abruptly*]: Am I unhappy?

THE COUNT: That you ask me that, Julia!

JULIA: Ah, the thought suddenly popped up in my head; forget it.

THE COUNT: My thoughts won't let go of you.

JULIA: What is the content of these thoughts?

THE COUNT: Sometimes I imagine that we came to know each other before I was bound to this banal person who has made my life a living hell . . . And before you . . .

JULIA: There's no comparing!

THE COUNT: Still I believe . . . but I'd better not say it.

JULIA: But say it! Now that you've made me curious.

THE COUNT: If we had seen each other back then and had talked . . .

JULIA: You want to say that I would have fallen in love with you.

THE COUNT: No doubt about it.

JULIA: How vain you men are!

THE COUNT: I am not vain.

JULIA: Everyone thinks they are irresistible.

THE COUNT: Oh no.

JULIA: But you just said so yourself.

THE COUNT: I don't mean it like that.

JULIA: How then? Tell me.

THE COUNT: Not I—my love would have been irresistible. My love!

JULIA: Oh, if that isn't a regular declaration of love, Count! You are forgetting that I am a married woman and in love with my husband.

THE COUNT: So you say, but . . .

JULIA: Do you doubt it? But it is the case. He is a marvelous man! Full of energy and life! When the door opens and he stands there, I think: "He is life itself," and I have to throw myself into his arms.

THE COUNT: And he?

JULIA: What "and he"? That's what he's like.

THE COUNT: But I know . . . I heard . . .

JULIA: That he doesn't love me? Who told you that?

THE COUNT: You did!

JULIA: I have never talked to you about my husband!

THE COUNT: Your eyes said it, the way you lowered your head, each movement of your hand, the sound of your voice, and your silences.

JULIA: Ah. You are trying to say that I asked you for a declaration of love? This is the last time you cross the threshold of our house.

THE COUNT: For God's sake, Julia!

JULIA: The last time, I said!

THE COUNT: If I could only be in the room next door! In the dark for all I care, I can hear your steps in the salon, and perhaps I can hear your voice, I close my eyes, and I can see your face behind my closed lids, smiling at me.

JULIA: In the next room and in the dark?

THE COUNT: Just to be near you!—What I said now and what perhaps frightened you . . .

JULIA: Not "perhaps!" You did frighten me!

THE COUNT: You regarded my declaration as vainglorious.

JULIA: Yes. Indeed.

THE COUNT: Horrible error! Who am I? An impotent enthusiast, nothing but that. The ancient name . . . Well, all right. But what of it? A certain education . . . well, yes, no one should make a fuss over it, as little as about pleasant manners. A special sensibility for matters artistic—the fact that I have a literally physical feel for the perfection of a line, of a sound, the nuance of a color? Two lines from a Lorca poem, and it happens that I break out in tears, I can't help it. But that of course is no reason to be vainglorious. That is a stigma. It just makes me lonely. Take a look at me, Julia, take just one look.

JULIA: No.

THE COUNT: Do you see before you a uniquely beautiful man? A silly thought, that! I look into the mirror and discover melancholy's shadow. Signs of secret deterioration of the once well-modulated features. I see the small twist of bitterness around my mouth, which I still manage to hide, barely, before the sight of the others. My smile is pained. Nothing of me is worth being loved by you, and you would be justified in casting your eyes away from me, as you are doing now, if that would be what would win you for me.

JULIA: I don't know what you are talking about.

THE COUNT: I am talking about my love, I am talking endlessly about my love, of my wildly courageous mad love for you. This love is my gift to you, not my insignificant person.

JULIA [*Holding her ears closed, whispering*]: Poison . . . Poison!

THE COUNT: Many are unable to love. They ask for love. As though they had a right to boundless love and loyalty. A man takes a famous beauty for himself and presents her: look at my beautiful woman, look at my tigress! And presents her chained. Look, she is mine! Look how she obeys me! But that does not mean he loves his tigress, he merely enjoys owning her.

JULIA: I don't want to hear it.

THE COUNT: How well you listen to me . . . How you have opened your soul up to mine! I penetrate into yours, I penetrate your soul.

JULIA: Leave me in peace! If he would suddenly come into the door . . .

THE COUNT: He is not coming! You don't matter to him! He leaves us together because he does not love you.

JULIA: He has great confidence in me.

THE COUNT: He has complete confidence in himself! Because he has seized everything, because he has made so much money—I don't want to know how!—he can't imagine that he might lose something once he owns it. He has no sense for what goes on in the soul of a woman. And me, he probably despises me.

JULIA: Yes! He despises you!

THE COUNT: I knew it. But he also despises you!

JULIA: Do you want to kill me with your speeches?

THE COUNT: He, he will kill you . . . And you won't be the first one whom he has killed.

JULIA: That is an infamy! You are lying. Oh how you lie! My husband didn't kill that woman!—Go, be gone, finally.

THE COUNT: It is a painful thought, I frightened you!

JULIA: Be gone!

THE COUNT: I understand that you want to be by yourself right now. You will reflect and will call me back. I won't let you down.

6

JULIA. FERNANDO KRAPP.

FERNANDO KRAPP [*Entering*]: Just imagine what happened today?

JULIA: Where?

FERNANDO KRAPP: I have to tell you, for you to have your fun.

JULIA [*Disturbed*]: I am listening.

FERNANDO KRAPP: Do you know what a duel is?

JULIA: Of course I do.

FERNANDO KRAPP: A duel! These days! Nervous little guys in a forest clearing in the morning fog, "choose your weapons," the whole rigmarole! That's not for me.

JULIA [*Frightened*]: You are going to be in a duel?

FERNANDO KRAPP: Are you frightened?

JULIA: Yes—so tell me!

FERNANDO KRAPP: You don't need to be afraid! Right, you know me.

JULIA: I don't know whether I know you or not.

FERNANDO KRAPP: Oh, the oracle has spoken!—No need to be afraid, you can't fool around with me like that: a duel! I am supposed to engage in a duel? Fernando Krapp? I of course sent the fellows packing. "Send me the bill and the matter is over."

JULIA: What kind of bill?

FERNANDO KRAPP: The doctor's bill and restitution for the pain and suffering, and whatever else he wants.

JULIA: Wants who?

FERNANDO KRAPP: But if he insists on a duel—let him come. I'll take care of him with a few slaps in the face and kicks in the pants.

JULIA: Whom are you talking about?

FERNANDO KRAPP: It was this . . . but now I've forgotten his name; I didn't even note down the fine gentleman's name.

JULIA: But how did the fight start?

FERNANDO KRAPP: He told a joke.

JULIA: A fight over a joke? I can't imagine that in your case.

FERNANDO KRAPP: It wasn't a fight. He told his joke and I smashed the glass over his head.

JULIA: Yes . . . and he was injured?

FERNANDO KRAPP: A few sprays of blood, barely a handkerchief's worth, that was it.

JULIA: But how horrible! Did he insult you that grievously?

FERNANDO KRAPP: The joke! The joke. [*Laughs*]

JULIA: Please explain. I am becoming more confused by the moment.

FERNANDO KRAPP: He is telling a joke . . . some kind of joke about a husband who comes home and, entering his bedroom, he finds . . . something like that. Anyway, his wife is lying in bed with a man, and the husband doesn't notice. And then I hear him say: "like Fernando Krapp!"—He says that you are cheating on me.

JULIA: Oh! And of course that made you furious.

FERNANDO KRAPP: Have you ever seen me in a fit of fury? Have you ever seen me lose my composure?

JULIA: No, never when you were with me. But in this case, it would be absolutely natural for you to become excited.

FERNANDO KRAPP: Ah, people, all they do is talk.

JULIA: At any event, you hit him for my sake.

FERNANDO KRAPP: For your sake? That would be ridiculous. For *my* sake! I didn't like the guy's smile, this thin smile is what I don't like, where you don't see the teeth.

JULIA: It should make me happy that you feel so certain of me.

FERNANDO KRAPP: But of course! Don't worry yourself!

JULIA: But . . .

FERNANDO KRAPP: No "but"—the wife of Fernando Krapp *is* happy!

JULIA: Yes.

FERNANDO KRAPP: People tell me that I should make my house off-limits to the Count. What nonsense! If that jerk manages to keep you amused with his delicate leaps and bounds, it is no matter what I think of him. I know that my wife is amused and isn't bored while I look after business. A lapdog! Does one toss a lapdog out the window? It might fall on someone's head!—But seriously: you would throw out the Count yourself if he becomes dangerous to you, that is, if you became interested in him. That he cares for you is self-evident; everyone cares for you.

JULIA: I already forbade him once from coming to the house, Fernando.

FERNANDO KRAPP: Really? [*Briefly taken aback*]

JULIA: Yes. But he came back.

FERNANDO KRAPP: So there! That is a good sign!

JULIA: Now we're seeing a lot of each other again, a few times a week.— [*Suddenly vehement*] You have to send this man away, Fernando!

FERNANDO KRAPP: This man?—"Man"?

JULIA: You have to make the house off-limits to him. For if I did, as you put it, become "interested" in him . . .

FERNANDO KRAPP: But Julia, you want to make me jealous! That's something you just made up, you live in a romantic world, and that confuses you! I believe you should spend a few weeks in the country, away from the city, that will do you good. Fresh air! And if you become bored we will call the jerk, why not? We'll go tomorrow.

THE COUNT: And the next day they drove out to the country.

7

JULIA. FERNANDO KRAPP.

JULIA: What am I supposed to do here all day long? Should I stare at the cows for hours at a time, who stand there among the boulders in the grass? And at the dogs tugging at their chains and growling? I can still hear the chains clanking, in bed at night, my eyes open, unable to fall asleep. And the maids screech all day long, in the house, in the sheds, or over there by the water, where they beat the wash. They screech if one of the farmhands walks past. They have voices of metal, ugly! I am scared of Alfonso, the half-idiot, running after me and taking off his hat and grinning.

FERNANDO KRAPP: Your nerves are in bad shape, Julia.

JULIA: If only I had some books or a few magazines! I am supposed to interest myself in reality, you say. What I see, bores and repels me. If only I had a book! Why didn't I take a few along!

FERNANDO KRAPP: Did I keep you from doing so? You agreed to my idea that we should seclude ourselves a little out in the countryside.

JULIA: Because I knew that you wanted it like that.

FERNANDO KRAPP: But I don't forbid you anything! Did I ever forbid you anything in your life? I am not a tyrant. I don't prohibit anything, and I don't demand anything from you.

JULIA: Yes. You don't even demand that I love you!

FERNANDO KRAPP: But Julia! Love can't be demanded! There are men who demand it from their women, and the women also agree to enter into this demand. They playact for their men, who traditionally expect it of a loving woman: a sweet tone of voice, a certain deep look in the eyes, endless and endlessly repeated descriptions of feelings, sometimes they are supposedly weaker—but have not entirely disappeared—sometimes they burst forth like volcanoes, sighs, whispers, deceit! And their men even believe it. Deceit!—You cannot demand love.

JULIA: But do you believe that I love you?

FERNANDO KRAPP: Not "I believe it"—it is like that.

JULIA: It is like that . . . it is like that.

FERNANDO KRAPP: You saw me back then. I showed you what I am like, from the beginning. You know what I am and who I am. And that is why you love me. It can't be any other way. The fine points of this subject you had better tease apart with your soul friend—not with me. Have him come.

[*Silence*]

JULIA: Don't you think that I noticed that you— [*Hesitates*]

FERNANDO KRAPP: Well?

JULIA: At night sometimes you visit one of the milkmaids. The fat one. Simona is her name! You have started an affair with her. I know that!

FERNANDO KRAPP: I made no effort to hide it. It's not important.

JULIA: In the horseshed, in the larder, in the broom closet . . .

FERNANDO KRAPP: Wild!

JULIA: How primitive that is!

FERNANDO KRAPP: Primitive, yes! I grew up on the manure pit, don't forget. I have a weakness for it. A simple sensual animal, dirty if you like. Yes, dirty, that's what I like! I throw her into the brook, clothes and all, and scrub her clean, and she puts her thick wet arms round me and pulls me down into the water, and screams with such delight it nearly tears my eardrums.

JULIA: So, you like that sort of thing.

FERNANDO KRAPP: Yes, but why are you making a face like that? What does that have to do with you?

JULIA: Perhaps it is beautiful, I am trying to imagine it. Perhaps I could also try to be like your wild animal.

FERNANDO KRAPP: You, Julia? Not you! You must stay the way you are. You are beautiful, you are graceful, you are complete.

JULIA: And you are a liar! It sounds like a declaration of love, but in reality it is an insult.

FERNANDO KRAPP: Oh my, your nerves again! I was thinking that they had improved.

JULIA: A man can do anything. Believe me, a man can cheat.

FERNANDO KRAPP: Who is cheating?

JULIA [Screaming]: You!

FERNANDO KRAPP: Julia! You look at everything at once as though it were a novel. This is simple, normal life. I don't give a damn about that tub of lard, even though I happen to like her for the moment, perhaps still tomorrow, the day after tomorrow, no more.

JULIA: I see, that's how you think it is!

FERNANDO KRAPP: And she thinks just the way I do. She wants to have her fun with me.—I am still your husband, Julia.

JULIA: Which is supposed to mean that I am still your wife.

FERNANDO KRAPP: Now you're coming to your senses.

JULIA: I am becoming infected by how sensible you are, Fernando.

FERNANDO KRAPP: Simona can only gain from me. I pay for everything, and this dowry will afford her a good husband. If she brings a child into the marriage, she can consider herself lucky—with a father like me. A man like me!

JULIA: Quiet. Be silent, quiet!

FERNANDO KRAPP: What a shame! Your neurasthenia isn't as easy to cure as I thought. We have to watch out that it doesn't get worse.

JULIA: You are not a man, Fernando, you are not a man!

FERNANDO KRAPP [Derisively]: Now listen to that, how did you hit on that one?

JULIA: No, you're not a man.

FERNANDO KRAPP: The ideas you have! And why am I not a man?

JULIA: I will tell you some time.

FERNANDO KRAPP: Fine. Tell it to me later on, or don't tell it. Keep it inside your romantic little head.

JULIA: I am silent.

[*Silence*]

FERNANDO KRAPP: You'd better tell me.

JULIA: I know that you don't love me.

FERNANDO KRAPP: Oh my God, are we starting that again! To love and not to love, all this jabbering. That is for your soul mate, please don't bother me with it.

JULIA: You don't need to say anything, I know it anyhow—from the way you are.

FERNANDO KRAPP [*Derisively*]: Should I bring you roses?

JULIA: Oh, roses! The garden is full of them!—It will no longer be a problem if the Count comes and goes as he pleases.

FERNANDO KRAPP: You have no problem with it, that is all that counts.

JULIA: Yes, I am entirely agreeable. Yes! Yes! Yes!

FERNANDO KRAPP: You're getting excited again.

JULIA: Why shouldn't I find it agreeable? He is my lover!—Are you listening? You understood it perfectly well, he is my lover! I am doing it with him, do you understand? Not as primitively as you with your Simona, but I am telling you, he is a very clever lover!

[FERNANDO KRAPP *remains silent*]

JULIA: Fernando!

FERNANDO KRAPP: Yes.

JULIA: You built the pavilion for me.

FERNANDO KRAPP: Yes.

JULIA: The divan with the Indian silk cover stands there.—Of course, we let down the louvers.

[FERNANDO KRAPP *remains silent*]

JULIA: Fernando!

FERNANDO KRAPP: Yes.

JULIA: Yes, yes, yes, yes—is that all you have to say. You're not going to kill me? You're not going to choke me to death with your hat like the other one? The Mexican?

[*Silence.* FERNANDO KRAPP *suddenly breaks out in fits of laughter.*]

JULIA [*Screaming*]: Stop it!

FERNANDO KRAPP [*Stops at once, speaks very calmly*]: It is neither correct to say that I killed my first wife, nor is it true that the jerk is your lover, that as much as his little finger has ever touched you. You are lying to me to enrage me. You want to turn me into an Othello. But that's not what I am, Julia! Will never be. If you are going to go on being obsessed by such fantastic ideas, lose all your defense against them, I will have reason to be seriously worried. We will reach the stage where we will have to lock you up in a madhouse.

JULIA: You are a coward.

FERNANDO KRAPP: My house is not a theater! We are not playing a play.

JULIA [*Screaming*]: Coward! Coward! Coward! [*Starts to cry*]

[FERNANDO KRAPP *leaves*]

THE COUNT: One week later Fernando Krapp asked his wife to join him in his study. There were two gentlemen present. Diabolically, he has also asked Count Bordavela to be there.

8

JULIA. FERNANDO KRAPP. THE COUNT. TWO PSYCHIATRISTS.

FERNANDO KRAPP: You don't know these two gentlemen, Julia. They are Professor Enrique Alvarez and Professor Doctor Hermannstetter, psychiatrists both—madhouse doctors, experts in their field. Professor Alvarez is chief of the Psychiatric Division of one of the hospitals financed by my Fernando Krapp Foundation. I am proud of the fact that they are the most modern and scientifically progressive clinics in the country.

JULIA [*To* THE COUNT]: But what are you doing here, Juan?

THE COUNT: I was asked to come here.

FERNANDO KRAPP: These two gentlemen will diagnose you and take you into treatment. There's something not right in your head, that is why I had to have this done. You will come to realize that, in your lucid moments, Julia.

JULIA [*To* THE COUNT]: We used to meet in other places, Juan. This is not a nice place for a rendezvous.

THE COUNT: It shames me. [*Looks down at the floor*]

JULIA: Why are you looking away? Look at me, Juan. It's me—Julia.

THE COUNT: I certainly recognize you, Madam.

JULIA: You don't usually speak in such a formal tone of voice with me.

FERNANDO KRAPP [*To* THE DOCTORS]: You can see, gentlemen, she still has this idée fixe. It started quite unobtrusively, but her condition gradually worsened, so that there was no talking to her anymore. I, her husband, could no longer talk sensibly with her! She claims, and keeps insisting, that this gentleman here, how shall I say?

JULIA: Yes, he is my lover! It is true, I admit it! If it is not true, let him say so.

FERNANDO KRAPP: Count, you hear what my wife claims. Help the poor creature by telling the truth. The specialists have to get a good picture of the situation. I must ask you point-blank: Have you ever had intimate relations with my wife?

THE COUNT: But no! No! For God's sake!

FERNANDO KRAPP: You see, gentlemen!

JULIA: What are you saying? You deny it?

THE COUNT: I do not recall ever . . .

JULIA: You deny what transpired during our afternoons in the pavilion? Those long stretches from afternoon till dusk. There we lay closely entwined on the divan. Naked. And once you came back at night because you couldn't stand it and I couldn't either, and you stayed until morning, to the last minute, as Fernando returned from his trip and was already calling for me here in the stairwell while you were fleeing through the veranda. You lost a button in your haste, a pants button.

THE COUNT: Milady . . .

JULIA: Fernando found it!

FERNANDO KRAPP: I found a button? You see, gentlemen . . .

THE COUNT: Calm down, Milady! Come to your senses! Please.

JULIA: What is that horrified look you are giving me? As though you had no idea what I am talking about.

THE COUNT: Please calm down, please!

JULIA: Am I lying?

THE COUNT: Lying . . . is the wrong word.

FERNANDO KRAPP: Your condition unfortunately is such that . . .

THE COUNT: Yes, so it is.

FERNANDO KRAPP: That you can't keep reality and fantasy apart. That's what you mean, isn't it Count?

THE COUNT: I feel so sorry for your wife—what a tragedy! If only I could help.

FERNANDO KRAPP: Don't moan and wail. The doctors will help her; that is why I asked them to come. You can depend on them.

JULIA: Good-day, Professor Alvarez, good-day, Doctor Hermannstetter! Oddly enough, I notice your presence only now! How nice that you will help me!

FERNANDO KRAPP [*Applauding*]: Bravo!

JULIA: But you can't help me.—[*To* THE COUNT] Just one more question, Juan! I am not mistaken if I recall your coming now and then to our house, and sometimes quite frequently.

THE COUNT: No, in that you are not mistaken, Milady.

JULIA: What did we talk about?—Let me think: we saw a cat leap up the wall and talked about whether animals, especially cats, have souls, which would be as immortal as a human soul—that is what we talked about. And then we looked up what different philosophers had to say on the subject, literally turning the bookshelves upside down in our research . . . But, as best as I recall, we did not reach a conclusion on the matter; or have I forgotten it?

FERNANDO KRAPP: About a cat, yes! That sounds credible.

JULIA: And also about life after death . . . And didn't I say that it sometimes seems to me as though I had already died?

FERNANDO KRAPP: What nonsense, here you're sitting among us, absolutely alive, Julia! The wife of Fernando Krapp.

JULIA [*Pointing at* THE COUNT]: And that one over there?

FERNANDO KRAPP: Count, now you tell her why you regularly visited our house.

THE COUNT: Of course, out of friendship for you, Mr. Krapp.

JULIA: What, you two are friends?

FERNANDO KRAPP: I have his palace, the rotten old palace, I saved it from ruin, that's what he means, isn't it?

THE COUNT: Yes.

FERNANDO KRAPP: My wife asked me to—otherwise I probably wouldn't have done so.

THE COUNT: Of course, I also came occasionally as an admirer of the honorable lady, with whom I was allowed to converse. It is unthinkable that a Bordavela would misuse the confidence of a friend, to deceive him, such a generous friend.

FERNANDO KRAPP: Like me? Is what you wanted to say?

THE COUNT: Yes, like you.

FERNANDO KRAPP: What? You think I counted on your behaving honorably? I could depend on your morals? That I am dependent on that? That means nothing to me. It doesn't exist for me. You turn your morality as you like, you turn it this way or that, the way the wind blows. That's what you're like. I know that, they are all like that who live only from what their head does, and claim to be the proprietors of the world's wisdom. As far as I am concerned, you might be the cleverest of cutthroats, a real wild guy, not the pathetic being I see before me. Even in such an eventuality, you could not fool me. Not for a second. Fernando Krapp cannot be deceived. Did you understand me? Is that what you wanted to say?

THE COUNT: Yes . . . that is about how I would have put it.

FERNANDO KRAPP: About like that or precisely like that?

THE COUNT: Yes, like that.

JULIA [*Starts to scream*]: And I am the madwoman, yes? I am locked into the insane asylum because you are afraid to tell the truth, you coward? He bought you! There, I can see you grovel on the ground, your tongue is hanging out, slobbering all over—a huge, greedy tongue! Crawl to him, your tongue wants to lick his feet, that is how greedily it trembles! Another moment and he will take off his shoes and proffer you his filthy feet, the feet with which he stood in the filthy cowshed! Lick his feet! Lick them!

FERNANDO KRAPP [*To* THE DOCTORS]: Gentlemen, I am sure you have already made your diagnosis. Help her, start your treatment, do what you can!

9

JULIA. TWO PSYCHIATRISTS.

FIRST DOCTOR: A horrible tragedy! What are we going to do Professor Alvarez?

SECOND DOCTOR: Well, Doctor Hermannstetter!

FIRST DOCTOR: Unfortunately "well" isn't going to get us very far, Professor Alvarez.

SECOND DOCTOR: Which therapy do you suggest?

FIRST DOCTOR: And you?

SECOND DOCTOR: Did you think shock treatment might be the preferred method in an instance like this?

FIRST DOCTOR [*Ironically*]: Well . . .

SECOND DOCTOR: We should be careful with that, at least not start it right away. Or pharmacology?

FIRST DOCTOR: Calm her down first of all would be my suggestion.

SECOND DOCTOR: We don't need to do that. The patient is completely calm! [*To* JULIA] Honorable Madam.

[JULIA *does not respond*]

FIRST DOCTOR: She can't hear us.

SECOND DOCTOR: She's exhausted from all this excitement, which is, as it were, normal.

FIRST DOCTOR: Absolutely.

SECOND DOCTOR [*To* JULIA]: Dear Madam . . .

[JULIA *does not react*]

FIRST DOCTOR: I am under the impression, Professor, that in this case we are of one and the same opinion.

SECOND DOCTOR: Which is?

FIRST DOCTOR: I don't need to tell you that.

SECOND DOCTOR: No . . . I think I understand what you mean. But what if the person isn't ill, are we permitted to have her in safekeeping, as it were?

FIRST DOCTOR [*Ironically*]: Well . . .

SECOND DOCTOR: I must tell you, something inside me resists the thought, I can't make my peace with it.

FIRST DOCTOR: But that's what we'll have to do.

SECOND DOCTOR: Don't torture me like that!

FIRST DOCTOR: I am torturing you? How do you hit on that idea? Me?

SECOND DOCTOR: It is horrible!

FIRST DOCTOR: Yes. But if we release her from the clinic, and say that she isn't sick?

SECOND DOCTOR: Horrible.

FIRST DOCTOR: Then the husband will kill her and this Bordavela too.

SECOND DOCTOR: Yes. On the other hand, I have a doctor's conscience!

FIRST DOCTOR: You have to realize that in this instance we are preventing a terrible crime.

JULIA: You are not a doctor!

FIRST DOCTOR: Terrific! Do you hear what I am hearing: "I am not a doctor!"

SECOND DOCTOR: Terrific! That way we would be free of the responsibility!

JULIA: You are Othello!

FIRST DOCTOR: I am Othello?

JULIA: I will sing something into your ear. [*She sings*] "The poor soul sat sighing by a sycamore tree"—You must know that? It isn't my invention.

FIRST DOCTOR [*To* SECOND DOCTOR]: Listen, just listen to this!

JULIA: Excuse me, I am mistaken. I really am not quite right in the head. That becomes evident from the fact that I took you for a Negro! Oh Julia! Julia! Open your eyes!

[THE FIRST DOCTOR *turned around to* JULIA. *It is* FERNANDO KRAPP. *He turns around again.*]

SECOND DOCTOR: Actually, our finding should be that Fernando Krapp is the madman! And we should proclaim it decisively and loudly.

JULIA: I disagree! He is much trickier than Othello! Othello is a moronic animal by comparison, which becomes evident in the decisive scene, right Juan?—Now you don't say anything. You deny me. We used to chat for hours in the pavilion! About the psychological problems of sentences that use the subjunctive. Fernando took a very different vengeance from Othello! Am I dead? He did not choke me to death—he would never damage property of his! And he did not murder you, either, Juan. I can see you in front of me! Please, Professor Alvarez—or am I again mistaken? Show yourself, you coward! Coward! Coward!

[THE SECOND DOCTOR *turns around: It is* THE COUNT]

SECOND DOCTOR (THE COUNT): Julia—I am in such despair! Julia! I tried to find the expression for it, in the form of a . . . I feel like calling it an elegy. However, the pain that the black heavy images afford me keeps me from penning them on paper . . . I am nearly sad for the words, everything is pain—I am afraid of petrifying! You know my ungodly disposition for catatonic states, Julia . . . Beloved Julia—who will understand me, if I should lose you, only you . . .

JULIA: You traitor! You failed to protect me! You are guilty. It is your fault that I was locked in here— [*Screams*] In the madhouse!

SECOND DOCTOR (THE COUNT): Oh, poor Julia, poor me!

FIRST DOCTOR: If we keep you here much longer, Dr. Alvarez, she will perhaps become really ill.

JULIA: Professor Alvarez, I have come to a realization and have to communicate it to you: this Mexican woman . . .

FIRST DOCTOR: Who are you talking about?

JULIA: Don't pretend to be so naïve! You were the one who drew up all the reports and read them to me! I mean my husband's first wife, the one in Mexico. It has become clear to me that he did not kill her

207

by force, he did not need to kill her by force!—I find myself in a state of awakening. He drove her to the point that she died of her own accord.

FIRST DOCTOR: I see!

JULIA: Do you love me, Professor Alvarez?

FIRST DOCTOR: What did you say?

JULIA: They all love me for my beauty. I am going to tell you now why I love my man, why I love Fernando Krapp. Don't run away!

[THE TWO DOCTORS *run away*]

JULIA: What devious intelligence it took on his part to get the Count to show me how pathetic he really is! I was blind, I blinded myself! But *he*. He saved me. He knew everything, saw everything, and made his diabolic plan. Did you say "diabolic," Julia? Yes, that's what I said, up there in the air there still stands the word! A diabolic angel saved me from the abyss. That's why I love him! I love him.

10

JULIA. FERNANDO KRAPP *is just entering.*

JULIA: Fernando, please excuse me! [*She falls down*]

FERNANDO KRAPP: What is there to excuse in you?

JULIA: I suddenly fell down. I am so weak, I've been sick such a long time.

FERNANDO KRAPP: No, no—don't lie there like that. Everything is all right. [*He lifts* JULIA *up*]

JULIA: Excuse me!

FERNANDO KRAPP: The doctors at the institution already told me that you are cured of your psychosis.

JULIA: I was so mad! So mad! And the lies I told in that mad state! Everything, just to make you jealous! That was the only reason why! Do you believe that?

FERNANDO KRAPP [*With total coldness*]: You asked me once whether it was true that I killed my first wife. Then I asked you how you could possibly believe that. What did you reply at the time?

JULIA: I said that I didn't believe it, that I could never believe it.

FERNANDO KRAPP: So I am telling you today. Just as you were unable to believe the murder story, was I ever unable to believe in that story about the Count.

11

THE COUNT

THE COUNT [*Reading a letter*]: "and as you have probably heard, Count Bordavela, my wife was released completely healed from the madhouse. She would like to speak with you. Come join us on Thursday, the day after tomorrow, so that we can clear up the matter altogether. My wife begs you to come; I insist on your appearance. I am certain that you will come. You can imagine that your nonappearance can have most unpleasant consequences. You know me, Fernando Krapp."

12

JULIA. FERNANDO KRAPP. THE COUNT.

FERNANDO KRAPP: Please bring us the tea, Julia! You can send the girl away, and the butler, too; they can have the day off. All evening.

THE COUNT: Tea?

FERNANDO KRAPP: No, no. Don't fear. I have no stomach complaints, I am completely healthy! You love teatime! Thus tea it is.—Are you sitting comfortably? You can sit down on the divan if you like. Julia, I am sure, will have no objections to your sitting on her pretty Indian cover.

JULIA: No, none at all.

THE COUNT: I am sitting very nicely here, thank you.

[*Silence*]

FERNANDO KRAPP: What a pleasant silence! Only this odd delicate noise . . . oh, that's your cup shaking in the saucer . . .

[THE COUNT *quickly puts the cup down*]

FERNANDO KRAPP: My hearing is especially sensitive, excuse me. I did not want to embarrass you with that.

THE COUNT: But "embarrass"? How so? No, not at all.

FERNANDO KRAPP: Oh yes, you're a man of the intellect, and me they consider a roughneck—so what. Julia, you poured the tea for our Count, and why not for me? Please, pour me a cup. I want to take the first sip so that the Count can see that you can drink anything that is served in this house without needing to be afraid.

JULIA: Of course. I know that you take sugar? [*She tosses sugar cubes into* THE COUNT's *tea*]

FERNANDO KRAPP: Of course, I don't read novels, belles lettres, and so on, only occasionally a few papers. Tabloids. That's where you read about the sort of things that happen in life, right?

THE COUNT: I don't know. I can't . . .

FERNANDO KRAPP [*To* JULIA, *merrily*]: Look at his face puckering up! He can't agree happily with me on that score, the man of intellect.—You sometimes read about incredible crimes there, you begin to wonder about humanity. Even I begin to wonder, although I, as a businessman, am someone who thinks that he knows what mankind is like. No one can put anything over on me, Count.

THE COUNT: No, certainly not.

FERNANDO KRAPP: You, too, think I am capable of anything.

THE COUNT: There are limits . . . there are limits . . .

FERNANDO KRAPP: All people can be bought, or not?

THE COUNT: I should hope . . . not.

FERNANDO KRAPP: One half has the money, the other has the intellect.

JULIA: Artists have to be indulged a little.

FERNANDO KRAPP: Who is talking about artists? Oh right: you write poems to while away your time.

THE COUNT: I sometimes make an attempt . . . to express myself.

FERNANDO KRAPP: I do that too! I say what I feel like.

THE COUNT: I mean: in verse . . . in free rhythms.

FERNANDO KRAPP: Don't let me stop you! If you have enough, I will have it printed.

THE COUNT: That would be . . . a real honor.

FERNANDO KRAPP: Nonsense—honor! What nonsense, honor! You don't have anyone who will print the stuff!

THE COUNT: There has been a certain expression of interest . . . a publishing house . . .

FERNANDO KRAPP: So much the better! Then I'll buy the stuff, and we'll cram it—how many copies are there?—into Julia's pavilion. Excellent!— Well? Are you happy?

THE COUNT: I am thankful for your interest.

FERNANDO KRAPP: Crime thrillers is what you should write! Murder stories! You'd be able to sell those a lot better.

THE COUNT: Unfortunately, that is not my genre.

FERNANDO KRAPP: Just imagine, the other day I read about a husband who cut his wife's lover's throat, severed a head sprouting intelligence until its last moment, from the body!

THE COUNT: Evidently a psychopath . . .

FERNANDO KRAPP: As you like. Then he cut the body into little squares and fed it to the chickens. All that people found was the head.

THE COUNT: How hideous!

FERNANDO KRAPP: He has a chicken farm.—Here's another story, not that I want to bore you . . .

THE COUNT: No, not at all.

FERNANDO KRAPP: Julia was impressed! She usually doesn't read these reports in the boulevard press, and that is just as well. She is supposed to busy herself with pretty things. An attempted murder of a husband, it all came out. However, the couple made up, and they sent her lover, the hairdresser, packing. The point is, the hairdresser hung himself.

THE COUNT: Mr. Krapp . . . I would like . . .

FERNANDO KRAPP: I am boring you! Or you are becoming impatient because you still don't know why I asked you to come here?—Julia!

JULIA: I asked my husband to have you come here because I must ask your pardon for the insults to which I subjected you.

THE COUNT: But Julia, I don't know what you're talking about! You didn't insult me once in your life.

FERNANDO KRAPP: Impossible, Count Bordavela, that you would not be aware of the situation, a man of your intellect.

JULIA: Yes, I put you into an impossible situation. I feel very sorry for it.

THE COUNT: You confuse me . . . I really don't know . . .

FERNANDO KRAPP [*Interrupting* THE COUNT]: Watch out!

[*The startled* COUNT *does not know what to say*]

JULIA: You are so polite and tactful and want to spare me.

FERNANDO KRAPP: But you must understand that a person who has done damage to another person, and feels guilty for having done so, wants to beg for forgiveness.

THE COUNT: Of course, Mr. Krapp, but what damage? What injustice has been done to me?

JULIA: Of course I was ill—my brain! That is why I pray for an extenuation.

THE COUNT: Please don't torture yourself, Julia.

JULIA: No, I want to speak. I want to pull all my courage together and make a clean slate and not prettify anything, so that when I have received your forgiveness I will feel truly free.

FERNANDO KRAPP [*Roughly*]: Come on, hear her out.

JULIA: In my crazed state I claimed that you were after me, had made secret overtures to me, that you had whispered heated declarations of love into my ears, and that you had succeeded in heating up my feelings more and more.

THE COUNT: Is that what you said, Julia?

FERNANDO KRAPP: And that finally I had given in. Oh, what a state I was in, completely crazed. How could I say something like that!

THE COUNT: Oh, I feel so sorry.

FERNANDO KRAPP: Yes, it certainly is most embarrassing for you.

JULIA: I said even more than that! That we had done the most shameless things, even on this divan, many times, again and again. That sometimes you came at night when my husband was away on business. How horrible, that I claimed all of that! And put you into such a dreadful situation! The idea was stuck so fast in my head. I am sorry that you had to let yourself be interrogated about our alleged affair in the presence of the doctors. That must have been a revolting moment for you. And yet!— Forgive me if you can, please.

[*Silence*]

FERNANDO KRAPP: Do you accept this apology?

THE COUNT: I must admit . . .

FERNANDO KRAPP: Yes or no?

THE COUNT: Yes—I forgive you. I forgive you both.

FERNANDO KRAPP [*Crudely*]: Watch what you say; *me*, you have nothing to forgive!

THE COUNT: No, that is true.

FERNANDO KRAPP: You are so excited. Calm down! Now it is all cleared up.—You see, Julia, it was right to do it like this. [*To* THE COUNT] It suits the direct character that is mine not to cover up unpleasant matters.

JULIA: Fernando, I am so glad.

FERNANDO KRAPP: However, if for some reason or other you should be tempted to misrepresent these matters, Count . . .

THE COUNT: Certainly not!

FERNANDO KRAPP: Who knows. You get around a lot and talk . . . Perhaps in "free rhythms" . . . I suggest you don't. You know me.

JULIA: Oh, the open window! I can hear the birds twittering in the hedges!

THE COUNT: I believe . . . I am no longer needed here . . . [*Turns to leave*]

FERNANDO KRAPP: Stop! I wanted to ask you, Count Bordavela, to come again, and as often as you like! Even when I am not at home; that shouldn't deter you. It would make a very poor impression and lead to rumors if our relationship broke up too suddenly. Right, Julia?

JULIA: Yes, Fernando.

FERNANDO KRAPP: The two of you probably still have something to say to each other . . . under four eyes—what you don't want to say as long as I am here. I shall leave you. [*Walks off*]

13

JULIA. THE COUNT. *They sit in silence. The Count is looking worriedly at the door.*

JULIA: Stop looking at the door all the time!

THE COUNT [*Whispering*]: What if he's listening?

JULIA: You don't need to whisper.

THE COUNT: I lost my voice there for a second.

JULIA: Fernando Krapp does not hide behind the door to listen to what we have to say!

THE COUNT: Well, after everything that's happened.

JULIA: Really now, Juan. You don't need to be worried.

THE COUNT: I worry? Julia! I don't know who I am! If you weren't sitting there and said "Juan" to me, if you didn't address me with this name, which I associate with my person, Juan Count Bordavela—a person whom I believe I know—I wouldn't know . . .

[JULIA *smiles*]

THE COUNT: I have a recollection of this person. Not that I admire him particularly or liked all his character traits, not that. Still, I didn't find him disgusting. But now, Julia—I am revolted by myself, I'm nauseated by myself! [*Cries*] You can see what has become of me, of this human being whom you once loved.

[JULIA *remains silent*]

THE COUNT: I am overwhelmed by sadness.

JULIA: No, Juan.

THE COUNT: You still have some hope? After this play of ugliness and lies and calumny, do you still believe that we can find the way back to ourselves? That our pure feelings might come alive again? After this gruesome scene?

JULIA: What scene are you talking of, Juan?

THE COUNT: I see myself standing there, miserable and defenseless, the two doctors as witnesses, who of course understood only too well the game that was being played, how I was being forced to deny you—this gruesome scene, where I was so deeply humiliated—and you too.

JULIA: Oh, my poor Juan.

THE COUNT: I thought we would never be able to look into each other's eyes again.

JULIA: That is what you thought?

THE COUNT: How incredibly strong you are, how strong!

JULIA: Yes. Because of my love.

THE COUNT: You—are giving me back my life. Hope! Everything.

JULIA: How stupid I was! And now finally I understand everything, the mistakes, the confusion has left me.

THE COUNT: But what if he is listening behind the door! That you, Julia, had to beg me for forgiveness!

JULIA: It was self-evident to me.

THE COUNT: Julia—now I no longer understand you.

JULIA: It was entirely as you wanted it, wasn't it? When you confessed that the whole love affair was a delusion of mine, and I finally apologized. You were right, there is no need for you to worry.

THE COUNT: But Julia! Even now that we are just the two of us, you want to go on denying that you knew my feelings, that you returned them, that you were my lover?

JULIA: Please stop it.

THE COUNT: But I know it for a fact! I know it.

JULIA: It seems that way to you, dear Juan. It is driving you mad. [*She laughs*]

[THE COUNT *runs off*]

FERNANDO KRAPP: Fernando Krapp was the victor. Of course. She loved him with all the strength of her heart. Then death came and took her away. First it took her beauty. Then her courage. Then her breath.

14

JULIA. FERNANDO KRAPP.

FERNANDO KRAPP: You let the little haircomb slip out of your hand.

JULIA [*Whispering*]: Oh, I didn't even notice.

FERNANDO KRAPP: It weighs little more than a feather, bends as I touch it.

JULIA [*Whispering*]: Give it to me.

FERNANDO KRAPP: Suits me too! That way, I can tame my forelock.

JULIA [*Whispering*]: Yes.

FERNANDO KRAPP: You're not laughing.—I could make faces too, you know!—Old monkey. Look at me! Or: a lion is roaring . . . All I can think of is animals. Don't human beings make enough grimaces of their own! Gargoyles! Think of grinning Alfonso of whom you are always afraid! Doctor Hermannstetter told me about a madman who used to run through the streets absorbing every expression he happened to encounter, impressing them on his mind—obsessively! Then he would hide in the dark hallway and quickly imitate each and every one of these expressions so as to get rid of them, the way you disgorge a putrid meal. Just imagine that!—Here is your little comb.

JULIA [*Whispering*]: I can't bear the hair falling in my face.

FERNANDO KRAPP: I will get you another, covered with diamonds.

JULIA [*Whispering*]: I am dying, Fernando.

FERNANDO KRAPP: No, no, no!—Don't talk nonsense! You know I can't stand it.

JULIA [*Whispering*]: Just take a look at my face.

FERNANDO KRAPP [*Screaming*]: You are not dying! That can't be! You belong to me! I won't give you up! I won't give you to anyone! Not even to death! The lousy crook!

JULIA [*Whispering*]: Oh how you love me! Say it! Say it!

FERNANDO KRAPP: But you know it!

JULIA [*Whispering*]: But you never said it out loud, not once! Perhaps it will return the power of life to me.

FERNANDO KRAPP: And at that point the bands of steel around his heart suddenly gave way, and he talked for the first time of his love to Julia, he couldn't stop, he cried doing so, screamed and sobbed. He seized her weak, extinguishing body, pressed it to himself. He lay down beside her on the bed and kept repeating: "Take my life! Take my blood! I won't surrender you to death."

JULIA [*Whispering*]: You are crying. But I am happy.

FERNANDO KRAPP: Thus she died. Days afterward, they broke open the door, they found Fernando with Julia. He must have lifted the dead woman out of bed and carried her nearly to the door. There he collapsed with her. Only then he cut his veins. Thus he died without letting her out of his arms.

Totenauberg
(Death/Valley/Summit)

ELFRIEDE JELINEK

•

Translated by Gitta Honegger

Translator's Note

•

Elfriede Jelinek was born in 1946 and grew up in Vienna, where she studied music and theater. She has written, roughly, ten prose pieces (most notably, the controversial novels *The Piano Player* and *Lust*); nine or so texts for the theater, among them *What Happened after Nora Left her Husband, Sickness or Modern Women,* and *Wolken.Heim,* a montage of variations on texts by Kleist, Hölderlin, Heidegger, Hegel, and Fichte, peppered with excerpts from writings by the terrorist Baader Meinhoff gang, and most recently *Raststätte* (Restroom), a feminist deconstruction of the *Cosi fan Tutti* themes of mistaken erotic identities, set in the restroom of a highway service station; and countless radio plays and several screenplays.

In *Totenauberg* (which premiered at the Vienna Akademie Theater, the second stage of the Burg Theater, September 18, 1992), Jelinek tackles one of the megamasters (or perverters) of German thought, Martin Heidegger, juxtaposing him with his former student and lover, Hannah Arendt. Jelinek is not interested in a psychological exploration of the relationship between the Jewish emigré intellectual and her idol turned Nazi but in juxtaposing what she calls "planes of languages"* as opposed to dialogue. Her stage characters turn almost literally into figures of speech.

Jelinek's portrayal of the philosopher Heidegger is based primarily on his essay, written after World War II, *The Question Concerning Technology,* in which he summons up all his linguistic tricks to come to terms with his Nazi utopia. With merciless humor and her own savage joy in language games, from etymological transformations to the cheapest puns, Jelinek demonstrates how the rhetoric of the most self-consciously politically, morally, religiously, and fashionably correct picks up on philosophical and linguistic "Heideggerisms," which easily convert into the slogans of a newly emerging elite of nativism, evolutionary perfectionism, ethnic chauvinism.

The play's title, *Totenauberg (Death/Valley/Summit),* is derived from Todtnauberg, Heidegger's beloved Black Forest mountain retreat. It only takes a slight adjustment to reveal what's in a (compound) name and to set

The translator extends special thanks to Manfred Laubichler for his invaluable help with Heidegger's philosophy.
*See my interview with Elfriede Jelinek in *Yale/Theater Magazine* 25, no. 1 (Spring/ Summer 1994).

up the ironic context for its most famous inhabitant and the central tenets of his philosophy. In that philosophy, nature/home/dwelling function like Duchampian "hinges" in a construct that enshrines the native and excludes the foreign—with catastrophic consequences, as the play points out.

As a scathing critique of the German language, the play presents nearly insurmountable problems for the translator. Unlike the equally problematic translations of Heidegger's texts, a play intended to be understood in performance cannot use footnotes nor apologize for the impossibility of developing equivalent word games. For example, *Wesen* as a noun can mean "essence" and "creature"; *wesen* as a verb means approximately "being," "existing," and is one of Heidegger's favorites, an antiquated word now completely out of use; its transformations are *Anwesen* (an estate), *gewesen* (the past tense of "to be"), *verwesen* (decay), and so on. There are also the distinctions between *Sein* and *Dasein* (literally, "being" and "being there") and terms like *Gestell* (framing), derived from *hinstellen* (to place), leading to *hingestellt sein*, "to be placed there," and ultimately the noun *Gestell* as a construct, which, both in an existential sense and in its technical meaning, is a key term in Heidegger's explorations of technology. *G'stell,* in popular Viennese usage, is a (sexist) term for a "great body." The root, *stellen,* permits transformations into *bestellen* ("to order"), *verstellen* (literally, "to obstruct"; but also, as *sich verstellen,* "to disguise oneself," "to pretend"), *anstellen* ("to stand in line"; also, "to employ"), *entstellen* ("to distort," but in Jelinek's Heidegger context, it could also mean "freeing from the *Gestell,*" as a physical contraption, in which she has Heidegger literally trapped). *Holzweg* (the singular of Heidegger's book title *Holzwege,* meaning "a path cleared in the forest") is related to the term *Lichtung,* "clearing," which in turn is related to *Licht,* "light," so essential to Heidegger in its metaphysical connotations. In idiomatic usage, "being on a *Holzweg*" means "barking up the wrong tree."

Equivalents had to be found. At times the choice had to be made between approximating the effect of a particular word play and its larger meaning. The English language does not generally allow for dazzling new formations of compound words or the transformation of verbs into nouns. It is much less flexible than German in the creation of new variations and combinations of linguistic roots and much less hospitable to ambiguities in meaning, which Jelinek exposes with feisty anger in her native language. If it has become almost a truism that "a Heidegger" is possible only in the German language, the problems of translation inherent in this play ironically highlight the most devastating aspects of Jelinek's cultural critique.

Gitta Honegger

Totenauberg
(Death/Valley/Summit)

CHARACTERS

The Old Man
The Woman (middle-aged)
Elegant Waiters
Elegant Ladies and Gentlemen (in evening clothes)
The Elegant Young Woman (in evening clothes)
[Skiers (in colorful outdoor gear)]
The Young Mutter
The Typical Professional Athlete
The Two Lederhosen (in lederhosen and Tyrolean hats
with characteristic chamois-hair brushes)
Cross-Country Skiers
The Old Farmer (white-bearded, in local costume,
smoking a long pipe)
[Corpses of Mountain Climbers (in colorful outdoor gear)]
[Corpse 1]
Cheerleaders (in colorful alpine, but
distinctly American, costume)
[Corpse 2]
[Female Violinist]
[Male Pianist]
Travelers
Hunters

●

Bracketed character names shown above indicate those characters who appear onscreen only. The film sequences must be made by the director (at most, with the help of a cameraperson). For this purpose, the director should choose a mountain such as the Matterhorn, Montblanc, Rax, or Schneeberg. The film may be, even should be, shot quite amateurishly.

The figures of Heidegger and Hannah Arendt should be indicated by only one small characteristic (e.g., for Heidegger, perhaps by his mustache).

(Bracketed dialogue indicates cuts made for the first performance, at the Vienna Burg Theater.)

Out in the Country

THE OLD MAN *sits in the lobby of an elegant luxury hotel, dressed in a rustic-looking ski outfit. He is strapped into a kind of body frame* (Gestell), *which follows the contours of his body, only much larger. He is inside his double, so to speak. In the background, a movie screen. On it, snow-covered peaks, an alpine pasture or something like that. Sitting on the bench in front of a mountain cabin,* THE WOMAN, *in urban traveling clothes, her suitcase next to her, ready to leave.*

THE WOMAN [*speaking from the screen to* THE OLD MAN. *Some time during her monologue, she comes onstage from behind the screen, alternately speaking the text herself and listening to herself talking on the screen.*]: There you sit now. [Tucked inside your double. A far cry from what you were to your mother. Not to mention your father—his wet finger stroking the exposed parts of the forest.] The sun falls through the holes in the branches, but your heat—it has become harmless. Once you were the lover; now women throw their sticks at some other prickly old nuts in the treetops. Now nothing simply drops into their laps. Now all they do on their benches is sit and knit, needles nestled in their hands. You're cast out from such nesting, which is resting. [Youth, their bodies gleaming with glamour, gather around the buildings. Music penetrates the heart. Rapturous. Rupturing.] And you complain because people are laughing at you! [Students became useful under the whip of that unemployed tanner's apprentice, who shaved their white T-shirts with pumice and gave their hides a good tanning. Precious blood spilled everywhere.] What an effort to scratch a homeland out of the nightmare once again. Let's start with the insignificant, the small: Aren't the words needed now smaller than any you could ever possess? And you yourself make a nice little picture, a "representation"! Don't fit into the fine but phony suit of this phony landscape. Music that acts up against us. But its loudness is just one of its bad habits. Listen to a song, while you sit there, noticeably unnoticeable in front of your cabin to let yourself be grasped in toto by the seekers! They want to hear one single word, and what do they get? The whole world and how to appear in a modern vehicle to transport oneself to who knows where.

And always arriving at the same place, home sweet home, to be honed and cloned: Heimat! [Slowly you beat your retreats, which have always been there even before you pulled up your sled on the chain of your body. Too long you've forced yourself upon the Holzweg, your timber trail of modern Dasein—those being there were barking up the wrong trees! A lot of costs were cut in the making of you! But there's plenty of skin, almost too much, I see. Curling along the edges, sagging around your face. The stakes are high. Let yourself be swept away by what's been lost.] Young people stuck in a uniform's chill, with the child's gym shorts still sticking to their legs. All of a sudden they had discipline, disciples of the future. [They have been, and they would have been. Nature finally took them in. Their arms reaching out of swamps toward foreign land, which always belonged to someone else! So they were placed inside themselves.] That's education, and they owe it to you. Allowing them to call out daily for the man who was able to scare the hell out of their Dasein, their being-there.

Look, how people today pursue their recreative battles! And you dare say that nature rests, stretched out shamelessly in front of us, in our better suits, or better: pursuits. Out into nature! Technology doesn't let her be! Forcing the brook out of its bed and the river of history back into its course, whence it surges up again and again. We are the target, the eye of the bulwark. But we also have an inkling of what's beyond. Actually, it's been ours for a long time. Haven't we held onto our title on the shakiest of grounds!

Everyone endures the measure of his being. But look: My face is no longer suited for pleasure either! Remember, please, what a seductive blueprint you once were: Man set into silence. And if he is the Grund, the ground of his being, then he is God, in ten lectures. I can see it now: in a minute you'll bow to the audience. They are buying their tickets already, their fingernails scratching the marble in the lobby. They paid for their tickets, now they want to learn fear as they race across the country's highways, each one a climax of *being*, the wrong way into one-way lanes. I think they turn back, afraid of one-ways. To the moor! Register at the ranger station, Hochmoorsoldaten ohne Spaten, "High moor brigades, without their spades," hiking sticks instead, their grinning skulls lowered to their knickers. Grease shines around their mouths, the sun in their eyes. The forest! Thinking is dealing in used cars! Please memorize the many models existing in one era.

Now look at all the passersby who will enter in droves to hear you. Look! Go ahead, take a look! Every other person throws out the sight of you! And they no longer trust their ears either. No one buys anymore this utter absorption in what one is. What one eats, yes! Eating has always been a pleasure to you. If you can't make the world, at least you can destroy it, right? The only thing that's happened to you: the parents. The holy grandfather in the straw of Hölderlin's stable. The Black Forest! The light that shines! [The Alps, which you cross like a protruding vein wrapped inside your age—how beautiful! Falling like grass, wringing hands like trees. Oh yes, those ahead of you—one thing at least is certain about them: they have been. Passed you for good, across the bridge, look there, close to the cross at the summit! Your sandwich wraps rustle in your hands. Now they stop. Look!—They're talking to each other, but they aren't waiting for you! How that hurts! The father jumps up from his place.]

They were the seeds scattered over the ground in order to dwell. Death tore them out of context. Finished! Suddenly you are no longer one of them. The cord has been cut. Your parents' death turns you into someone else. Yes, it's you! [What terror to find all heavenly views obscured! The mountains serve you as stirrups. Whatever there is, is there to highlight you.] Your thinking atrophies inside you. A little bench to sit on would come in handy, wouldn't it? So that the crowds can pass in front of you. Man however is alone. Restlessly, his poisonous kind roots in the earth. No one wants to be like the other, and you too stand only for yourself.

In the meantime, how often did you return, weathered, from the country inn, where you were admired as a child for every trifle. Translating from the Greek. But now—great things took off from you and got lost that way too—now it is you who gets lost, among the children of pretty, protective mothers, who are so fussy about the way they dress. You didn't expect that, did you? [That some day there will be some whose every steps are covered by a roof, so to speak?! That the Alps will serve as a children's camp, a wildlife reserve.] That technology would work out so well, future generations won't be needed anymore, for everything is *Now*. Translate, it's getting late! Greatness, is it still braving the storm or already buckling under questions? [All over. And rebuilt, from scratch. So everything's calm and pleasant again, and there you sit. Ready, once again, to host. All prepared, once again, to sell the void to the crowds who bought their tickets—which in turn will have to be voided.]

There you sit. How many strangers have you impressed in all those years you happily traveled through people's minds? Who still thinks of you today, the day after? Well, aren't you a funny bundle, always carried by others! Why don't you carry your own self for once, will you! You'll have to wait a little longer for death on this bus that takes you back to yourself, where you have waited all along like a good boy. Where you had been hingestellt, set up, as they might say. In reality, you never moved. You are! No longer a child. [You're getting pushy now, because earlier you were showered with gifts.] No one wants to stay where he started. But inescapably he ends up there. [Scattering like snakes, under your guidance, your people rush to the runways and up in the air, there to stay, as they claim. Not even birds would dare to say that about themselves.] Where did you leave your language, in which you learned to stand up to nature? Oh yes, lateness mattered at a time when one was still expected. The self is the core; no, the whore; no, the Who of existence. Das Wer des Daseins. Death is the Where of existence. Das Wo des Daseins. He makes of you (and us too) retreating serfs, a few spasms of life still twisting their bodies, if one stands in front of their cages and tells them the bars mean nothing. They are still nice and clean. Big and smooth like Lake Constance. But beware of them if they find the door! Then you too might be without a job, eating wurst. Because they might not listen to you in your passionate desire to be a *self!* They'll step on your hobnail shoes in which you tear through the landscape until it shakes you off again. [Or you move to the dining car, where you step in place while nasty travelers in Italian shoes try to kick you in the butt. Stasis and movement in one.]

How often, by the way, did you risk something that might have caused your death? In truth, you were a coward, you friend of the family. While the fraternities threw themselves into the playsuits of war to fight for their stay. The furthest you can see is this luminous lane lined with chestnut trees, yes, yes. Why don't you bend over! Give it a try!

[THE OLD MAN *has been desperately trying for a while to get out of his frame*]

You'll have to try a little harder. The self in absolute isolation is senseless. Yes. Well then, this luminous lane doesn't matter, I can also describe it to you—with chestnut trees running to your left and right like mean dogs. Away to the bright mountain lodge, in the back of which people expect a beer garden. But only you are there! A red hot think tank marring the face of the landscape.

Listen to it roaring in the distance! In the face of the ocean, people immediately slap athletic equipment on their bodies. The landscape you sit in
resounds, cash registers and cassettes sing along. How about here, on
your bench, in your blind? You hear nothing? So, give it a shot—make
man start all over, no, shout all over, no, shoot all over, until the game is
splashed all over the morning frost, leaves bending under the juice of
death. The skiers shoot out from their starting stalls, look at yourself in
the mirror. That's the kind you are! Go ahead, shoot! The edges crunch in
the firm snow. Showing off technique that passes for substance. Today
you would have to actually have substance to be the only one of your
kind. If you were a child, you'd still have your swimming wings, remains
from mother's body, flapping from your upper arms. By means of an
illness God wipes your little mug, in which you wanted to make yourself
resemble him. You are not like him; that makes you waste. Turn yourself
in, throw yourself out. I could waste my time saying something nasty
about you; I'd rather keep silent. I stick to my memories; they swept the
meadows of my mind, turning them into a smooth surface. [A face above
the fence, a great time for skiing and a late winter sun. Now time also
pulls on your frame, which is completely bent out of shape.] If once upon
a time you were together with the ones you loved most, myself among
them, now time has declared you finished once and for all. You are
dismissed. [Dragging your poor feet around the attic, a raging homeless
man, that is to say there is a roof above your head, but it leaks. Sit still,
will you! Someone else wants to relax too, squeezed in the chair next to
yours, some pitiful beverage in his fist. You aren't missed by anyone,
while a hand pulls you sharply by the sleeve as you scornfully smash a
little creature at your feet.] May I introduce you to death so you'll finally
be dragged out of the shining light, that dangerous Black Forest moon-
shine cherry schnapps puddle. Doesn't matter, they were also moonlight-
ing when they dug heaven out of the ground. That's where the deceased
lie, only in death did they cease to lie. It is now 8:31 P.M. Your lecture is
about to begin, and no one can see a thing. Start to speak after the beep.
The bleep. Go ahead, speak!

[On screen, soft nature, nothing shrill. A pond framed by reeds exuding an air
of danger, but also calm. THE OLD MAN has succeeded in tearing himself out of
his frame; now he drags the frame's pieces around with him, staggering here
and there. Enter ELEGANT WAITERS and several ELEGANT LADIES AND GENTLE-
MEN who have come to hear the Old Man's lecture. The Waiters serve
beverages to all. THE WOMAN sits by herself at a small table, drinking coffee.]

THE OLD MAN: Die Natur ruht. Nature rests. [The weather turns, once again it turns against us after we just bade it farewell in the hope not to run into it again too soon. Not a good friend, represented by the picture of a stormy pond.] That calm in the forest, in the sky does not mean the end of motion. Nature comes into being as we walk. We are her middle, we are her means that make the light fade all around. Our equipment points to the way we live: beams of canned spray all around us, on our hair and shoes to protect us while we are intoxicated with ourselves. At the same time, we tear open the air, we, the livestock that can't be rescued from our own breathing. Poisonous wandering. [We are included in the experience, and what we experience becomes an object we catch in our nets, by the meter, by the minute.] Instead of going places, we have our film, video, and photographic equipment. [We turn out well only because of it, the first visitors in the early morning hours, because we want to make good use of the day, and they're already pulling on our teats.] We, the crowds! We're piling up! [During presentations of folk music, as it is frequently called, old women shake themselves out of the magic boxes of their bodies until they end up as puddles under their seats, swaying to the yodels of the Zillertaler Schürzenjäger.] We tour the sights only to deface nature with our faces. Armed with information, we charge through the famous formations and return reformed and recharged. But everything that we say exists is always an illusion, illuminated in the light of the clearing. We are the There. The di-stress of our sudden appearance has long been prepared in a seemingly pacified world.

Now everything is falling. We bemoan the holes in the air, but still we stuff ourselves mercilessly with what has been, with what has been nature before. [Juice runs down our chins, from our chintzy home videos. We seem to believe that's the way to induce wildness, war into our flesh we beat into our partners while driving ourselves farther and farther into isolation.] That blind spot, wilderness, is supposed to cut us free, in one stroke, from our dull being. We turn nature into us, we transform nature to become us so it suits us. We get us some freshness into the house, preserved in a can. [That's the truth about our beauty, stored after it passed.] Nature owes us her coming, and in turn we must thank her that we may come and leap across bubbling brooks. Now let us go mourn in the wetlands where they build power plants! They can't do that! Only through our mourning does nature come into being. It is the thought of her end that wakes her up. We, her new frontier, are coming to terms with her. Only in her death does she find life. Wasn't there someone else who did it that way? What does God say and why?

Is this need for nature the need of the absence of need? Does our mourning lift us to everything lost that we have also made our own, that landscape condemned long ago? [It belongs to us more than the unharmed land. We lose ourselves out there, yet we turned out better than we were before, when we had nothing but our bathing suits and could throw ourselves fearlessly into the sun.] We've settled comfortably in all that loss, because need has brought us together. [What is ours grows in our lamentations.] There is no room for the need of others. [What we need are those trees, that arid brush, those dead toads: If they weren't endangered, we wouldn't find them so endearing! We are no longer alone, we get a sense of ourselves in things larger than ourselves; that's what we like.] We are the rescuers, we know how to give the things we have destroyed a new shape: our own! We have learned to watch out for ourselves. We, the wildlifeguards, the wetlandlords [We are coming. But we never arrive. Because there should always be the expectation of our coming.] We are the saviors who want to be there, everywhere. Wrapped up snugly in their nativeness, they sit there armed with their organic Agent Orange juice against the destroyers; getting clobbered by their clubs, they bounce right back and sing a song to their guitars [breaking the law of silence with their voices, which never need to stop for breath]; all covered by prime-time news—see how nature itself takes cover under their bodies. Nature's slipcovers. Like rubbers, they slip themselves over nature's grandeur and hold it together with their own selves. Those dead rubber chickenshits!

If there's enough light, the cameras start running. This is how they inscribe themselves into life. Microphones stuck in their faces like nose bags, they complain into the light, the void; they should disappear right into it. Before the light gives up and vanishes inside itself in mourning.

And already they're back on their asses, on their couches: meat counters of the television set. Because nature doesn't want to see *them!* So they look at themselves. But now's the dawn of a new day. And the experience turns into sentiment, to each his own, right. Everyone adds to his sentimental NOW account, which has earned him high interest over the years; so he jealously guards it against his next-door neighbor. Everyone has his own story, kept under recycled wraps, which have some defects but can be seen from afar. Announcing ourselves far and wide: we, in the middle of

Europe. [Our experiences haven't prepared us for reality, but we can function as its henchmen.

And still they sit on the floor like plants, and they don't shy away from anything, there, at the campfires, near their camp leaders, whom they point out. The small pool of light in front of them creates a clearing, in which they finally can be seen through the TV cameras. No, no, it's the other way 'round! Without the clearing they had cut for themselves, the light wouldn't even be seen! It wouldn't hit them. And they couldn't radiate to the living rooms.]

The opening of the land—shouldn't these really be quiet events? Does the word have to show off so shamelessly? In lamenting what has been lost, they become creative, but all they create is always only themselves. Horrible, their awakening! Heavy steps in the swamps. How they inflate themselves with enthusiasm! A victory for environmentality! Let's go! They won another small victory, and nature wins over time, which is older than her. Those sit-in champs! Gather around them! It's time that nature finally finds itself. She is just beginning, and when she begins to feel herself she should feel brand-new. They'll take care of that! Mourning the moribund, they seem to have made themselves immortal. All together. All together now.

[*On screen,* THE OLD MAN *and* THE WOMAN, *he in rustic outfit, she in urban skirt and blouse, are climbing up to the cabin. Onstage,* THE OLD MAN *has fallen; he lies on the floor, partially covered by the pieces of his frame. Two* ELEGANT WAITERS *and one or two* ELEGANT LADIES AND GENTLEMEN *try to help him back on his feet, but he keeps falling down again and again.*]

THE OLD MAN [*Almost into the floor*]: [Terror is what's shared by all. Mercifully, they descend upon the land. Saliva foams around their bridles they always balked against. They talk incessantly.] To each his amen corner, where they can blend in with the people, swaying, singing along, kneading themselves into the yeast. Planting their roots inside themselves. Calving, on all fours, like cows. Holding their brood up to the policemen's clubs, with which they want to keep our species well beaten. That dough stretches beyond ourselves. Those processes darkening the planet can't be engendered by individual people. People are only the executive organs, who must eat their cake too.

229

Those eco-protectors can never simply throw out their Being; desperately, they keep holding onto themselves. Speaking for everyone else. Never each for himself. Always for all. Terrible, but doable. They don't let nature find herself—they have to wake her up. At full blast. Every appearance has been surpassed by them, before they have ever seen it. And that hole in the stratosphere is more real to them than anything they see. Their hiking shoes step in the tracks of others. Nature always is just beginning, but to those people she has to be what has always been. The closer they get to her, the more hopeless it has to be. That's what they live from. Nature withdraws, but they go after her [with their brats, whom they batter to butter themselves up]. They don't beat around the bush, they grab her like some private business that belongs to them forever! Nature is horror, but they fix it on their camping stoves, everyone gets his piece, cut out of the void. They have no idea what's coming, because they think they've known it all along. And as they mourn, they're already figuring: Should nature awaken, they'll step out into the light with her, letting nature throw her revealing light on them.

The cameras glow like dawn. Every view is written down. [They never come out of themselves; yet they think they are the conquerors, albeit of those conquered long ago: everybody always knew that. The visitors' glances pile up high while opinions pile up on the poisoned ground like food on a plate that's loaded with side dishes. Just as they have been replaced by their images on a video screen, they want to replace the landscape with themselves. The more they tune into what they see, the more out of tune it will sound. They disturb so much not because they constantly obstruct the view, no, what is there to see gets instantly reduced to their own experience.] What has been forest turns into a picture. What has been mountain, turns into a picture. Nature becomes an object; an item ordered from the menu: scribbled on a waiter's notepad, prepared, garnished, guaranteed, served. Oh yes, they want that path in front of them to be cleared. Do they think someone will run ahead with a broom the way they clear the ice for a curling game? So that the track they throw in front of them gets smoother and smoother. Or it turns into a ski jump high in the sky, to set them into proper relief.

[A WAITER *and* THE ELEGANT YOUNG WOMAN *try to help* THE OLD MAN. *The Elegant Woman talks to him comfortingly.*]

THE ELEGANT YOUNG WOMAN: The woodcutters are ready. They consider their work, work on nature. But there are people sitting in front and on top of the trees to put them out of work. And those national park sitters have the greater task. They establish the space in which the wetlands actually become reality. Really. It is they who ultimately make the landscape, those New Age sitting bullies in their designer sweats. [Their time-share cabins are nice and comfy.] They cast themselves upon the land and the sky is also overcast. After all, that is where those who have passed on are joined in seclusion. And those down below pass judgment on good and bad pollution. How do I avoid the paths traveled by other wanderers? Would we have ever experienced our nativeness without those nature guards, who have planted themselves firmly in everything they own? And for our wholesome offspring we, the wet nurses of the wetlands, claim everything that should no longer be claimed: Spring water! Rain forests! Moors! The rivers that run through! Virgin woods and peckers! Tufa tortes; peat pies! Isn't it the tourists who create our foreign countries, without which we would always be at home? Only by going away and finding the same everywhere do we arrive back home again. We want to be in foreign lands to be lifted beyond us, to stretch across the unknown. Every place we go is worth our reflective gaze. Avoid what's close, and distance will call. It would also be possible to stay at home and create the foreign right there, but no, we have to get away to create a home for ourselves.

But I ask myself: Do we mourn the death of nature just to make her into something alien right here in our native land? Two solitary distant farms, if they still exist, still consider themselves neighbors, while in the city the closeness of door to door can mean a vast foreign territory. The closeness of neighbors does not depend on space and time. It is space and time that prevent closeness. If we want closeness, we have to carry it within ourselves. Yet we tear into each other with tender teeth and destroy what's home to the other. And the wilderness always is too wild, and sameness is always too much the same. The land greets us with gestures in the shape of monuments, lighthouses, citadels, cloisters, but the reason we understand them is that we know them from back home and can claim them as our home abroad. And all that foreign space keeps turning us away. Therefore we construct the foreign among ourselves and rise above it like the sun, the last control over the earth from outside. Aeronautics has made it possible to project ourselves, inject ourselves everywhere; concrete injected into the swaying soil. Not at home, yet home. We stay inside ourselves. Who can deny us what? Where does nature get her power to always be more than those who live in her? Healthier, more beautiful than they. She is our environment. It is her function to serve as our backdrop, which sets us off as the stronger ones. But our might is man-made. Nature is everything that makes itself. What are we doing there? She is everything there is. She excludes conflict because she is in everything. Why should we now fight for her intactness. That fight will also be tracelessly absorbed by nature. The place under the apple tree where we used to rest has become much more open since we cleared it. What if that landscape didn't exist anymore? Even the result of complete destruction would still be nature, because nature is always all there is. And it is precisely this unity of contradictions within nature that propels us outside of nature, because we want to be transported. Anyway, you get a much better view from afar. Then why do we complain about all that destruction? Because we want to sit outside in our damaged, jagged places, so that we don't have to be nature, but rather: pacified, satisfied *in* nature. I say, the visitor wants to appear as a mere appearance, an apparition apparently, while nature must be absolutely real. So that the visitor can let himself be embraced by reality, which in turn illuminates him as an illusion. And everything thus illuminated is already rendered obsolete by what we know. We don't look. We know! We know! Is it out of selfishness that we still want to go into the woods? The enormous star-studded heavens and a storm outside. Shouldn't we rather stop all our experiments and view the world as it is, in its exemplary greatness?

Death/Valley/Summit (Gesundheit!)

Onscreen, SKIERS *wedel down the slope. Onstage,* THE OLD MAN *sits on the floor and wraps his whole body with an endless elastic bandage.* THE YOUNG MUTTER *in a summer dress, a sort of feisty rustic waitress, enters the stage with an infant. She gives him her breast. In addition, she spoon-feeds him baby food, pouring it all over his face. It drips all over her and her infant and spills on the floor until she has a sloppy pile of mush in front of her.*

THE YOUNG MUTTER [*Bending down and licking up some of the mush that's spilling*]: I am healthy. [A souvenir in the heart of the forest.] A self-aware being! Only she who embraces distance is able to create a child. But people today have only the tastes from day before yesterday on their tongues and they can smell only as far as day after tomorrow. It's not just my *self*, it is also wholeness to which I aspire. I am whole. I am all I. Solemnly I discharge myself into the brush, and instantly I refill myself.

232

Where I am, the woods are no longer stripped, because I quickly descend upon them with others of my kind- and decent-ness. Nature has been assigned to us, and now we want to have it equipped with all the beauty there is. A journey that's finished right from the start.

I exercise the privilege of the species by coupling wisely. Nothing left to chance. Only wanted children and their older siblings, the trees! [Be the tree, not the axe!] I am planning to nurture my child and me toward a climax that interacts with the world more smoothly than the hand with the watch. [Yes, temporality and I, we get along well.] My descendant must do everything as well as I! Better! What has been is no more. [I tear all remembrance out of my body, because I am thoroughly now, yet I am also concealed in what has been and consigned to what will be. I am forever illuminated by top value. And I won't be quoting from Hölderlin for at least five years. Nature has every reason to shy away from us, but we don't shy away from her. We understand her and store her in our unfertilized, unsprayed bodies! We become what we speak. Animals don't speak, but they become us. Anyway, whatever knows how to speak, knows about its death. Right? Losing the soil, we would lose the ground on which we stand.] I never dream secretly, I say it openly: I do not permit myself to neglect myself.

This child was not born of a whim, it is my life. This child was planned, I chose its father with great care, that's the least I can do. Responsibility toward nature! Only quality women have something to give to the world. I am well-read, I am well-bred. I have desires for my future without shying away from taking possession of the present. As long as my child is well, it may live. Just wait until it is strapped to its schoolbooks, offering everyone an insight into its self! Corporations are courting it already, it's already moving on its own. As long as it is dreaming itself into the future, it may be here and now. It may wake up again, the loudest of all events, filling up my life. This way, our hopes are rightly fulfilled. It has the right to ask me for nourishment; I would gladly give it the best I have, which is my dynamic language. It's so loud, there's no doubt when I am about to appear and everything disappears all on its own. I made this child fit for athletic feats and cosmic feasts. It shall rise like an early breeze and get bigger and stronger. It is healthy. I am his. I am his I. It will want to become the kind of consumer who brings high quality to bloom. I have thought through my relationship to him very carefully. Under this roof, there's only room for those who have a taste for vitamin riches! Good health über alles! We owe that to the world, so it won't owe us anything.

I want this child to be me! The world must perceive us as completed, finished: that is to say, we're completely finished! Killing a snail or a day-old infant with a little morphine does not thwart any desires, because animals have no desires. If this child were sick, that is to say, a potential person who is not aware of itself, it wouldn't need any support. It wouldn't be conscious of anything anyway. Those born cripples try to get, or at least let, an ego that can neither be amazed nor frightened by itself. They just hang around, a shape unaccustomed to life, not planned like that by life. Luckily, they have become rare. I am absolutely delighted by medicine. If my child weren't dreaming now of staring at some fabulous commercial some day, food in its fist, bandages around his assorted athletic wounds, free from worries about the common welfare, I would have made sure it was cut off long ago! I've acquired it right inside me. Health is its privilege as well as mine.

I'm not random, after all! Not for nothing do I stuff the raw diet of my organic cheerfulness into this foreign element, which throws itself with a vengeance against the pier of my self; eroding it. Yes! I would kill it! Because it wouldn't take advantage of its solid stock, which is me! [It wouldn't be sacred, for despite all my loving it would never be like me. That's the source of all blessings.] Like me! Exactly like me! Addressing itself to the future, like me. Cheers! If it were different I wouldn't give it a nickel for its loyalty. If it weren't at home inside itself and my ambitious consciousness, in the sense that it couldn't wait to get on a plane and be someplace else, as fast as possible, I'd cut it short before it could race to the stadium and sing national anthems. Because it would spend too much time not being. What a waste. [It wouldn't even be able to recognize the emblems of real importance on its jogging suit. It wouldn't make any sense. Wouldn't recognize the signs sparkling on all the equipment. Couldn't read the bar codes for all things lasting that weren't grown: they enter man like a bar and stay there longer than he. The goods that keep the globe in its place. I am entitled, because I am healthy! I demand equal health for the child.] I want to put it in its proper place. Any bottled springwater asshole has the right to listen to the language of reason. This child shall learn to understand me, bottled inside his amniotic fluid. [If it were dense, it would be a completely different matter.] Now my love emerges in the jungle of my being. Awakened, like nature.

THE TYPICAL PROFESSIONAL ATHLETE [*Enters stage. Carries a small TV set and speaks into it.*]: It may be said that when a person is killed we are not left with a thwarted desire in the same sense in which I have a thwarted desire when I am hiking through dry country and, pausing to ease my thirst, discover a hole in my water bottle. In this case I have a desire I cannot fulfill, and I feel frustration and discomfort because of the continuing and unsatisfied desire for water. When I am killed, the desires I have for the future do not continue after my death, and I do not suffer from their nonfulfillment.

(Note: Thanks for ethics, Peter Singer!)

[THE ATHLETE *puts down the TV set. Exits.*]

[THE YOUNG MUTTER *continues to feed the infant. On screen,* SKIERS *somersault over moguls, their jumps and turns getting increasingly difficult.*]

THE YOUNG MUTTER: Without roaming, no homing. [Oh no! This child rests so securely in itself, it could, if it wanted to, cross the ocean in the boat I rock. It can leave any time to get itself some foreign goodies.] One must embrace order as well as the other, then stand up, speak out, and score. Or else one gets punished! That's living! Real living! Recreational living! [Its goal: Never look around timidly! *We* are what's most interesting. From time to time, we get sloppy. But no one stares us down because of it.] This child belongs to me. I know how to listen to my own creation! It screams. I can wrap it up and bring it along: A smelly little pee-nut buttering my bread. Good baby! [The other travelers are amazed how zealously I strap it to myself. I myself have abandoned myself to the simple, the seemingly simple: to the calm glow, which makes us both important.] One day this child will want to get out of my home. I can offer my baby the afternoon sun and a warm upward breeze: still, others will have heard about it! And that's good. If it didn't have itself, I would have it all myself. I catch it and increase its fortune. This child is too young to get away from home. I am waiting at the front door, I humbly accompany it. Its path is set: The tablecloth is already laid out, knives and forks are on the way, so the child can ingest its life out of cans and styrofoam, to the battle sound of the landmarks, the trademarks.

Here I am. I want to be with him every moment, but I must stay [—I just bought all new furniture—] within myself. He'd never get away from my services! No, sirree! [And he better keep the receipts for everything he gets here.] Or else I'd be on his heels, in my high heels and kick him, skirt up to my knees, right out of his space. This child must have his ticket ready for the holy places where all things sacred are kept: the sacred skiing equipment, the sacred surfing equipment, the sacred big game hunting equipment, the sacred real experiencing equipment. He has to learn to hold his own ground, because I can kill any person I made! He must know what he is about, a tough skiing tour, unconscious white fading into a sea of white on the frantic incline for more! More! [As unconscious as the landscape in its winter transformation.]

I am my child's dairymaid, his dairy queen. I reach greatness through him. [Maybe I should have never made myself this gift?] Now I commit to this child. [Content with almost all there is, wedeling down the hills, rubbing hands, and voila: the imprint of the real thing: the stamp of a discotheque, where people are jailed. Or the lift ticket, a strange bundle around our necks. Jellied. The view of the landscape mirrored in the plastic that entitles us to enter. Just as the night sky in itself is nothing. Only in the mirror of water does the night become an object.] I committed this child. I commit to this child. Through him I become more. Reality is kept fresh in the deep freeze and well described on the package: a colorful little picture showing in vivid detail what's rising inside— terrible, shapeless haze, brought to a boil in the pot.

[Onstage, THE TWO LEDERHOSEN *enter. They put tape on the floor, creating a cross-country course. After a while, one or two* CROSS-COUNTRY SKIERS *appear and run along the taped course. The Lederhosen work hard to get ahead of them with their taping. Onscreen,* THE SKIERS *disappear from the screen. Screen now shows, very discretely, an old documentary of Jewish people gathering for their transport; one has to find a very civil sequence. For a long time, one simply sees, in black and white, people in old-fashioned clothes who begin to gather in a square. Nothing brutal! The scene must come across as very simple, yet not quite ordinary! It might be quite harmless, if somewhat irritating.*]

THE TWO LEDERHOSEN [*Speaking in rural accents, they split up the text randomly. When they are finished taping, they scrub the course.*]: From time to time, we take ourselves out of the game. At the same time, we keep growing thanks to the demand for us. We winter wonderlandscapers and expert export wine makers are fond of opportunities that serve our private interests. We avoid thinking we saw what they had let us see. The sky's the limit for the kind of dwelling we offer our foreign tourists. As for us, we gather under our own umbrella. Nature projects and ejects. She threatens us and throws us out into the open, so that our foreign members get hurt and are picked up by helicopter as her most attractive robbers. Cruel Mother Nature! Forgives nothing. One step off the trail, and instantly she punishes our "essence" with its reality! Death! Everyone is entitled to at least one appearance bleeding from the palms of his ski poles, staring at us horribly. Someone is always after nature. However, thanks to modern sports, we appear in many more places. Nature as our house to keep in the horror. No one who falls thinks of us when he drops into the dusk. There's no secret in this clumsy wilderness we keep clipping until it suits us and our guests. By protecting nature, it belongs to me like the sea when it is calm. And with the purchase of a ticket, I set out cheerfully, on the road to myself. Nature wants to win! Our prefab wooden porches hide the perfectly pruned hedges of our lives. To others, we are foreign. They come to us, take us in, and feel at home on our trails. Vice versa, we follow their ways and their will—into destruction. They want our death. And we follow them to their death! We follow them, and instantly we are separated from our loved ones, who become strangers to us. One season, and we don't recognize them anymore on the foaming porches of our village inns, in the overflowing outhouses on our mountain tops, from the thunderous outpouring of our native marching bands. Nature wants to be with us every moment; she can't take absences. She fears the void! [She offers us her spaces for our feasts, and we look around timidly praying to animal fibers that they'll agree with us.] Nature wants us healthy! Intact! Shameless! Natur. Out in nature everyone is only what he produces. And everyone can only produce what he is: dead and living in his own grave or mad and living beside himself. The madman walks distanced from us but in the same direction. But not you, not you! You come to us, don't you! We'll make sure to preserve your eternal childhood right here—until you start to rot!

[Onstage, one of the CROSS-COUNTRY SKIERS falls and remains on the ground. THE LEDERHOSEN interrupt their work, get a sack of lime, and pour it over the man. THE YOUNG MUTTER takes off her summer dress, puts on a dirndl, and gets a tray with beer mugs. She puts the infant on the tray. Collects dirty dishes, piles them on the tray.]

THE YOUNG MUTTER [While executing her chores]: This child is something. If it hadn't turned out this time, I would have objections against his future but impossible happiness. I wouldn't get it registered at the motor vehicle department. But this one is healthy! Little bones are interred in its body, ready to jump to their resurrection as an upstart, a gymnast, a jumper. I keep myself abreast of him and I breast-feed him. I spend myself. What sense would it make to save? [The steps I take are reasonable. I meet myself, cheerfully and future-bound forever, I am setting my line, the animal on the hook glows dimly. The thin thread ahead of me becomes my path.] I need to accomplish my work as master breeder. A free ride in the front of the bus for the fittest! I am the intervention into alien life after preceding epochs of mental excellence—or at least average.

One must intervene; listen to me. There are two kinds of retardation. There are those who have been some kind of person at some point! They kept themselves under cover, which their teacher had carefully wrapped around their heads. Consider the difference in the condition of their mental inventory! It's comparable to a random heap of stones that hasn't yet been touched by a sculpting hand, as opposed to the ruins of a collapsed building! The latter preserves the memory of the blue twilight fading into the mental night: Those next-to-last people may stay with us as a constant question of how much it will cost us to keep them properly heated, lit, and ventilated. The others, however, those hundred percent pure idiots, are the ones we polish off right away so we don't have to keep chewing that horrible stuff in-between our regular diet of reality. We advocates of the sugar-free life. We'd better undo them before their births! We DNA-enriched mothers know how to do that. We pull them, unconscious, though consciously produced, out of ourselves. They have no ground to stand on; the least of us, our own. Otherwise, they'd get everything dripping wet with themselves, all over the carpet! Their caps were meant for better things than their curly, but curiously dead, heads. Several generations of nurses would look pretty stupid taking care of these deadweight existences! Because it isn't permitted to leave the locus of the self. Find your place within yourself and stay there! [It's simply not possible that these people go and watch television in any old ex-cathedral.] Next door, the nurses curl their lips and turn off the respirator.

Now this child of mine—take a good look—is mentally alive like a freshly split atom. It is no burden to the community. Only to me! This child doesn't have to learn to do without. [It has a future, finely chopped, which I mark for him in the shopper's guide and schlepp here, all by myself. The simple has become even simpler.] A child who is not conscious of itself, may be brought to an end. This denial of life doesn't take anything away. This denial brings us something! Another can live in its stead! We must learn to protect nature from us. Gesundheit über alles. Standing tall like a Tannenbaum! Keeping out anything unhealthy! Keeping oneself in a savings account! Snow! In the city it turns to dirt, adding to the jungle of un-nature. But there's always a dewy new morning to keep us fresh.

What does the day have in store for us? Backpacking, a repetition of what scares others? Mountain climbing, an imitation of what puts us above others? Finding a place to sit down and eat our disappointments, while the view ahead restores us again. Origin comes a long way. We are livestock, we keep ourselves in stock, because we are native in our selves. *Being* is the product of everything that is. [We hand our coupons to the cashier. Discounted items make a great impression upon us.] You will recognize us by the things that surround us, shiny white herds whose dairy products are much in demand. We couldn't be more real than those branded names of what has been, marketed on the TV screen. They always precede our actual arrival. We want to fill up with freshness! We consume ourselves. The only goods we touch come from our own stockroom, and we hope it is intoxicated with feelings rather than with toxic fills. But what do we let seep in instead? People we didn't order and didn't want. [We've got a soul, which we discover in a midsize sedan, but it never overtakes us. We keep ourselves under bushels of light, where once we shone, all on our own. Yet, this time we weren't noticed as we were passing, we, of all people, always trying to meet things head-on. Nothing was left of us, the whitest products, not even the washing instructions. But now it is day.] We know our price. As a maid, I need this child. [I am too much. Look at me overflow. I, the Dragon Lady, have littered all over.] Filled with ambition, I speak as a mother, whose eyes and hand define the visible. I produced something that was thinkable, and now it thinks itself. This child hardly starts to wander, and right away his shores remain behind. I wave to him, but he pulls away from me. It seems only a short time ago that I nurtured him. This child is aware of himself, and he is right. This child is unfinished in many ways, but he can grasp himself. He keeps grabbing himself to check whether his new gym bag with the tennis racket's still there. What a piece of birth! Filled with life.

But how is nature doing today? It's chugging up the driveway and has almost made it all the way to us. And here we wait for her with our banners and busses, to explain to her the detour into a national park, where she must be tamed: we, the people who camp out and are also only partially conscious. [At the moment we have no further wishes. We are well on our way out of oblivion.] But the National Guard, dispatched by the Interior Ministry, mounted on their subcompacts and left to stand there, aim their rubber equipment at us, until we bounce, happily like balls, right out of the screen. We are a plot, we are being performed. We are a curtain, we are being dropped right in front of our eyes.

[*Onstage,* THE TWO LEDERHOSEN *sit down on the cross-country track they built. They cut off little pieces of the lime-covered* CROSS-COUNTRY SKIER *and eat them leisurely. They take beer from the tray of* THE YOUNG MUT-TER, *drink it, wipe their mouths on the sleeves of their jackets. Onscreen, the documentary film shows people in old-fashioned clothes being humiliated.*]

THE TWO LEDERHOSEN [*They alternate speaking, partly with their mouths full, so that much of what they say can't be understood, some of it only after they swallowed. They clearly have a rural accent: rural vowels and virtues in their language.*]: Something in nature always goes for food. That makes her chipper and chubby. As to what we just said, this is what we mean: Masses of peoples are adrift. The borders are open. They are hurled at each other as if they were their own pictures in an exhibition. Nothing to hold them back. They look down from their balconies and quickly find their place among their kind. The sun shines on their cars. They go for broke! Becoming the kind of person that transcends itself! Harvesting what others have planted! Hitting the jackpot. Just watching the sun, they lose their money. [With dark patience, they still carry around their truths, but those cherries are already full of worms. No store admits them to its stacked shelves, its shelved selves.] They want new things more plentiful than anyone ever divined or devoured. [They sell themselves right from their cars, but they've already sunk so low, their balls are tossed about like a boat in high seas.] For example, at an altitude of 4,000 feet they want to have their little bench to sit on. That's what they lived for, worked for, every single day of their lives. While their wardens rent their mountain lodges exactly half a meter above them. Last night, at our expense, they appeared as martens and ate up the insides of our car! [We predators have our worries, too, but many more varieties.] These people are just exhausted right now from not having anything for so long. [Their midnight excursions won't add anything except a few poetic perversions leaving their imprints in the snow.] In their seclusion they've been away from us for too long. They are the borders they cross. How pitiful when poverty wants something! In the meantime we hurl ourselves screaming across the deep snow. Those boards under our feet, our stage, the world. We built it ourselves! The smallest contraption we could con out of nature with a little cunning. And it works! The foreigners come here in droves. What they still have to learn: If you want to be rich, you must be able to outdo yourself. They have always parked their busses someplace else. Today they are still able to loot their history and count on our pity, but tomorrow we'll settle accounts! At least we stole our entire history! And much sooner! We who live here don't ever look at the landscape, we experience it through its worth to others. We are self-sufficient. [Some day these foreigners, too, will have to become hosts to the new; that is when they will own themselves. When they have something cooking. Their neediness has been corralled for so long, rubbing its back against the fence.] We don't need to destroy their views; let them convert them into our currency. We print our own views and even sell them in viewmasters. We are self-sufficient. Still, more would also be sufficient. But there are those foreigners who force their way across the border to board with us: they only know the kind of deprivation that wants to *have*. We, on the other hand, don't want anything, because we *are*. We are here for our guests, who speechlessly watch the Alps self-ignite. Nature demands it from us, and we demand it from her. We expand in our wealth, which we donate exclusively to ourselves. People come from far away just to take a look. [They want to give themselves to the unique, in the hope that something will happen. They open up right out there in the open.] But those who can't pay won't hear the mountains ring. The rock will stay sealed like their past when they were powerless. They live without zest and want without zeal. They push a button, but they get no picture. They just don't get the picture.

[THE OLD FARMER *enters stage, listens for a while, shakes his head, and exits again*]

THE TWO LEDERHOSEN: Let's hear some live music, now! The color print, the color screen are not as nice. [Good things happen only if one stops wanting.] Those foreigners will never learn! The more they want, the less they can stuff into the corpses of their egos. The air that makes the day glow blue is not enough for them. They want to have, without understanding the essence of wealth. All wealth is within oneself, underneath a big overhanging roof, with everyone else shooting on top of it. Every shot a hit. And the view gets better and better the higher one climbs. We have been kindled in the mountain air for so long, one day we'll come down as full-blown fires. But those strange foreigners just don't see the flames flare up under our flaring loden capes. Their silence wasn't one of seclusion. It was filled with their greed to experience us! That's foreign to us. We had a much quieter childhood. [Our being was let loose like the thick mush that was dumped so generously into our cribs.] That's how we arrived at our superior *essence,* which looks like us, so that there's something left to scare us. We keep looking. We keep spreading. We are the true guest rooms, the real rest rooms. We gather in our seclusion only to offer different kinds of accommodation! With or without excuse and refuse. But no fraternizing, please. After all, they must remain strangers and pay for it. We open our ways to them, we are the marked trail, we are truth and life. [But we aren't deep enough into winter that we have to share our stock with them.] We even are the ride that takes them the wrong way. [The factories entrusted with healthy fruit; already native juices start running out of our mouths. You can take us right in front of the TV, you don't even have to take us outside to extract the milk teeth of our wishes with a thin thread. For the time being, the outside stays where it is. It's not going to run away from you! We've got all the gas you need. Twilight falls upon us as if it lost its consciousness. We open more inns, as if we had conscience. We are surrounded by car dumps, where all that rubber is getting hotter and hotter, rubber meant to protect us from each other, while we get at each other all the more violently. Yes, this rubber protection covers all members standing in line.] We are hot! Throngs of people have been lining up at the border for the past twenty-five hours. Bunches of people glistening with expectation; the berries picked in the morning light. Now the sun is burning down on them. Those lines of cars, especially at the eastern borders! With people looking out at us who look brand-new for once. They've been strangers to themselves for too long. They don't want to be strangers anymore, anywhere. So they expect us to hide them in our childhood. They want a brand-new memory from us. As soon as they come down they get up right away and drive their greedy beast all the way down again. The next best thing to native earth is Astroturf, but that's still rolled up and blocking our entrances. Good speed! Pretty soon they won't even understand themselves! They want the best but don't want to wait for anything that takes its time. We also had to wait for thousands of years until the mountains were ready to be mounted and stuffed into our pockets.

They have to buy all that video equipment to throw some light on themselves! [Why can't they just appear as darkness, which is content with itself!] Constantly checking on us, whether someone accidentally stole us before they had a chance to carry us away themselves! No. Absolutely no. They cling to us and think they only last as long as we take care of them. They don't even dare to sleep, they are afraid they might be gone again. All that noise in our quiet childhood! But they don't yield any interest. We pursue our own interests. We have photographs of us that show only us. Because we are the ones who are really secluded, and we make a good living from it. [Our customs are for our farmers! Nature trails are beaten our way with the whip. This river doesn't cost anything, as long as it leisurely moves along its way. But if other customers wish to see it flow, whose cash we want to flow, they'll be flooded with customs and costumes, a sea of troubles for the unaccustomed!] We can set our price! And never too low. In return we sing to the zither until a blizzard shrouds the evening. What they want is to dwell in our land, spreading all over, and dwelling on what has been donated to the world, which is them. Packets of food and clothing. We forgive them the articulation of their wishes as long as it is us they want. [The voice of nature comes to you on this machine. Listen to the bird's beep! It may be yours.] We even forgive them their dangerous journey; in fact, we offer one thermoblanket and free bumper stickers to everyone who gets stuck with us for good.

Home World

Onscreen, part of the mountain in close-up. On the slope, fragmented CORPSES OF MOUNTAIN CLIMBERS. *Next to them, mountain-climbing equipment, ropes, assorted picks, etc. The corpses are partly decomposed, some are only skeletons. Onstage,* THE OLD MAN, *partially wrapped in bandages, builds a toy railroad onstage, in front of the mountain, including an appropriate little village.*

THE OLD MAN: Can I see from here how others skipped to the top? How about myself, has my full weight been lifted into the purity of space? With no ground under my feet, only a chasm in front of which people lose their self-sufficiency. Der Ab-Grund, the ground way down, a chasm. It unites space with time, making men finite, that is to say, they can't rejoice over having finally reached the top, because right away there is another abyss between themselves and their gaping mountains. They fall, and space and time, Raum und Zeit, merge as death. Zum Tod. Many would do well to hide; they disturb the eyes of the beholders. They should learn to avoid them, vomited as they were from their countries, ungainly as they had become, they had nothing to gain there. They think they can make a go of it here, if they make our various virtual realities actual, if they worship and ship our wares in an unchecked frenzy. [If they steal our ventures and drive them right through all checkpoints into the river, onto the dead-end track.] We exclude them all the more rigorously. Let them return to their impoverished rooms! Left to their last wills, this is what they expect from us: there, in the fog, Europe's new skyline rising high. Eastern art in the showrooms. Those shitheads! [We demand health insurance policies, which make us sick, but anyway. . . . They, on the other hand, lost in our order, like to reflect but also expect to burst into being once again.]

The column advances. The forest in the fog. But they stew in their own smog, in the traffic jam of the displaced. [They can't remain inside their memories. Their long self-denial hurls them far ahead, out of the present. They don't have anything left to recover but must keep themselves under cover.] They should have turned back sooner, those amateur mountain climbers! But they did not like the thought of returning home. They wanted us as friends, but our ground does not give way. It doesn't make room. This lust for altitude, where there is only crippled growth: dwarf pines, stunted grass! But it is precisely the endangered things that kindle our fears. We try to embrace them. But they suddenly feel at home everywhere. They have become their own travel agents. Those unneeded needy think they can buy us by invading our presence, like an army entering the darkness. Recruits of dusk, their sleds loaded with merchandise that they keep lugging up the hill to drive them in a dangerous downhill race toward their warehouses, in which both disappear: those good sports and the goods they rescued at great pains. They relieved us from guilt. We encircle them as their shepherds. We bark at them as soon as they dare to articulate their precious wishes. They never get closer than the next, the fifth column of cars, with which they try to penetrate the meaty layers in our window displays. So they waver back and forth as to who they are: bright cheerleaders cheering their team and at the same time forced to represent the team itself. The speakers rattle. No one around who can pronounce the name of their club. Fans of their own teams; here they remain strangers trailing us. [But they didn't bring us anything but an enormous appetite on their tongues. Now the flank gleams in the rising sun—the peak of passion—and time keeps picking on it like a mad dog.]

[*Onscreen, the mountain slowly gets brighter in the morning light*]

How I wish for unrushed people who stick out in their own times, because they get to work way ahead of time; letting themselves be handled slowly, deliberately. They should be happy! In the meantime, those foreigners are already followed by the hikers, who think they are much more at home here. They are foul, like balls. But they won't smuggle themselves in! Stretching the human skin to greatness. Where does that get us? Under the lampshades of welfare. But Mother Earth is not there to protect us. Let alone them! [And certainly she won't have any fun. Her trees are uprooted. Thinking digs its furrows inside us.] This soccer-playing foreigner in our stadium, for example. Trying to become local by being loyal—to us and our accomplishments, which are plastered all over the walls of our athletic armories! All that stunted growth must be cleared! The foreigner avoids his own kin; they keep listening for him long after he's gone and don't hear from him as soon as he's gone. He found work in a shoe store. Those remaining behind are severed forever from these wanderers, like scabrous parts who dare to eat from plastic plates with plastic spoons and get stuck in the green mold of their stock.

[*Onscreen, colorful garbage is emptied from the side of the mountain: cans, packaging, etc., that ends up on the* CORPSES]

We look at these people through the eyes of the guest, while it is they who are the real guests. We—that is to say, knickers, kneesocks, hiking boots. We are well equipped. [Nearby, other party guests, struck down by the foreign that seemed familiar much too soon: nature, into which they were lured.] No light will make this stranger a brother. No sound will make us understand him. [And the point of our edifications is a completely different one: our edifices pull nature as close as possible, while distancing the people: as soon as they arrive in order to dwell, they are thrown right back into nature again. Their faces turned to the sun, sunscreen splashed all over, sunglasses blinding their view.]

How so? Friend and foe scorn the radio, I mean *ratio*—both have long become one and the same. Ever since, they've been taken by the hand and led carefully by something grand, like a can of Coke and a second can of greed. [So they stand there, retained by life like a pawn, which they themselves could not redeem.] Gambling's their game. Yes, yes, give it a try! It's all the same now. Living without meat would be too much for them. There is more than enough beer and more than enough people; I don't think their unborn children will look good enough to let them be native born, which they must be to qualify for the discounts offered by Vienna's municipal swimming pools.

[*Onscreen*, CORPSE I *rises, bloody bandages hanging from him, revealing terrible wounds*]

CORPSE I: Forgive the disruption, but . . . We were driven in here like animals, before we had a chance to carefully consider the offerings in the mail-order catalogue. Driven into a foreign experience. And right away we are supposed to make do with what we had all along. But our frugality has long been extinguished by this great selection in your windows, behind the sausage counters, on the cheese wheels. Actually, your awesome skills in marketing any kind of detergent should be enough to deter us, but quite the contrary: it attracts us. It attracts us! [Images of ourselves appear enlarged in the windows; we are attracted by our own beauty, I mean, by the offer to increase our beauty, if needed. All those inventions for our own good! Layers of lotions and colors shield our faces, while our bodies are protected by fashionable clothing. Landing smack in the middle of a foreign way of life, we wouldn't have been able to stop in our tracks.] Like a nervous herd smelling land, we left our families; for too long they have made our homes in the kind of seclusion from where there is no way out. We barely took the time to say good-bye to our beloved. Out into the fashionable cool! We no longer have to watch the words we say! Like our relatives we left behind, they can't be held against us anymore. We have learned to submit to the superhighways, which we patiently talk into tolerating us on top of everyone else. Now we foreigners leave the dark cold of our childhood, which has ruled our lands far too long. It's too early, the stores are still closed. [Who would want to listen to us? So, on to new rooms and boards. Like heavy thunderstorms, those faces of the farmhouses. Carved works, their frames spitting us out even before they finish their insulting speeches.] We can't be reproduced—take a look! You won't ever find another one like us! Doesn't that make us precious and dear? Expensive? Our partying a parting. Even our shopping sets us apart from the stronger boys and girls who push us aside. They have outgrown their costumes, before we had a chance to grow accustomed to ourselves. Like cattle on the way to the slaughterhouse, we had to leave everything, butchered by nature, who forgives nothing. [Why should we protect lakes and rivers? They're just

246

waiting to run right over us!] What we were can't stay with us, even as a beginning. They don't accept it! Since we can't go on living our own history, we are taking theirs! We cannot tolerate that our dear souvenirs—madonnas in the snow, the elks at the shore, those plaster visions—are already forgotten in our new beginnings. As if we could experience everything new in one single moment, so that nothing will have ever been. We have been made over from scratch, but the care given to children, their clothes, sport, and transport, will never include us. May I please have this instrument?

[*He takes an ice pick and starts hacking into* OTHER CORPSES, *while he continues to talk, breathing heavily*]

Thank you for at least opening nature to us! [But why did you close it so quickly again? We were shown what is considered the most magnificent, beautiful sight in the area, but why are there graves dug into its flanks? Oh, yes, I know: The mountain won't open up all by itself!] And how are we allowed to fit into it? [Once again, in the only shape we know: we, the cozy spots in the shade, torpedoed by nature with great success, crumbling, dripping into the ground.] A place of nothingness. The mountain doesn't seem to need us. We fail at the sight of it. From the beginning, they only wanted to sell us trinkets, never tickets of admission. That doesn't make us more manageable! They and nature go back to the same old covenant! This is the township of what town? Small steps are no longer enough for us! We want to catch up! We want to catch this place in our shopping nets! Its golden essence shines through the loops of our bags! The one and only thing to which we want to entrust ourselves! And what did it get us? [On paper, this place wouldn't be the same, it would have been left unsaid. Just a map, in which to fold our homeland so we could bring it along.]

We are the man of this century, the emigrant who is capable of misery several times in his life. It is our nature to suspend ourselves so they can show us something else as the new model for our dripping bodies. But the new is forever hidden to us. Luckily, people protect their property so carefully from us. They are right: They'd lose it if they didn't prevent us from staying! Because taking in this vast expanse, if only at a glance, also means wanting to possess it, from one end to the other. Just look how I ended!

[*He leans on his ice pick, breathing heavily*]

But it won't bring you any luck either that the thought you planted was actually realized. It wasn't only us you cut off! [This expansive plant stands also as your admission that every good view must instantly be blocked by you.] Your ugly blocks—this dam, the dike 300 kilometers from here—actually serve to protect everything that had been visible before—the open view of the river, the valley—from our arrival, doesn't it? You veiled all that, so we would see it and then again not see it. So that we would see it in what has been. Even now, in your slide shows in the parish house next to the Chamber of Commerce, you maintain a dialogue between us and your lost landscape. You don't ever speak for yourself. You let flowers and perfume do the talking for you.

[*He lays his head on the ground and is silent. Onstage,* CHEERLEADERS *enter. Goad the audience as during a sports event.*]

THE OLD MAN: You think you can have nature as your ultimate wrap? You are not entitled to such a big dwelling. The other way around. You are nature's container. You preserve it for us for later. For you, nature is only as big as you can grasp it as your personal quarters. Only from where you stand does it seem we might finally be able to sleep!

[*Onscreen,* CORPSE 2 *speaks, as he stays lying on the ground*]

CORPSE 2: I am speaking for all who are victims like myself. First of all, one has to abandon oneself, believe me! Anyone who can't be grasped easily will be immediately questioned as to what he means. They look into our wallets, and immediately we are questionable: Do our intentions match our choices? The faces we make! One day I got up, warmed up some snow, dropped my candy wraps on the floor, my excrements right next to them, put on a smile sweet as candy, determined to become a stranger on earth. All I wanted was a two-room apartment for one more person than the one I had become. The sandwiches intended for the afternoon remained wrapped. My being had its home, my sensuality its sense. That is to say, I wasn't real. For years I decomposed with great effort, out in the cold. [I never existed. Amid bits of orange peels and pulp, between bytes of pulp fission, instead of the burger patsy and the brand name products at my filthy feet, I finally stepped on myself. Ouch! A popular manufacturer sponsored me, and now my presence represents something that took a lot out of me, while I never took in anything. I am my product. I am packaged inside me. Dare to be different.] Let me be happy! [Like a tarpaulin, I am spread out on the mountain slope.] I am quite close to being forgotten. My family no longer puts lights in the windows for me, the deceased, and for all their other dead, who, besides the particular circumstances of their passing, were lonely and unnoticed. We are a collapsing billboard. Whatever women we spent our nights with, all we ever wanted was ourselves. Sport! Wandering about still is the nicest aspect of human homing between any work and its haven: those marvelous gadgets we have fastened around ourselves. What happens when we listen to a singing nun or another popular performer? People smile as if in a fever, turn around, and slam themselves shut.

[*Onstage*, THE YOUNG MUTTER *enters as the rustic waitress, steins on the tray. She bandages the* CORPSES, *while the* CHEERLEADERS *continue their exercises to department-store Muzak.*]

THE YOUNG MUTTER: Sign our petition for an environment that we have cleared completely. Among the many nations desired by those who want their turn being desirable, we are one of the first. Even though we haven't paid half of our debt to history. Our dirndls and lederhosen are almost new, starched to a crisp, and once again everyone likes us just for being ourselves. [Decorated like leading cows, we appear in the early morning dew on our mountain highways so that we can be duly admired. Pure nature; it thrives on never changing.]

Our country. Our home. Those foreigners are foreign because they are on the road. They are attracted to our shelves stacked with quality labels, which would fit them well too, so they think. [So that their mirrors would finally let them in; but the product won't play along, and they are thrown back into the water. But we! We dwell because we own. Searching for us, they settle here—but always only as wanderers.] They won't become us. We'll take care of that! They should move on, but they keep looking for us; and always, they look for themselves in us. By having a goal, they become wanderers. Their goal is not to be at home. Sign here, so that we too can stay inside ourselves, where it is most beautiful. Those foreigners do our work, and suddenly everything will belong to them. They are getting fresh. [They'll be sorry, they'll be history. We keep them behind our chocolate bars. While we were working on our tans, the stores filled up with people asking for us a hundred bloody times. But we stay outside for the time being. The sun rises, so we don't have to explain what we've been doing up to now. You can tell from our clubs and bars that once again we settled for what we own. We and our teammates prefer to rest on that rather than on our sexual organs, which are too slippery for us; that we stored our togetherness in food coops, like cheese. We smell of ourselves; that we keep our secrets like our juicy herds dripping from the lead of labeling long before they reach the domestic hearth in beefed-up color brochures.]

We are close to each other, we belong together. [Coming home, we keep going. And we put a stop to all that homecoming by denying it to others. We have risen far above ourselves and turned into mountain ranges. We can't be resisted, we constantly offer ourselves in super sales, but we don't give away a thing. Even our memories are tied to us, like ships. Woe to him who unties himself, we'd have to face our past, which up to now we saved like provisions. We'd have to go on with it, knowing full well there's something dark behind us, an eternal night, spurring us on. Yet we are the ones who are finished. Closed borders, open minds. We take to the streets, but we don't take a liking to anyone. Hurry back into the house. It would be nothing but a desolate vessel if we didn't have nature surrounding it.] Our country. Our home. We mustn't lose anything that belongs to us, especially our health. And nature: Rather than offering it to foreigners to dwell in we'll do the dwelling ourselves. Yes, those foreigners aroused in us the need to dwell! How lucky, we've already accommodated ourselves.

We aren't giving away anything. We always come home, where even our teeth can be replaced. [And only in our homecoming do we realize again and again that we were just lurking nearby, ready to bounce back, raging with anger. What a nice surprise: We came into possession of ourselves. A bingo game, in which we always win. The others still have to learn how to play us! It takes our breath away.] We take great care keeping silent about our past; that way we can't be excluded from it, either. [They can place us anywhere; there's no backstabbing. There's nothing there. Never was! We are the legitimate winners; now we pull all kinds of stuff from the shelves, as consolation prizes that can't console us.] And this great era keeps pulling us, but we don't move.

We are honest because we keep still and wait until someone comes close to us. Then we fall back on ourselves, like a healthy thrashing. Under the punches of natural disasters, we became the seals imprinted on the landscape. Houses in floodplains. Pregnancies without counseling, within the steel-woolen dwellings of churches. After all, it is us who dwell here. [We should recognize our own tracks behind us! And this is where they end. This is where time comes apart, this is where we've come in order to go back.] And no one else should ever think of coming to stay.

We are our own sons, homely, homebound, and always coming home. The one who's coming and the one already there. Those foreigners won't become our neighbors! We prefer to become the sights for them to look at, like furniture. It's us, always. It's us, no less. Let them become friends but remain strangers. Let them shortly bow to our dwellings; but we know how to safekeep ourselves. We don't have to get off, because we already arrived where we have always been. Since we have made ourselves comfy and lasting, we can outlast what's coming and outwit what's changing! [Our country, our home!] As long as we're here! Now, look at those creatures crowding the arrival booth! Gathering to squeeze in with us. We are close and closed. There's no mystery to those strangers' arrival; unsteadily, their busses are approaching. [Iron clasps snap for their worn-down heels. But we are our own best friends, our own fathers and mothers. Resolutely, we keep ourselves open, like greedy beaks. We vacate horrifying beds, in which we sleep on top of snakes, forever insulted, waiting for some light underneath the shady rock that a jaded wanderer turned around. Pale, transparent worms and bugs come crawling out from under.] And we matter once again, at long last. Busily, we carry their suitcases; how strange our nature, as we discovered. We're easily accessible, and no one will be let in.

[THE OLD MAN *gets up from underneath the pieces of his frame. With great effort he puts on his skis and starts a cross-country hike, while the* CHEERLEADERS *and* ALL OTHERS *onstage sign the petition for a clean environment.*]

THE OLD MAN: We, on the other hand, have our say and go away. The dogs bark invitingly, but we escort ourselves. And we throw the waste of an animal's life in front of our guests. They want their meat fatter and fatter. Well-fed, the guest gets up, one among many, even though he has been accommodated courteously. He wasn't born yesterday! He sets foot in a restaurant only to save money. No money, however, should be saved on him. His feet are twitching even in his sleep; he keeps his eyes open to pick up new stuff even in his dream.

The borders are also open: our slits to reach for our home-canned goods stored in cracked jars, safe from all outside interference. And every man is well spent here. We have opened our big events for him; we are his festival. Europe is expansive, but slowly it's getting dark. He is welcome. He moves through the dusk. His most faithful pal doesn't run beside him wagging his tail, he drones right underneath him. [He does not pay attention to those passing him relentlessly. Everyone gets ahead of him! The motor speaks softly. And because he stays in perpetual motion, he eliminates any possibility of staying, once and for all.] And his chances? No chance! [He emerges from his hell of bloody limbs on the highway, death still before his eyes. His suitcase, torn open, placed carefully in front of him, facing the wallpaper landscape which he likes.] Suddenly, everything comes to a halt. [He is joined by friendly, curious people, helpless animal-loving existences.] Since everything is possible now, the foreigners are caught for our benefit, trapped in their staying, which will never be for good. They're here, that's all, and they look up to us. [The sky above us likes to get upset too, and they come upon us like the usual, endless misfortune. Our waitresses resent the time wasted in the traffic.] They are paying off. The guest doesn't know us. He has hardly arrived and already he is trapped in the mementos of his being here. He leaves us to his memories of us, since not even we have met ourselves. We live in his slides, his videos, his photographs. While he harvests for us the clouds from the sky and the light from the mountaintop. Nothing decreases, but nothingness increases. What feels homey will never be home. And those who could never get out from their homeworld, they look at us gratefully: all beings essential to our well-being. Slabs of butter, links of sausage have been generously slammed on their breakfast trays. All skin and bones stuffed into the garbage can. [Casually, all the clothes they wanted appear made in the frill-filled windows. They wouldn't dare complete the picture with their swears about the devastating weather.] They laugh about everything and shamelessly make a show of themselves. For once they really enjoy themselves. [Music keeps them riveted to their car seats.]

They got rid of their opinions and in their place slipped into much too tight local costumes sewn with red-hot needles. Europe is running low on fireproof material. Gratefully, they accept us in order to become one of us, to be banished with us. We planted mushrooms especially for them near the edge of the forest. Berries and insects maintain a welcome silence that is broken only by the machines transmitting information about us and the surrounding areas of recreation and preservation, so that they won't drive away but stay. After all, our government-administered foods and drugs have just been freshly squeezed from nature! Nickels and dimes are accepted.

[Only a few stay home. Looking pretty stupidly at their views. Two strokes get you further than one. No doubts arise. Only birds are up in the air. On the ground, all the animals we let live for a while and all the paying guests we want to live on forever. Rural festivities glue us together. So, now we are sufficiently entangled; we even let them peek into our home lives! We appear with open hearts, take off our shoes, and step on land. And now, please make room for the next! We made the beds; they are sticky so that we can stay together a little longer. It's cozy. Our raised brows sparkle with worldliness.] We look hip and native. Yes, yes, that's us. Check us out! We take checks. You better pay us well! Don't be shy! Use us as you please!

Innocence

Onscreen: the interior of a rural castle: horns, antlers, stuffed birds on the walls, everything quite exquisite. The FEMALE VIOLINIST *plays, the* MALE PIANIST *accompanies her.* THE OLD MAN, *elegantly dressed, sits, listening, in a big easy chair among* THE ELEGANT LADIES AND GENTLEMEN. *Onstage: the toy railroad, and especially the little village, set up by The Old Man have suddenly grown very big. They have grown in scale, as it were, so that the tallest building, maybe a church, is now several meters high, the other buildings are accordingly larger. After awhile, a constant flow of* TRAVELERS, *carrying luggage, cross the stage. They have to squeeze past the buildings at times. In contrast, The Old Man's frame has shrunk, so that he has to sit in it cramped, as in a child's chair.*

THE OLD MAN [*to* THE WOMAN, *who again is standing next to him with her luggage, wearing her traveling suit*]: You can't call this earth anymore! They tear the roots from our graves in the forest. We warm each other in snow-covered cabins, nothingness piled up high. Above our heads, nothing, inflated water. [A substance, through which we let ourselves be driven, eyes focused on nothing but the abyss, an effort as tiresome as working the land. Yet it gets us temporarily excited.] Through skiing we become the crown of our Dasein, our being-there; exhibiting ourselves to others. [But we're only entitled to do so if we return our innermost self, that unsold merchandise in our stores, where we bought it to begin with.

253

It no longer fits our well-groomed appearance.] Now skiing is the definitive interpretation of us, as a work. Strange apparati grow out of us, and we fight to protect ourselves from each other. And to win. Never racing downhill side by side, except in parallel slalom! Better one after the other! It measures time that begins and ends! Our opponent's most intimate trait; the hissing air around him scratches our cheek. We forget everything in our skiboard skycabins, fenced in by ski tips. That is our world. [As soon as we step out into the world, into the light, we immediately have to get attention, a lovely property, a proper prayer for speed, packaged in waterproof clothing.]

Deeply, we imprint ourselves in our stuff. That's plenty of ground to carry us safely. Nature! In the cities, where even the most casual stroll is a matter of studied technique, we still feel lost. [Amid the lawn mowers and water sprinklers. We've guzzled too many Lights, lightning strikes us, so off we go again to the country, the future tied to the roofs of our cars. Let's go.] In the cities, we get used up, in nature we use ourselves up.

Greasy paper and empty bottles line our homecoming celebration. We were honored, taken out of the package and thrown away. The challenge continues; we must practice our sport every single day. [We don't yet fully know the treasure we have in ourselves, surely not in all its details. We must keep going, brightly and briskly.] We are alive, enjoying ourselves, there is only the atom bomb, the broken reactor to make us sick! No need to worry about either; it's cars that will kill us.

[THE WOMAN *has opened her suitcase, looks through it. As she speaks, she pulls out a dirndl, holds it up against herself, then starts to undress slowly, gets the dirndl ready to put on.* THE OLD MAN, *crouched in his frame, starts to kick, trying to squeeze his way out. The Woman sits for a while in her underwear.*]

THE WOMAN: There are worse things than the busted reactor: the crippled embryo encapsuled in the maternal body. It could be its own sickly nature that made him so unnaturally small! Let it stop its lament and get lost. We want to remain wholesome and holy and congratulate ourselves on our beautiful voices that cheer us on between slalom poles or hurl commands at the dogs in the brush. Until we are torn out of our comic books and forced to face the sun with painted lips and blow-dried hair.

It's enough to be able to tell yourself that you won the downhill race and right away you are on the way to yourself! You've been there before, last year in fact, and surely, there always must have been someone who had been there before. A man who lets us see his funny side, the other he can keep to himself. [After all, his jokes are entitled to get us hot in our tubs and whirled in our pools, where those awful MC's jerk their hips and shoot water from their guns.] A cabin party during the cabin fire, throats screeching with gaiety: the clinking of glasses mingling with the forest. The shouts get louder and louder as if, clandestinely, we have already claimed the land. The county sheriff takes charge of what's real. The prelate in the hunting cabin with beautiful women slipped over him. [Not for nothing is he full of charming qualities; fat-assed flatteries thumping about far away from his church, pulling on their leash, spitting in their muzzles, rubbing their hands, and smashing glasses and teeth as they attack something new.] From his order he embezzled the trifle sum of a million. For good.

Also, the state senators and district councilors, their concrete, shrill reality, the way they thunder down the dirt roads with their iron-pumped bodies, lowering their horns and blowing up their own asses for added resonance across the land. [Watch out, now they are exploding. Slushy paper flies about like clouds. They squat on the ground, but others are bleeding to death for them.] Discretely, they receive an envelope slipped to them by a slippery nouveau riche Autrichien. Cadavers roll through the grass, the pine needles groan, and in consideration of all the beauty they will still have room to ingest, those lords of the land, those supermen, throw up at the edge of the forest. Women have also been handed to them, they don't control themselves, they yell beneath them as if they too were part of Being. Under heavy layers of fat, the bodies moan as they discharge their loads.

Nature is powerful because it is beautiful without having been beautified. And it belongs to those people! Vowing that they, sole owners of the soil, will continue to exist forever, they hold up to each other the sky and the deepest abyss as if warding off a demon with a crucifix. They vow to each other that they will exist forever and deny pushy intruders all nature. Those simpletons would only destroy the wonders. [They can't be handed anything, it would only turn against them. Motor sleds are hard to handle and unpredictable, the way they go. Those poor people in their shacks! I have an inkling they are not what's far away but rather what's coming.] Unfortunately, there are more and more of their not handpicked kind. [How ridiculous their clothes! Henpecked, that's what they are. The prelate seduces his women to graceful motions, his light ecclesiastic cloth clinging to his body. That's what makes him attractive; what a devout man, how nice it is to see him dance, nibble, and neck! It ain't cheap. But nature is worth it to fool people and fell women right at the edge of the chasm. Innocent eyes peek from the faces of jumping deer. This ecclesiast has embezzled the trifle of several millions from his order; now everything points to him. As the evidence gets out, people point at him and shout "good riddance." He's a real hotshot and welcome anywhere, if at all. Showing off in his Land Rover, that son of a gun! He regrets the light in the trees, the trunks are getting dark, bundles of native costumes crouched behind them, wooden, snot-nosed; several of them tied together, they relieve themselves in droves, well fed, well liked as they are.] And we get an idea of what's yet to come: the new day. Such a quiet event simply doesn't fit here!

[THE WOMAN *puts on the dirndl.* THE OLD MAN *manages to get out of his frame; he approaches The Woman. Taking advantage of the moment she pulls the dress over her head, he sneaks up on her to embrace her. She wards him off, friendly, but with determination. Onscreen, there are again the people from the old movie, moving along in an endless line. Onstage,* HUNTERS *enter, aiming their rifles.*]

THE OLD MAN: [Nature is our only passion! There is much to accomplish. Maybe we'll have a chance to read in her embrace. The farmer works himself right into her. Pine trees stand tall against the storm. The river roars in the autumn night. It is enough to call out oneself to meet oneself. Simple as that. The storm rages around the cabin. Snow. Is there anything that simple? Something easier to forget? I, for example, tell myself everything, but I don't believe me.]

Is it necessary that everywhere we go we find ourselves present already, in our indelible tracks, which alas turn everything into a desert? Technology throws us into the arena, we are blown about, shit hitting the fans, and there we are, looking the same as before. Greatness can come only from one's own country and only because it belongs to us and no one else. [The foreigners disturb us in their enthusiasm over everything coming their way; they don't know how to choose. But nature knows how to chasten them. That's what they want, after all! So they get chased about a bit, that's all. They don't let the farmer guide them, who has built in two more rooms, AC, and shower. Those foreigners! Dragging their horrible selves into foreign lands where the wind howls; where they can be a little better than foreign. To this end, they packed mother's delicious native buns in their traveling bags and knapsacks. They too want to fill themselves with all the good stuff! And to go with it, some wine from our region, for which we win prizes. And demand high prices. At worst, they'll smash a napkin in our face! We are content. Behind our four-wheel drives on our soft country roads, we avoid those detourists. A technique we have perfected; prudently, we proceed behind the wheel.]

And we have a place for our own terrific "essence," which darkens the sun: home. Because we have it, we never have to think about what happened. It did not! [We are here, we stay and forget everything else. We are innocent when we arrive at the cabin, cleansed in one of nature's washes. Her raging bristles brushed us well.] Quickly and thoroughly, our Black Forest deeds and tortes can be buried inside us. Sweet trifles! [Barrels of schlag against our temples.]

In nature there is innocence, and there always is another day. It did not happen! It is beautiful in the forest, our hearts belong to all beings. But we'd rather forget what has happened! [Our cars work well and make us free. We've kept ourselves reined in for too long. We never reflected. We simply acted. But now our thoughts, taken off the leash and barking loudly, could go much farther than ourselves.]

The blood stays in the ground. It doesn't talk to us. We don't lick it off. Our thinking can't even shock a bird in the tree. [And yet, wherever one steps, a horrid, ghostly world. A march into history; and yet we've never been there!] Do you hear the steps? As if in a barrel filled with grapes we once stomped in foreign *being,* until the red juice bubbled up underneath our soles.

In our blindness we have reached beyond ourselves, and sure enough, someone was already there! And right away the battle of appropriation begins: of the small dairy, the umbrella shop, the bookstore of the neighbor. It all belongs to us now, and it won't happen again! We won't let anything happen to it. We'll never outdo ourselves by taking action. That's done with and, thereby, undone. We shall never be beyond the reach of our thinking, which is always right. [In the meantime, we can let ourselves be seen in the light that makes us look better.] Whatever has only been said is not real. And saying things is always only a beginning. And we are rocked to sleep on the soft wafts of our precious furniture, reassured that history cannot go on until it has caught up with us. [I mean, it cannot go farther than the depot, where we stock the provisions for our superiority and survival.]

[*Onscreen, nature, in bright light, almost overly clear. All the beauty worth its money dipped in glowing daylight. Onstage,* THE OLD MAN *tries to kiss* THE WOMAN, *who resists, softly but determinedly. She kneels down before him, fastens his skis on his feet, his cap on his head, and so on. She does this as she is talking. After attaching a starting number to his body and strapping a knapsack to his back, she sends him off to the slope. A soccer game can be seen on one or more TV sets, with hardly any sound; all one is able to hear is the faint roar of the crowd over some action on the screen. For a while, The Old Man skis about somewhat undecidedly, then he lets himself be drawn into the events on one of the TV screens; he stops, watches the game.*]

THE WOMAN: How lucky for you that others had to experience death for you! Herds of humans were torn from their comfort, while your mountain rivers roared. Death tears the individual out of all connections to his kind; thanks to death, one can have one last solo performance. All alone. When all is nil, we drop out of the world at large and enter the world of home, where we can sit all alone on a bench, peeling an orange. [The first cigarette after the strenuous climb!] In earlier days the whole world was in every individual. *You* have made sure that the whole world was destroyed in every individual by becoming guilty. [Horror becomes reality, gaping wide; it stretches and looks leisurely at the crowds in front of the ticket booths, inching patiently toward the empty bleachers; there is a scream, the teams enter. One can root for one side only and make it last longer than the other, the opponent's. A storm comes up howling and cheering for the home team. Junk and scraps of paper fly about. Clouds of dust fill the air. The stadium is a house of terror. The people grow larger than life, they roar, the storm blows their coats up in the air. They lift their arms, those perpetual crooks, drunks, and dupes. Then they fall into each other's arms, the robbers, cops, and criminals, because their team seems to be winning. Or not? In the clouds of screams, one can see the ugly very clearly! From far away, everything seems possible; up close it doesn't look so good anymore. The self, turned conscience, put itself in the place of humankind and, being oneself, in the place of being human. Now the hats are flying.]

By killing masses of people, you have denied them that one moment, at the point of death, of stepping in front of the curtain, all alone, to take a bow. Even death's Nichten, that turning to nothing, the last chance to quickly pass on one's guilt like a handful of marbles, has been suspended by you. Because there were too many in this house of dying. You had to stuff them in! Doors shut carefully, even fearfully, locked against the outside and the inside! And no inside could be any quieter now. [The crowd is holding its breath. The tie, two minutes before the final whistle, won't last forever! The first lone wolves run down the stairs, to beat the others to the busses. Not to have to push one's way through heartlessness, while running to the toilet. People pay careful attention to their favorite players. Those terrific little human factories built for them by the creator of the products written on T-shirts and pants; this gorgeous touch of home amid the gore. Those stars who present themselves as human as you and I. How thoroughly thinking has changed the world! People seem happy about so much presence: the team plus thousands in the bleachers. They got themselves ready for the arrival of the victors but actually contributed to their disappearance. Anybody there? The gigantic field is totally deserted! The screams must be coming from somewhere, it occurs to us, while we listen to the terror. The sun was shining mildly just a moment ago when we sat down and opened a bag of chips.]

Now you stand on top of the mountain. That's where you escaped to. And what do you find? A somber hallway. Before terror can creep in there as well, let's populate it quickly with a race: get into your sacks, everyone; make sure you pull them all the way over your eyes. And instantly, we are comforted by the grace of the winner. Stay on your course, you master of Being. Can you hear the yelping behind you? It's snapping for your thighs!

Now, once again: You are standing on the mountaintop, the sun rises, you listen; and there are the other athletes; facing sadly declining steps, they pull out of their sleeves and waistbands all the tricks they worked so hard to acquire; losing promptly, they get clobbered with peels. But you have reached the top. Just imagine! And present an image of it! And then the people slip away from you, one after the other, in the rough climate of their own downhill races. They shoot right by you.

[THE HUNTERS *aim at the screen and start to fire without a sound*]

Your technology, that dark place with which you are obsessed, didn't create anything new. It made millions of people disappear! History suddenly ran backward, a hand appears and once again hands over the dead lovingly, as to a waiting mother. Strange movie, in which the person who was just laughing cheerfully is now robbed of his Being. [Didn't he just buy it for himself, popcorn, light as a feather, in a paper cup soaked with the spittle of rapture. Out of nothing, make more!]

You have spooled these people in the frantically running film of history; it doesn't make any stops; one has to jump on and off. Yes, it has become quite evident, you didn't quite master this technology—people actually disappeared! They became matter jumping up, waving, briefly made visible in the glowing beam of the projector, one second, only a fraction of one second, brought out by you, big and glowing in a somber light, and instantly used up. [Jumping over the edge of the snowbank. Don't be sorry! That sort of people is sometimes sensitive to the weather, like an entire forest! So let's get rid of them!] You had to start them up, over and over again, as it were. A perpetual, millionfold, repetition. And before they are allowed to finally see what's been left behind, they are the ones left behind.

[THE YOUNG MUTTER *enters again with her tray, filled with steins, body parts, and children's heads. She serves* THE HUNTERS, THE WOMAN, THE MAN. *The Old Man still stares at the TV set, fascinated by the soccer game.*]

The whole world, that's your stage, made of boards, like your skis, burnt behind you. No more trace of these wretched wanderers. [They've initiated this delightful concert in your and our great name, mailed the tickets, cheered the conductor. No through traffic here! Kindly park in the designated areas, even if you've been driven about like scattered clouds. A swim club can also be great fun.] People always like things present; the snow is marvelous; greetings to you and your family; and have a great race! [Nothing happened. We all wish our traces would only be a faint sound, a noise that lasted for a long time, but now no one hears it anymore. Consequences imprinted in the snow but now blown over.]

One more push off the poles, bounce your knees, look into the abyss, the goal of so many who suddenly want to do as well as the downhill champions; that is, to experience the world they just conquered for one last moment as both a beginning and an ending. A short fight for appropriation and affection, a short skirmish, a swarm of questions, and then the dive into nothingness. Sport! We have long waited for sport to move onto the TV screen. Someone has to make sure people disappear from the streets into the houses, out of the way and on their way! You don't remember, do you? You don't remember, do you?

[THE OLD FARMER *walks by. He has been listening for awhile; now he shakes his head, pointedly and seriously.* THE OLD MAN *sits in front of the TV set. His feet continue to make half-hearted skiing motions.*]

THE OLD MAN: The fear of asking questions lingers over the West. [It captures the candidates onto T-shirts, holds them on their worn-out ways, and forces them back into the torn nets of their goals, where it's all about their elimination. Everything will be taken away from them, even the way itself.] No trace, no beam of light coming through the slits. But when I call into the cabin for someone I knew, all I see is a door closing. The forest doesn't look right; everything I loved and believed in has fled. What's coming is not here yet. Nothing happened. I heard nothing. I don't remember, and getting ready for what's coming—which paralyzes me, the clean-cut amateur, even before the race begins—I kindly put out a pair of slippers. [That's all that those pros of profit will find of me when they come knocking at my door.] The hardness of granite, the Ur rock, should not discourage you! The seasons open and shut the landscape. I am only talking. Tired of thinking, all I want in this apparent void is sleep. From the cabin it is possible to wander in many directions. [But in any case, everything, as I said, will be taken away from you. Including your name and photographs. And what has been has no more bearing.]

[THE WOMAN *(in her dirndl) has watched* THE FARMER *the whole time. Now she approaches him, takes off his knapsack, pulls an axe out of it. Then she leads him behind the TV set, gets him to crouch behind it and talk into it. In the meantime,* THE OLD MAN *gets up, takes the axe from The Woman, and starts to chop wood on a chopping block without making a sound.*]

THE OLD FARMER [*Talks from behind the TV set, in a leisurely rural lilt, like out of an old Nestroy production*]: Cyclone B wasn't really a new product; only its application to humans was new. It has long been used as an

261

insecticide. The deadly chemical was produced by one company only, the Deutsche Gesellschaft für Schädlingsbekämpfung (the German Association for Pest Control), known as Degesch. Forty-two and a half percent of the company belonged to Degussa, a third was owned by I. G. Paints, 15 percent was owned by the Theo-Goldschmidt concern. The company's most important property was the exclusive rights to produce Cyclone B. The law required that, as a pesticide, it had to contain an odorous substance to alert people to the gas. Now the management of Degesch had to worry that the desire for a nonodorous Cyclone B would endanger Degesch's monopoly. The patent for Cyclone B has long run out, and Degesch could maintain its monopoly only on account of a patent for the warning odor. The removal of the warning odor would call forth undesired competition. But in the end, there wasn't much fuss, and the company had to remove the warning odor.

[THE WOMAN *helps* THE FARMER *to his feet. He bows clumsily, sits down quietly on the bench, and smokes his pipe.*]

THE WOMAN: I didn't have a choice. Pack up and leave. I may say this took some courage at a time when courage collapsed in everyone. Just entering the cold hallway. After all, one never knows what's around the corner— someone who has been standing there for a while or the door of a stranger opening. Whatever was buried in the forest soil, I could no longer pay attention to it. Others looked for mushrooms and found nothing but death. But now it's time to celebrate! We have found each other again! Go ahead! Throw the bones over your shoulder! Let the trees roar! Why not!

[*Shrugging her shoulders, she sits down, pulls her needlework out of her bag, and starts to knit*]

THE OLD MAN [*Angrier and angrier*]: This is the world of my work! To experience how the landscape changes. Everything has its own presence and duration. Then it's time to wake up. The abyss closes. The sun rises. The hills are alive.

[*Onscreen, the mountain slowly gets darker*]

Rapture erupts. The tourists watch us and applaud. Those Trapps trapped by music! Slowly, the pines keep growing. The meadows glow. The brook bubbles. Amid all that's real, we show up at the convention and cast our vote. It never was us.

Awakening nature finds herself and we find her. She needs us urgently! She almost perished. But we also lose our way. The moment of dawn is the most beautiful. A beginning, nothing has been. Nature can't help feeling new when she begins to feel herself. Water falls in the autumn night. Snow-covered surfaces seem solid and severe, as if nothing had ever been there. Snow buries everything in us, even the memory of the dead, which can never be a true memory because it also demands forgetting. So we stay at home, propped up, held back by poles, which are there only for us who grew up here, to grow along and away.

[*He starts to thrash around with his axe. The body parts on the tray are hit first; then the rest. He can speak only with the greatest effort.*]

We lie scattered along the foothills, in the shade of a low roof. Like light-bulbs, hawks are screwed into the sky. A vacation, if successful, is work on nature. The cattle step forward to make themselves available to us, serving us and our loved ones. They are watched closely, but who watches out for us? Lightning strikes, our farm goes up in flames. We're gushing out; still we want to stay until the first snowfall. Only then we too will have never been there.

THE END

Mommsen's Block

HEINER MÜLLER

•

Translated by Carl Weber

For Félix Guattari

Editor's Note

●

Mommsen's Block was first staged at the Nitery Theater of Stanford University's Drama Department, November 30, 1994. It seems to be appropriate that a text that reflects on the life of a great academic historian should find its first audience at a university.

Theodor Mommsen (1817–1903), one of the great historians of the nineteenth century, was a professor of history at Berlin University beginning in 1858. He won the Nobel Prize in literature in 1902 for his *History of Rome,* "an unmatched recreation of Roman society and culture," as the *Concise Columbia Encyclopedia* notes. His major work was the fruit of his exhaustive study of ancient coins, inscriptions, and literary texts. He also was a liberal politician, who passionately opposed Bismarck, the conservative chancellor whose politics triggered the Franco-Prussian War of 1870–71 and created the German Reich. The Reich united the previously sovereign German states but its formation also planted the seeds of World War I through Bismarck's insistence on the annexation of Alsace-Lorraine.

Müller's text is brimful of references to historical events and personalities, from Caesar, Augustus, Vergil, Tacitus, and Nero to St. John, St. Paul, Dante, Humboldt, Marx, Nietzsche, Dilthey, Kafka, Toynbee, and Pound—as well as Bismarck, Mussolini, Eisenhower, Shukov, and Ulbricht. Two events obviously inspired the author in writing the piece: the first publication of Mommsen's fragmentary notes for his university lectures and the replacement of a Karl Marx statue with one of Mommsen at the entrance of Berlin's Humboldt University, which was Mommsen's academic home when it was Friedrich-Wilhelm University (named after the Prussian King who founded it, in 1809, at the initiative of his secretary of education, Wilhelm von Humboldt). The Socialist government of the former GDR had changed the university's name to Humboldt and replaced the Mommsen statue with one of Karl Marx.

The text, however, is not only a reflection on European cultural and political history or a comment on the present predicament of unified Germany's eastern parts. It also explores the perplexing difficulties a writer braves when trying to capture the intractable complexity of historical events in the pages of a book or on the boards of the stage. It also may be read as Müller's reckoning with problems of his own when redetermining an authorial position that had been defined so clearly through the crisis of Socialism and the fratricidal tradition of German history, which he saw embodied in the antithetical economic and cultural systems of the two German states. Moreover, the Berlin Wall was always cited by Müller as the most concrete manifestation of our age. That wall has disappeared, and with it went a paradigm that informed much of Müller's work.

The text is open to many other viable readings, and it raises a multitude of questions while refusing to offer easy answers. Appropriate to its thematic multivocality, it is equally open in its formal structure. There is no effort at creating anything like a coherent dialogue. There is a continuous slipping into and out of poetic language, into and out of prose, with a generous sprinkling of literary and historical quotations that invoke the whole arch of European thought, from classic Rome to the postmodern present. Even if at first sight this text doesn't appear to be written for the stage, it actually offers an abundance of options for performance. In its form, it continues a line of experimentation Müller began twenty years ago with some sections of *Gundling's Life Frederick of Prussia Lessing's Sleep Dream Scream* (1976) and that he pursued further in *Hamletmachine* (1977) and *Explosion of a Memory* (1984). In these works, Müller probed the limits of a theater where the displayed image and the spoken language are of equal significance. His revisioning of performance was not unlike the work of such contemporary theater artists as Robert Wilson, Bill Forsythe, Pina Bausch, and the Wooster Group.

Heiner Müller was born in 1929, son of a low-level Social Democratic Party functionary, whom the Nazis put, in 1933, into a concentration camp. In early 1945, Müller, who was still attending high school, was drafted into the military and thus witnessed the final convulsions of World War II. After the war, his father became a small-town mayor but eventually run afoul of the ruling Socialist Party's politics and only avoided arrest by defecting to the West. Müller stayed in the East, where he finished high school and worked briefly as a librarian before he became a journalist and began to write plays and poetry. His first performed play was *The Correction* (1958). Originally favored by the GDR establishment for his treatment of industrial production and working class issues, he was severely reprimanded for *The Resettled Woman; or, Life in the Country* (1961). The play's performance was prohibited, and Müller was expelled from the Writers Association for revealing "hostility toward party and state"; this was the year the Wall was built. For a considerable period, Müller's plays could not be performed in the GDR, except for some translations of classic texts. However, by the early seventies he had become a highly esteemed dramatist and poet in the

German-speaking countries of the West. During the seventies, his plays also began to appear again on East German stages, and by the mid-eighties Müller was regarded in East and West as the leading playwright in the language.

Starting in 1975, Müller paid several extended visits to the United States, and his text *Mauser* was premiered at the University of Austin, Texas, the same year. In the eighties, Müller began to direct his own plays; he also commenced a collaboration with Robert Wilson, who staged several of his texts. Müller has been strongly influenced by Brecht's work as a playwright/director; he also absorbed elements of Artaud's theatrical project and of the theater of images that made its appearance in the seventies and eighties. Müller's texts have been translated into many languages and are widely performed, especially *Hamletmachine* and *Quartet* (1981), his adaptation of the French eighteenth-century novel *Les Liaisons Dangereuses*.

In the spring of 1995, Müller became the artistic director of the Berliner Ensemble, Brecht's former theater, and it might be said that he inherited Brecht's mantle. Already suffering from cancer, he started his directorate with a highly successful staging of Brecht's *Arturo Ui*. On December 30, 1995, Müller succumbed to the disease, two weeks before he planned to begin rehearsing his new—and now last—play, *Germania 3*.

Carl Weber

Mommsen's Block

What authorities are there beyond Court tittle-tattle.*
—*Mommsen to James Bryce, 1898*

●

The question why the great historian
Didn't write the fourth volume of his ROMAN HISTORY
The long-awaited one about the age of emperors
Kept occupied the minds
Of the historians who came after him
Good reasons are offered wholesale
Handed down in letters rumors conjectures
The lack of inscriptions He who writes with a chisel
Has no signature The stones don't lie
No trust in literature CONSPIRACIES AND
COURT GOSSIP Even the silvery fragments
Of the laconic Tacitus merely reading matter for poets
To whom history is a burden
Insufferable without the dance of vowels
On top of graves against the gravity of the dead
And their dread of the eternal return
He didn't like them those Caesars of the later empire
Not their languor not their vices
He'd had enough of the peerless Julius
Whom he liked as much as his own tombstone
Even TO WRITE ABOUT CAESAR'S DEATH he had
When he was asked about the still missing
Fourth volume NOT ENOUGH PASSION LEFT
And THE PUTRESCENT CENTURIES after him
GRAY IN GRAY BLACK UPON BLACK   For whom
The epitaph   That the midwife Bismarck
Was as well the grave digger of the empire
That afterbirth of a counterfeit dispatch
Could be concluded from the third volume
Jaded had become in Charlottenburg—
Twice daily the trip with the horse-drawn trolley
In the dust of books and manuscripts forty

Asterisks indicate a line of text that appeared in English in the original play.

Thousand in the Mommsen house Number Eight Mach Street
Twelve children in the basement—THE COURAGE TO ERR
Which MAKES THE HISTORIAN   NOW I KNOW
ALAS WHAT I DON'T KNOW For instance Why
Does an empire collapse The ruins don't answer
The silence of the statues is gilding the decline
THE INSTITUTIONS ARE ALL WE UNDERSTAND
BUT HE IS TIRED AND QUITE DUSTY
The pious Dilthey wrote to Count York
FROM TREADING THE BACKROADS OF PHILOLOGY
INSCRIPTIONS AND PARTY POLITICS
HIS MIND ISN'T HOMESICK FOR THE IN-
VISIBLE EMPIRE His empire was what is manifest
In a letter to one of his daughters Mrs. Wilamowitz
He dreams of a villa near Naples
Not so he'd learn how to die Comes time comes death
And no grace granted A BLIND FAITH
FOR COUNTS AND BARONS Christianity
A tree disease that starts at the root
A cancer infiltrated by intelligence services
The twelve apostles twelve secret agents
The traitor provides the proof of divinity
And the trademark Saul a colonized
Bloodhound plays the part of the Social Democrat
Turned into Paul by a fall from his horse
Bellwether of the Unknown God
For Him he lures the sheep into the fold
For the selection Salvation or Damnation
Only for the maggots the dead are alike
A police informer the first pope
Only John in Patmos amid the fumes of drugs
The heretic The guide of the dead The terrorist
Has seen the New Beast that is rising
The dream of Italy is a dream of writing
The stimulant of moonlight on ruins
With the divine arrogance of MY YOUNG YEARS
THE YOUNGER ONES AT LEAST YOUNG I NEVER WAS
What remains is the DIVINE BLUNTNESS — A POOR
SUBSTITUTE* In the swamp the eagles Why

Write it down just because the mob wants to read it
That there is more life in swamps than
In high altitudes is known to biology
How should you make people understand
And for what reason that the first decade of Nero's reign—
The frustrated artist the bloody one
Music is highly priced during the decline
When all has been said voices are sounding sweet—
Was a happy time for the people of Rome
The happiest perhaps in their long history
They had their bread their games The massacres
Took place in the dress circle
And they achieved high ratings
A fire in the Mommsen house caused
Not by Christian zeal against libraries
As two thousand years earlier in Alexandria
But by a gas explosion at Number Eight Mach Street
Gave rise to the horrible hope
The great scholar might have written after all
The fourth volume the long-awaited one
About the age of the emperors
And the text was burnt
With the rest of the library for instance
Forty thousand volumes plus manuscripts
Rescued was the ACADEMY FRAGMENT
Seven pages of a draft framed by the fire
IN POINTED BRACKETS THE SCORCHED WORDS
OF MOMMSEN as the editors write
One hundred and twelve years after the fire
The fire is reported in the papers
The newspaper reader Nietzsche writes to Peter Gast:
"Have you read of the fire at Mommsen's
house? And that all his excerpts are destroyed, the
weightiest preliminary studies perhaps made by any living
scholar? It is said he repeatedly
plunged back into the flames, so that finally
force had to be used to restrain him who was covered
with burns. Undertakings such as Mommsen's
must be very rare, since a colossal memory

and a corresponding sagacity in the evaluation and
classification of such sources rarely go together
but rather tend to work against each other.—When
I heard the story it truly wrung my heart
and even now I am in physical distress when I
think of it. Is this compassion? But what is
Mommsen to me? I am not at all fond of him."
A document from the century of letter writers
The fear of solitude is hidden in the question mark
He who writes into the void has no use for punctuation
Permit me to speak of myself Mommsen Professor
Greatest historian after Gibbon according to Toynbee
(Or did he say beside him That ever gnawing fear
Of the praised that the yardstick is lying)
In life resident at Number Eight Mach Street Charlottenburg
Two three pages long For whom else do we write
But for the dead omniscient in their dust A thought
That perhaps doesn't please you teacher of the young
To forget is a privilege of the dead
After all you yourself have forbidden
The publication of your lectures in your will
Since recklessness at the lectern commits treason
Against the toils at the desk Even the AENEID
You wanted to see it burnt in accord with the will
Of the failure Vergil Immortality
Was forced on him by Augustus
Masterbuilder of Rome himself deferring completion
Because it conceals the abyss
The DIVINE COMEDY would not
Have been written or would be less enduring
Without his verdict against the fire
And I'd wish you could read Kafka Professor
On your pedestal in your marble vault
The bombs of World War II You know they
Did not spare Mach Street Spared
Was not your Academy of Sciences
From the fall of the Asiatic despotism Product
Of an erroneous reading and falsely called
Socialism after the great historian
Of capital Whom you didn't notice

A worker in a different quarry
Until his monument stood on your pedestal
For the duration of one state The pedestal is yours again
Before the university that was named after Humboldt
By the rulers of an illusion
(They never had read your Roman history
Nor Marx who kept mum about reading it
Had he lived longer one could have claimed
He envied perhaps the money of your Nobel Prize the Jew)
Ensnared in the knitting pattern of the red Caesars
Who scanned HIS text with combat boots
How do you clear a minefield asked Eisenhower
Victor of World War II another
Victor With the boots
Of a marching battalion replied Shukhov
The GREAT OCTOBER OF THE WORKING CLASS—extolled
Voluntarily with hope or in a twofold stranglehold
By too many and even after their throats had been cut—
Was a summer storm in the World Bank's shadow
A dance of gnats above the graves of Tatars
WHERE THE DEAD ONES WAIT*
FOR THE EARTHQUAKES TO COME*
As Ezra Pound perhaps would say the other Vergil
Who betted on the false Caesar he too a failure
Because the ghosts do not sleep
Their favorite food is our dreams
Pardon Professor the bitter tone
The university named after Humboldt
Before which you stand upon your pedestal again
Long after your death it is shoveled out
Right now from the suspected rubbish of the new
Blind faith that's not for counts and barons
Yesterday while eating in a four-star restaurant
In the once more resurrected capital Berlin
I leafed through the notes of your lectures
On the Roman age of Caesars fresh from the book market
Two heroes of the new times dined at the next table
Zombies of capital brokers and traders
And as I listened to their dialogue greedy
To feed my disgust with the Here and Now:

"This four million / Must come our way at once // But that won't work // But that won't be conspicuous at all // If you haven't mastered the rules of this game / You're lost You've seen that in the X case / He didn't master them // You've got to drum them / Into his brain or he's going belly up Too bad // Well I'm afraid / They're going to smash him against the wall Like a jellyfish // He'll hang there Just squirming and squirming // I figure he's good as a buyer During the preliminaries / But when you cut right to the bone . . . // Then he's got to hand it over // But then you've got to ask Are our hands strong enough / To turn the table // You've got to bring him into line // We have to bag him for Deutsche Bank // We'll haul him in for ourselves / As soon as I put the screws on / I'll teach him a lesson Then he'll make / Serious money."
Five streets away as the police sirens indicate
The poor are clobbering the poorest
And when the gentlemen turned to private matters Cigars and Cognac
Strictly according to the textbook of Political Economics
Of capitalism: "They wanted to send me / To a remedial school // My mother was hard as nails / Against all of them You'll get your final diploma / The faculty was always split / There were teachers who thought I was stupid."
Animal sounds Who would write that down
With passion Hate is a waste Contempt an empty exercise
For the first time I understood your writer's block
Comrade Professor facing the Roman age of Caesars
The as we know happy times of Nero's reign
Knowing the unwritten text is a wound
Oozing blood that no posthumous fame will staunch
And the yawning gap in your Roman history
Was a pain in my—how long still?—breathing body
And I thought of the dust in your marble vault
And of the cold coffee at six in the morning
In Charlottenburg at the Mommsen house Number Eight Mach Street
At your workplace fenced in with books

Library of Congress Cataloging-in-Publication Data

DramaContemporary : Germany / edited by Carl Weber.
p.   cm. — (PAJ books)
ISBN 0-8018-5279-X (alk. paper). — ISBN 0-8018-5280-3
(pbk. : alk. paper)
1. German drama—20th century—Translations into English.
I. Weber, Carl (Carl M.), 1925–   . II. Series.
PT1258.D68   1996
832'.91408—dc20   95-41870 CIP